VILLAGES OF MID-CHESHIRE

THROUGH TIME

Paul Hurley

AMBERLEY

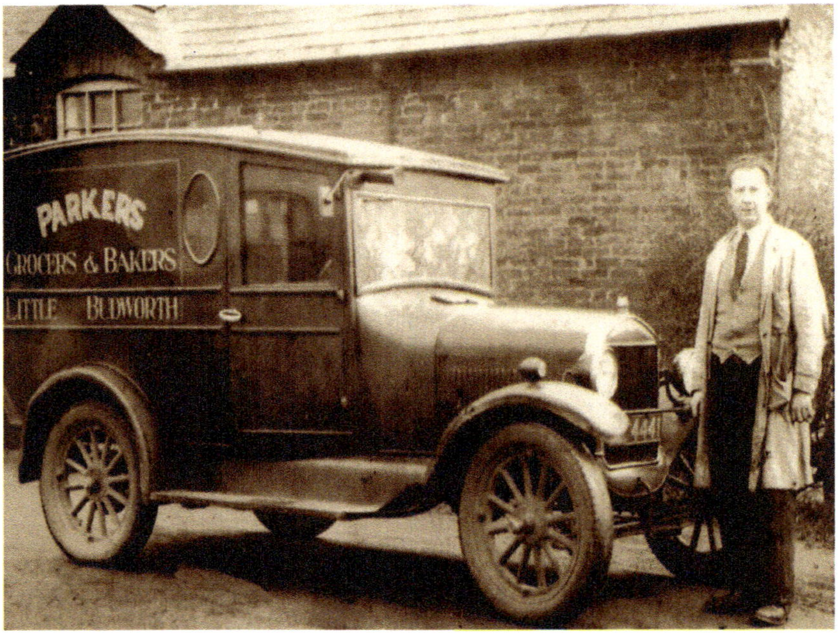

Brian Parker and his grocery van in Little Budworth *c.* 1920s.

About the Author

Paul Hurley is a freelance writer, author and member of the Society of Authors. He has written a novel and has written for newspapers and magazines. He lives in Winsford, Cheshire, with his wife Rose and he has two sons and two daughters.

Website: www.paul-hurley.co.uk

First published 2009
This edition published 2015

Amberley Publishing
The Hill, Stroud
Gloucestershire, GL5 4EP

www.amberley-books.com

ISBN 978 1 4456 5077 7 (print)
ISBN 978 1 4456 5078 4 (ebook)

British Library Cataloguing in Publication Data.
A catalogue record for this book is available from the British Library.

Typeset in 9.5pt on 12pt Celeste.
Typesetting by Amberley Publishing.
Printed in the UK.

Introduction

The Vale Royal of England is the impressive title held by Mid-Cheshire since the thirteenth century when Edward I named the new *Vallis Regalis* (Vale Royal). The abbey we now know as Vale Royal House was founded by Prince Edward, the future Edward I, prior to his accession to the throne. In 1277 the King and Queen Eleanor, together with the great and good, arrived to lay the foundation stones of the new abbey. In 1281 the monks moved from Darnhall to temporary accommodation on the Vale Royal site while the abbey started to rise around them.

Whitegate village was nearby and is named after the white stone gate into the abbey grounds. Many stories exist of the abbots of Vale Royal and their tyrannical rule. The history of the abbey had many episodes of unpleasantness and disgrace, which led to intermittent uprisings by the local people against the monks.

During the Dissolution of the Monasteries by Henry VIII the abbey and lands came into the hands of the Holford family of Holford Hall who, over the years, became joined by marriage to the Cholmondeley family of Vale Royal, later the Barons Delamere. Much of the massive abbey was demolished and the remainder was converted into an Elizabethan manor house in the late sixteenth and early seventeenth centuries. This in turn was replaced in 1833 by a new house designed by Edward Blore and a south wing was added in 1861 by John Douglas, the well-known Sandiway architect who went on to remodel Whitegate village and design some 500 buildings in Cheshire including the Eastgate Clock in Chester. There is now little evidence of the great abbey and the house has been turned into a golf club.

This book records in photographs some of the villages of Mid-Cheshire through the years; however, the inclusion of a village depended on the availability of old photographs suitable for print. In the case of Weaverham, I had the support of Mike Hornby, the Chairman of the Weaverham History Society, one of the best that I have come across. Other people helped with knowledge and photographs and quite pleasant raids were carried out on village pubs in search of photographs to scan. I apologise if a few of the old photographs are below the quality that I would have liked but they were the only ones available and I wanted to include as many villages as possible.

Britain is full of pretty country villages, and Cheshire is sometimes overlooked, it has a reputation as a wealthy county perhaps but not overtly pretty in a Cotswold sort of way! That is a misconception, Cheshire has many villages and towns that can compare most favourably with the likes of those in the Cotswolds and I have tried to show this, at least in the Vale Royal area.

Within these pages the reader can see just how little the villages have changed over the years and how many ancient buildings still exist to delight the visitor.

Things have to change but at the same time, some things stand still and history is kind. Many Mid-Cheshire villages have now been extended by the building of modern estates and those halcyon days of old have given way to busy roads that children once used as playgrounds.

The reader is invited to find time, relax and browse their way from Moulton to Church Minshull, Weaverham to Tarporley and Barnton to Hartford via the villages and places in Mid-Cheshire, stopping to enjoy the sights that were once to be seen and compare them with what is there now. Enjoy the book as I have enjoyed compiling it.

Acknowledgements

I would like to thank the Cheshire Archives and the Weaver Hall Museum and Workhouse for permitting me to use photographs from their archive, and Mike Hornby of the Weaverham History Society and Peter Craven of the Northwich Heritage Society for both the loan of photographs and their excellent counsel. I would also like to thank Barrie Johnson and David Michael Callis for information and photographs of their beautiful cottages, and Raymond Jones for his interesting story of his great great grandmother. To the managers of the Spinner & Bergamot, Shrewsbury Arms and Alvanley Arms public houses for allowing me to borrow photographs from their walls! To my publisher Jenna Whittle for her patience and guidance. Finally I would like to thank my wife Rose for her unlimited patience during the lengthy compilation of this book, not to mention her willingness to accompany me on expeditions into deepest Mid-Cheshire to take the modern photographs.

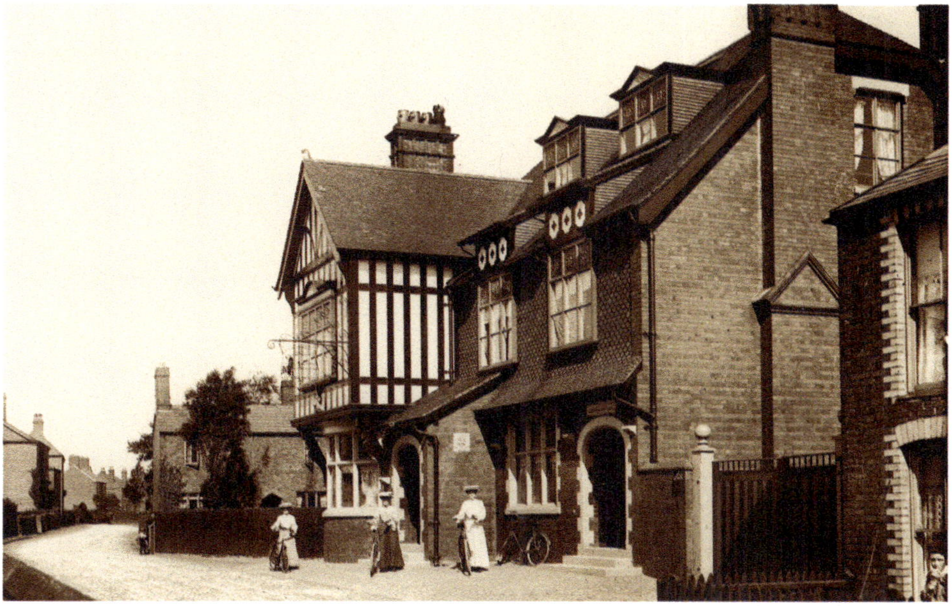

The Lion Public House, Moulton, 1896 and 2015

Until 1894, Martha Lyon (married name Jackson) ran a grocery and beerhouse on the site. Prior to this her husband had operated the business. Martha had the present public house built and named it, appropriately, the Lion, with a subtle play on her maiden name. She remained as landlady until the pub was sold to Ind Coope's brewery in the early 1920s. Moulton housed mainly salt workers from the many Winsford salt works a short way off via the railway tunnels. The tunnels are still there leading down to the River Weaver but the many salt works have now gone, leaving just one rock salt mine on the other side, which is now the main source of rock salt in the UK.

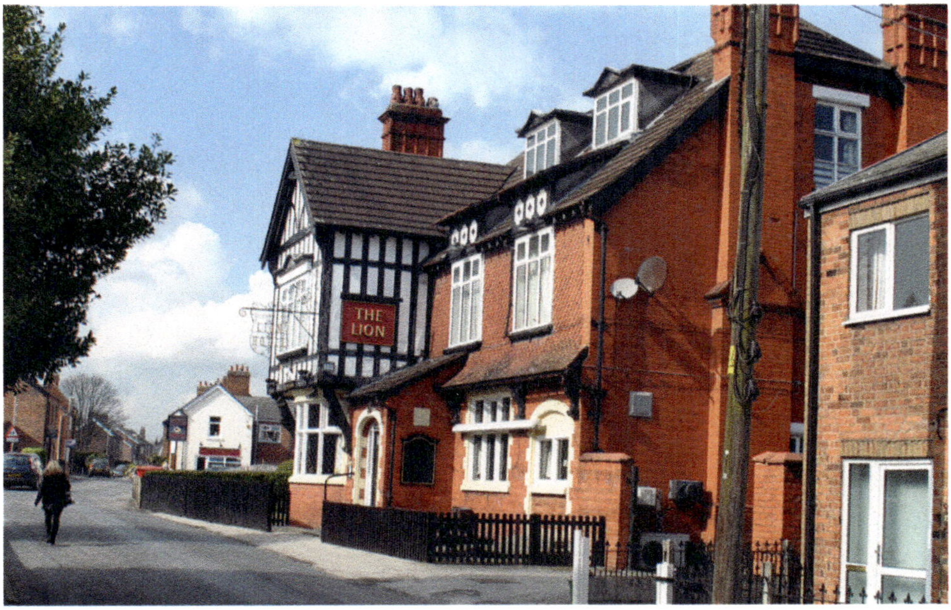

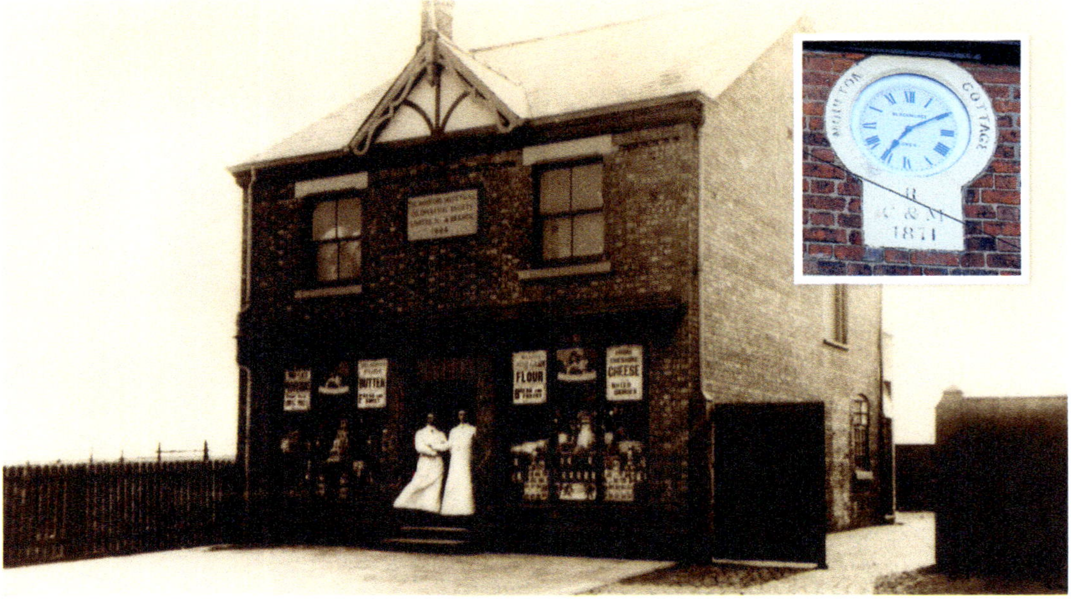

The Co-op, Moulton, 1920s and 2015

The Co-op in Moulton was opened in 1896 by the Winsford Co-operative Society to serve the needs of this growing community. The village is ancient, having been mentioned in the Domesday Book, but grew quickly in the nineteenth century to serve the salt industry. A very insular community then with a tremendous spirit, a cottage was built at the end of School Lane in 1871 with a clock on the wall to serve villagers who could not afford their own timepiece. Initially it housed a cobbler and clog maker's. The clock is still there, but times have changed and the locals now have their own clocks!

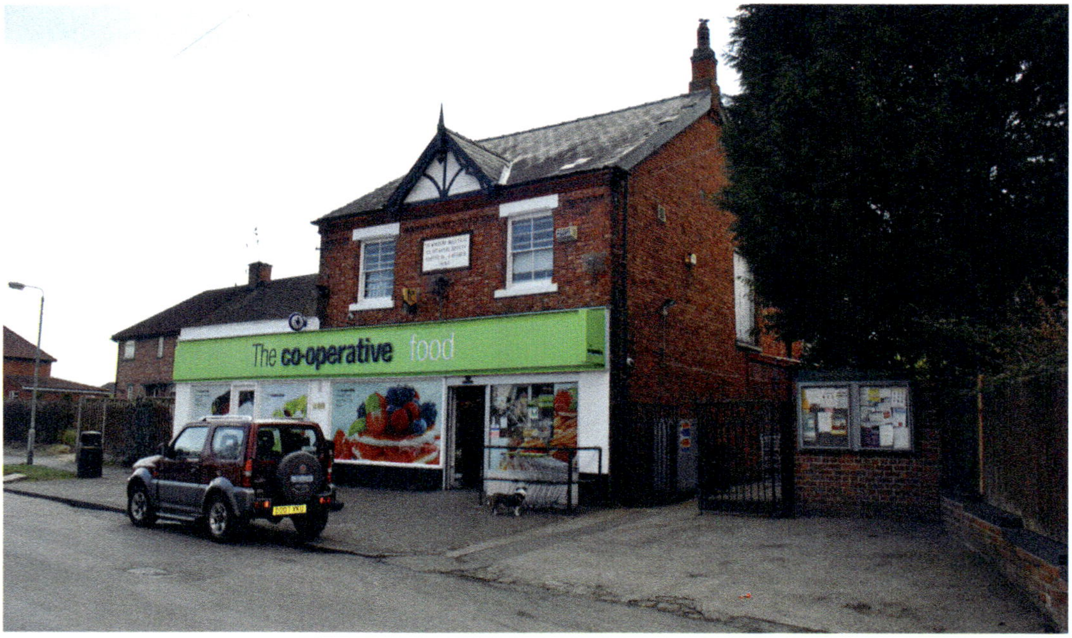

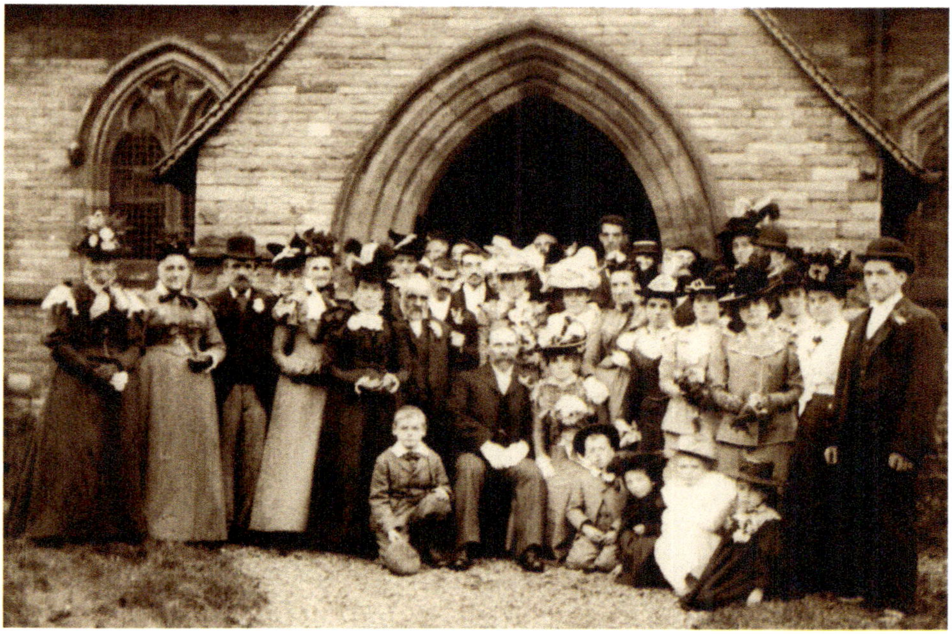

Moulton Church, 1890s and 2015

The foundation stone for St Stephen the Martyr's parish church was laid in 1876 and was consecrated the following year. It had been sponsored by the Revd France-Hayhurst of Bostock Hall. Here the Buckley family pose proudly for the camera in front of the main door. The village once had the busy Northwich to Winsford road running through it, but now its residents can enjoy a quiet residential conurbation surrounded by farmland while the Davenham bypass takes the traffic away.

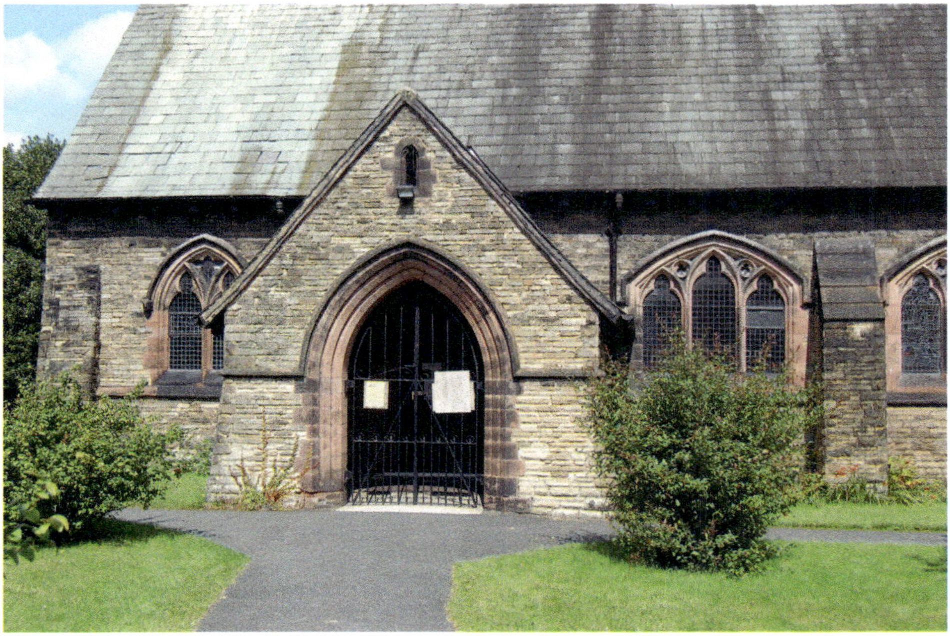

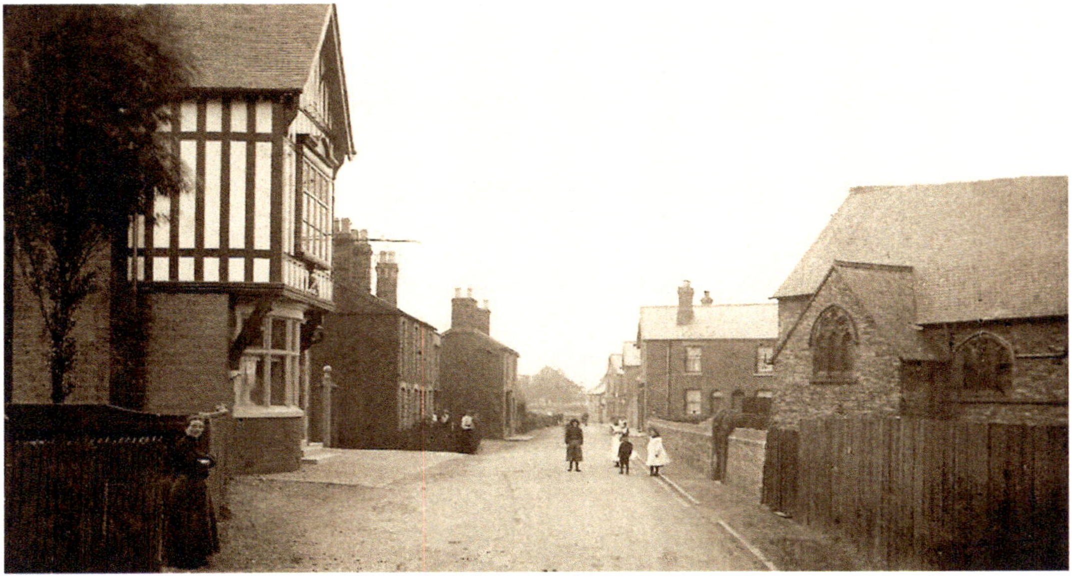

Moulton, 1896 and 2015

A view of the Lion pub from the opposite direction along Main Road with the rear of St Stephen's church on the right. Very little has changed over the years, possibly because the transformation of the village had taken place quite recently. Church Street and Regent Street on the right had been built by salt works owners for their employees. In the 1950s, salt mining changed from pumping brine to mining salt by other methods, resulting in a complete change for the workers. This led to the village becoming more of a dormitory village than one housing salt workers. In the 1960s, the village grew again with new housing developments and the population now stands at around 2,500.

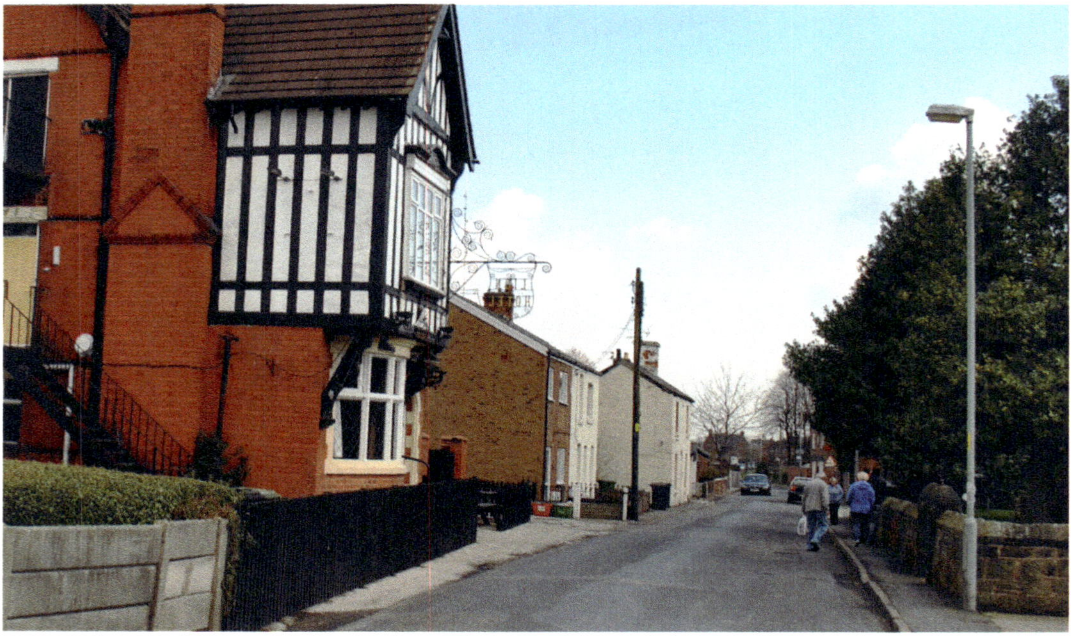

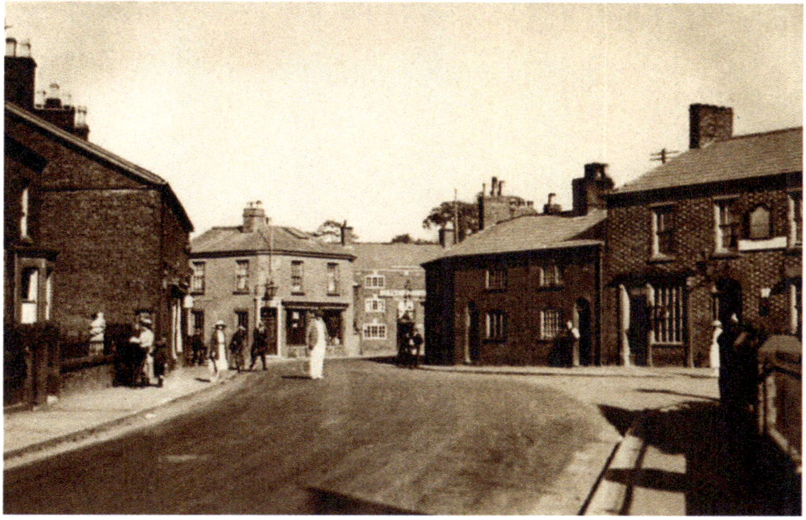

London Road, Davenham, 1900–1920 and 2015

This view taken from the Davenham roundabout side looks towards the Bulls Head in the distance and the Oddfellows on the right. The cottages after the Oddfellows have been demolished but the view is remarkably unchanged. The Bulls Head is an old coaching inn and has existed since 1764 and the Oddfellows, which started life as a private house, since 1851. Both pubs are listed buildings. Once a very busy road, this has now gained speed calming humps and has benefitted from the building of the long fought for Davenham bypass.

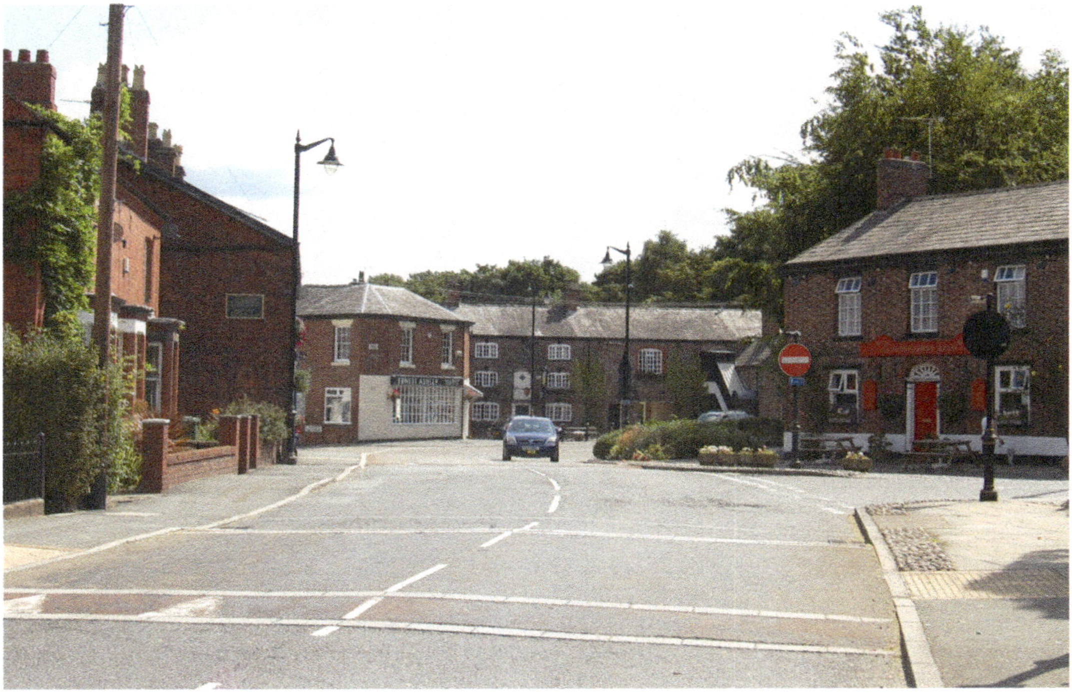

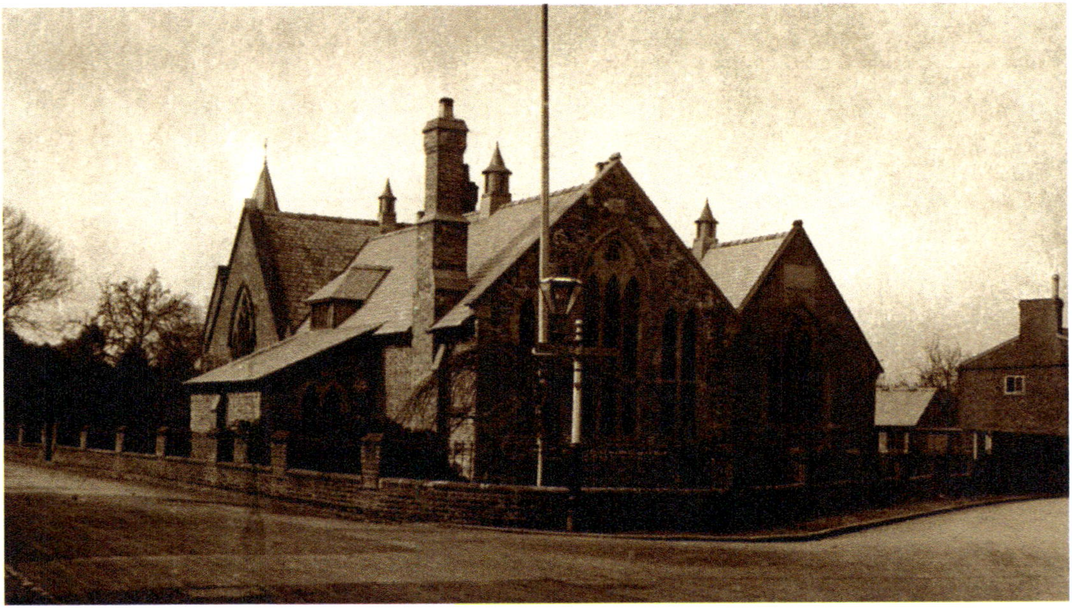

Davenham Schools, Early 1900s and 2015

This was once the main school for Davenham, built with the attached schoolmasters' house in 1856. In 1914, 340 children could be accommodated and the average attendance was 223. Mathew Earlam was the Master and Miss Mary Johnson the Mistress with Miss Louisa Horton as the Infants Mistress. The war memorial that can be seen in the 2015 photograph dates the old photograph to before 1 July 1921 when it was unveiled by Captain W. H. France-Hayhurst of Bostock Hall. When a new school was built in Charles Avenue, the old building was converted into flats. The building is now listed.

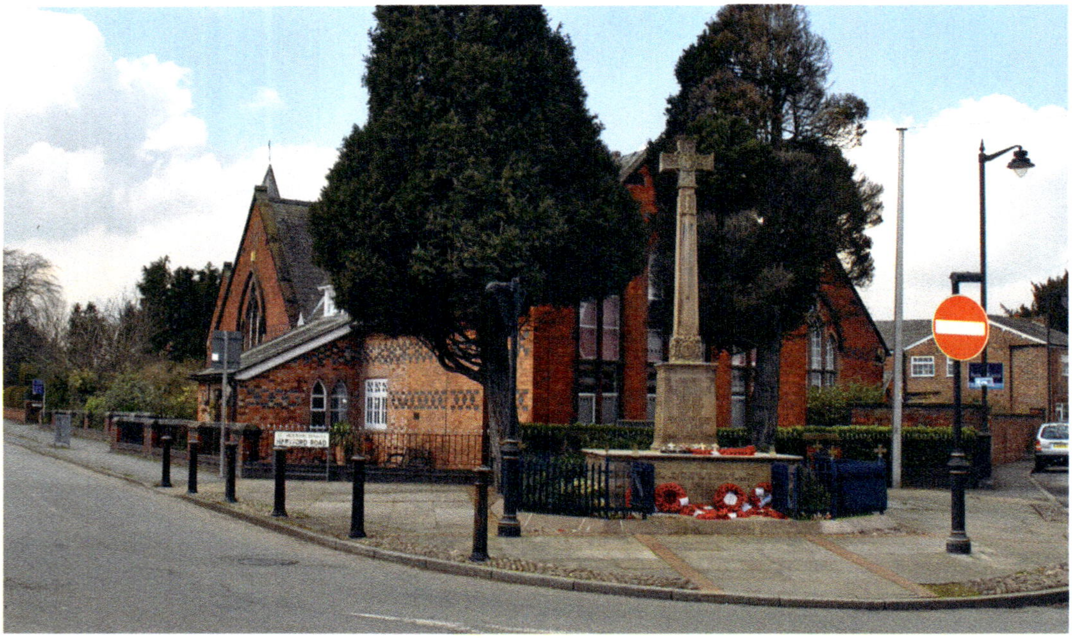

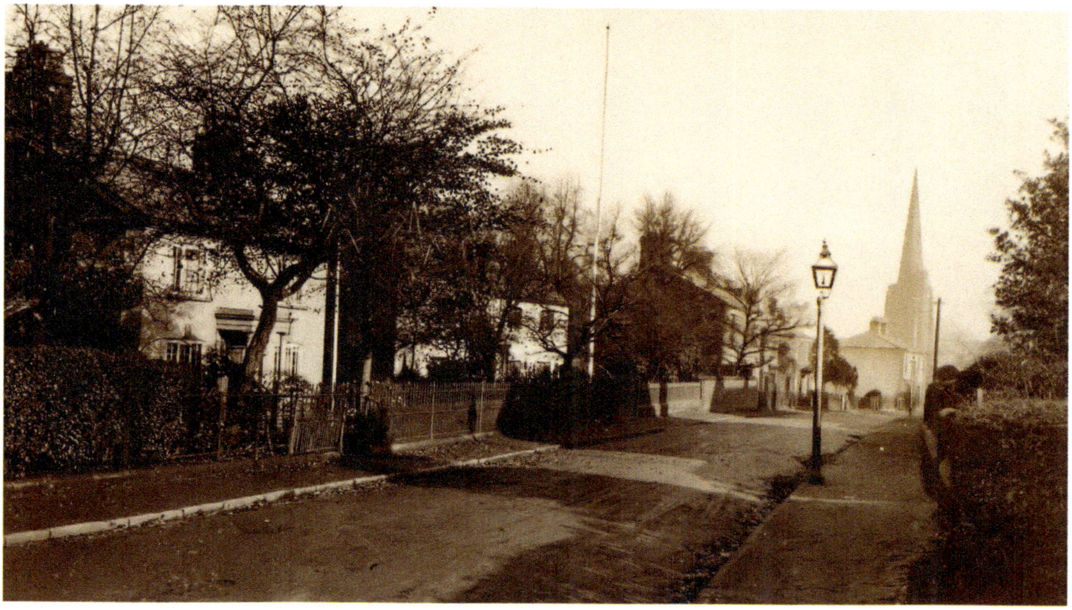

Church Street, Davenham, 1910–1920 and 2015

This street leads from the village centre into the countryside towards Bostock passing the parish church of St Wilfrid in the distance. The church was substantially reconstructed between 1844 and 1870. There has been a church on the site since at least 1086 and possibly earlier still; legend states that it was actually founded by St Wilfrid as he passed through Cheshire in the seventh century. The old photo, taken around the time of the First World War, shows it as a quiet and peaceful road. Apart from the many parked cars, this is still a quiet area. The houses on the left have now been hidden by a verdant vista of green beauty, perhaps due to the different seasons chosen to take the photographs.

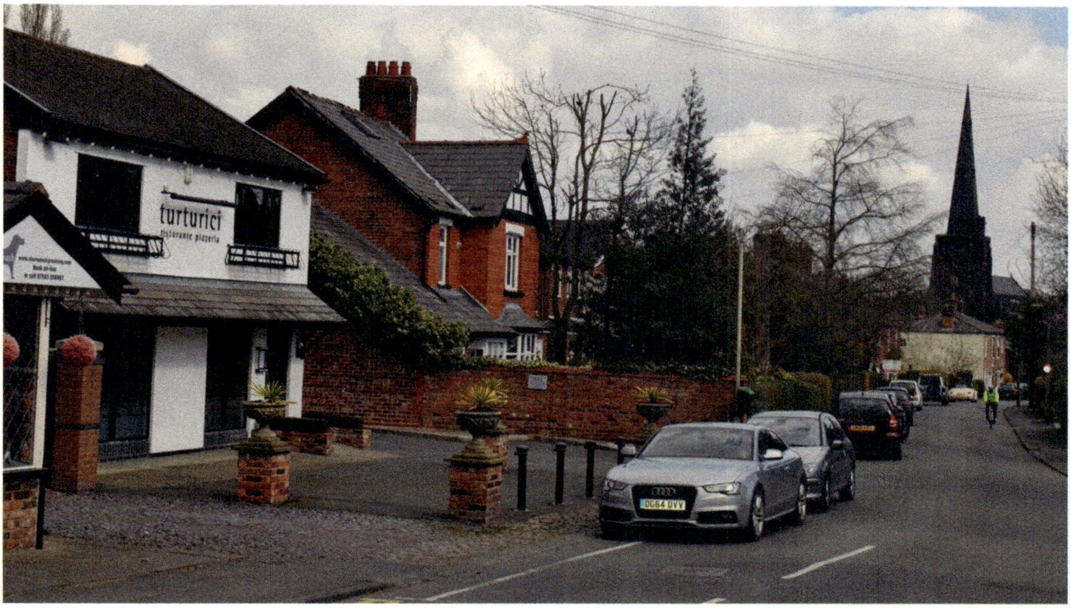

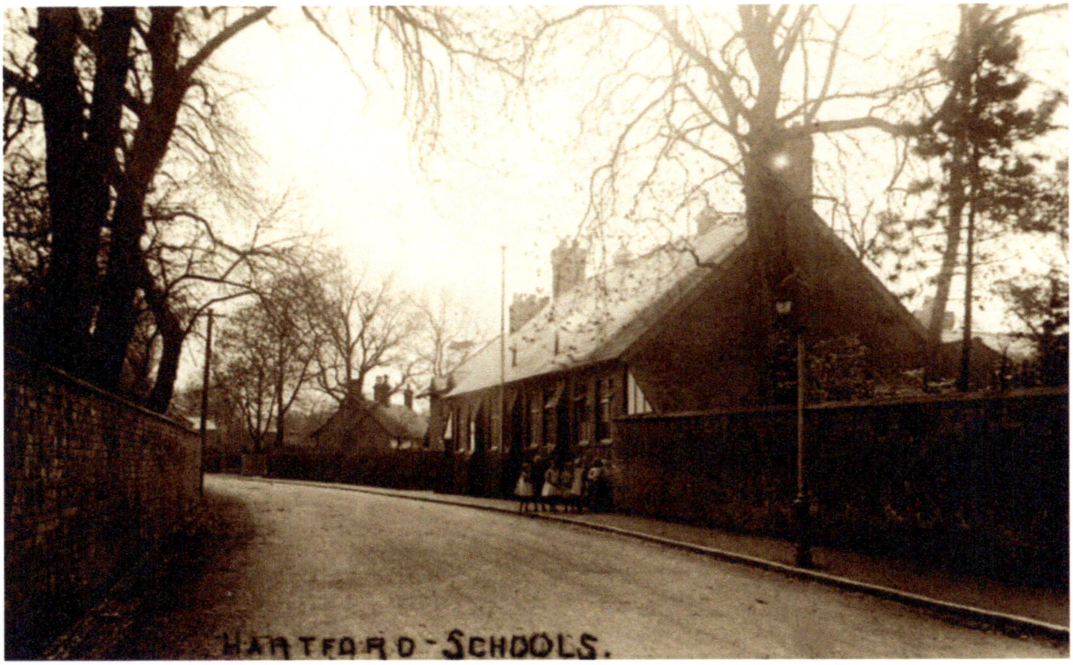

Hartford Schools, 1910–1915 and 2015
This was the main school building in Hartford and was built in 1833. Outside seven girls line up, five in pinafore dresses, to watch the photographer at work. The building now houses the Hartford Old School House Day Nursery. A more modern primary school is situated in Riddings Lane.

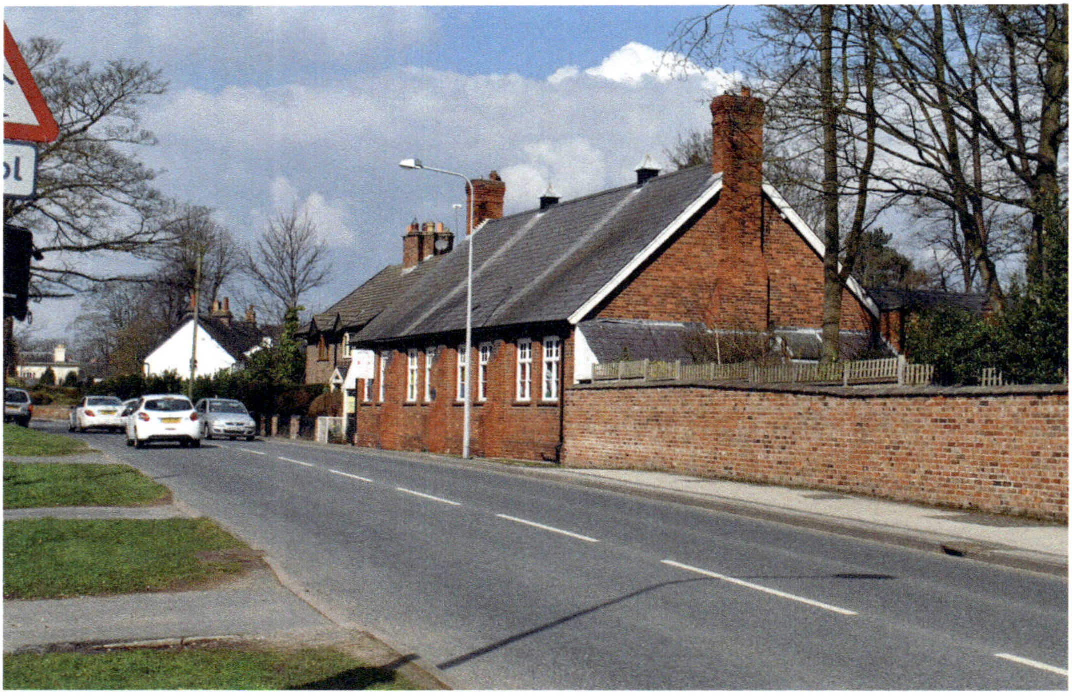

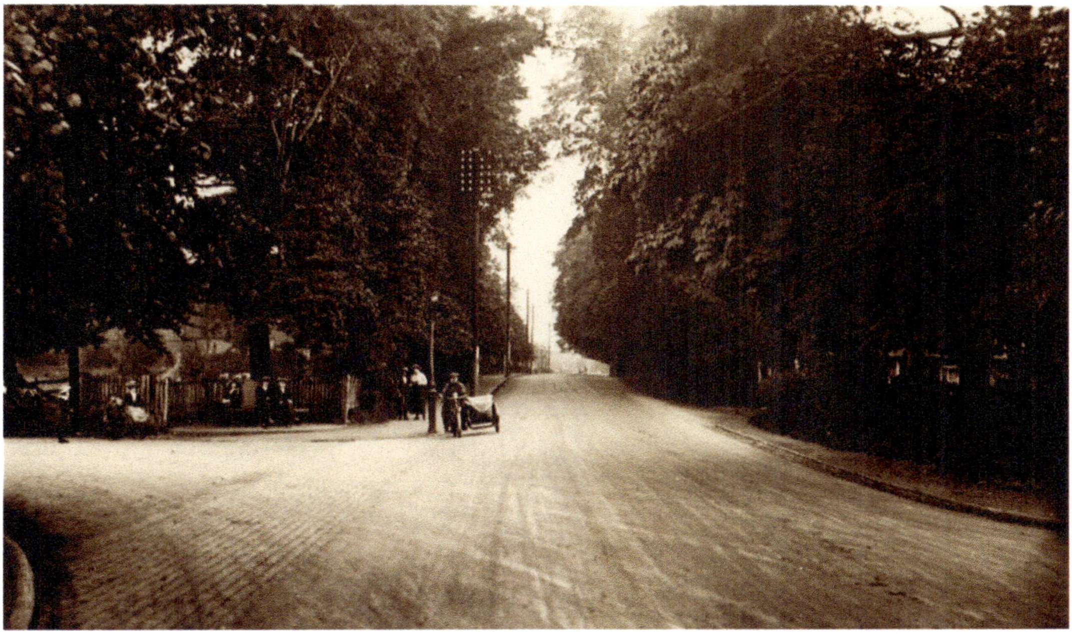

Cross Roads, Hartford, 1910 and 2015

I had to include this 1910 photo with its period motorcycle and dress. There is a woman in a three-wheel invalid carriage and just at the side a woman with a child in a perambulator. Quite a busy area with a seat around the tree occupied by locals stopping to chat. The crossroads were considerably modified in 2009; straight on is Northwich, left is Hartford Beach and right is the A556. The traffic on this road is still very busy and is likely to get worse when the houses that are being built behind the camera in the new shot are occupied.

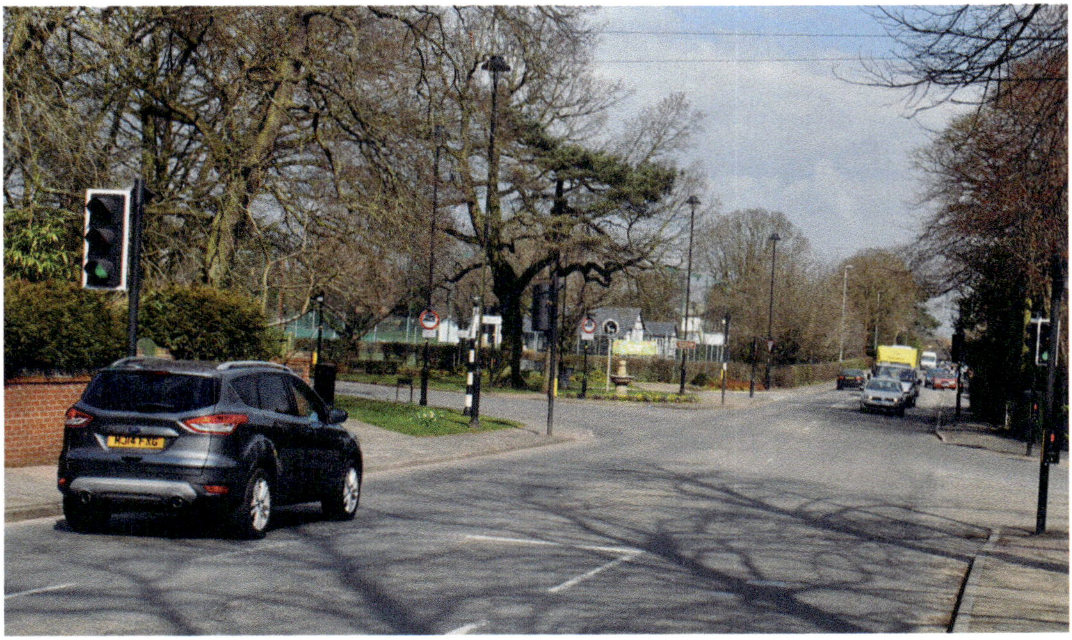

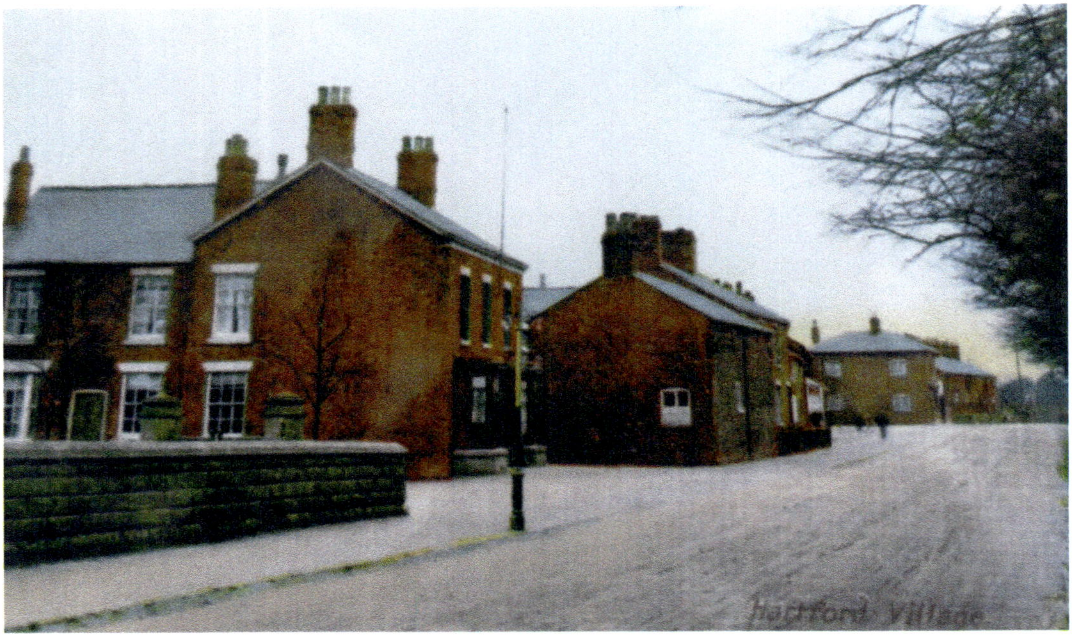

The Red Lion, Chester Road, Hartford, 1900s and 2015

The Red Lion was one of the seven pubs that could once be found in Hartford. It was originally called the White Lion, with the Red Lion on the other side of the road. In 1857 Greenall's bought the original Red Lion and closed it. The licensee Isaac Wilson crossed the road, took over the White Lion and changed its name to the Red Lion. Simple really! The old Hartford fire station, with its well and buildings for the horse-drawn fire engine, is now used as the pub's beer garden. The box for the bell can still be seen high on the gable end of the next building along.

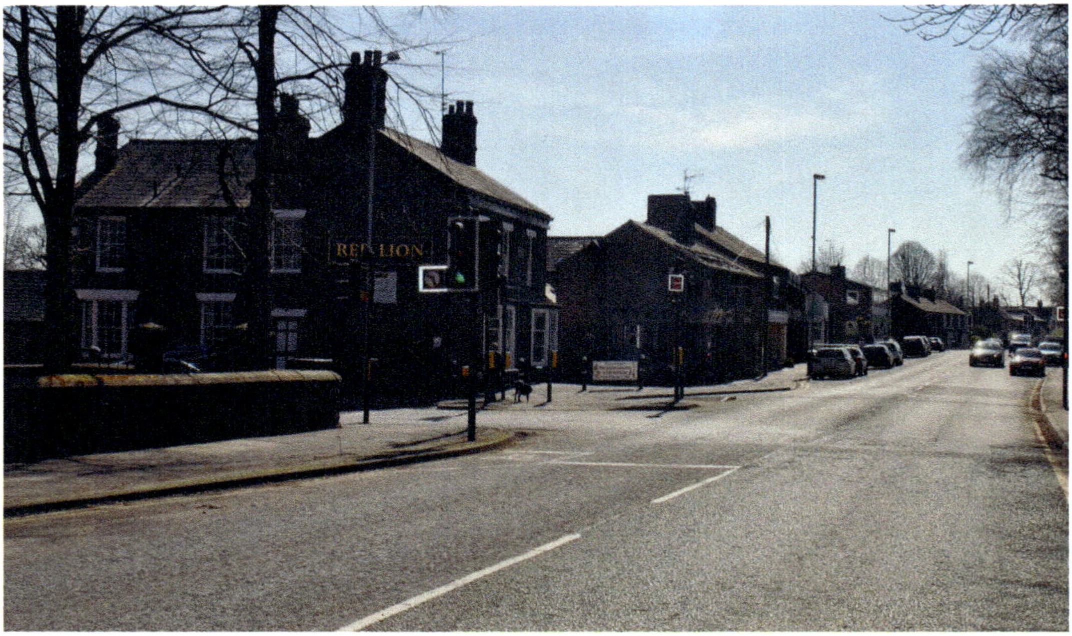

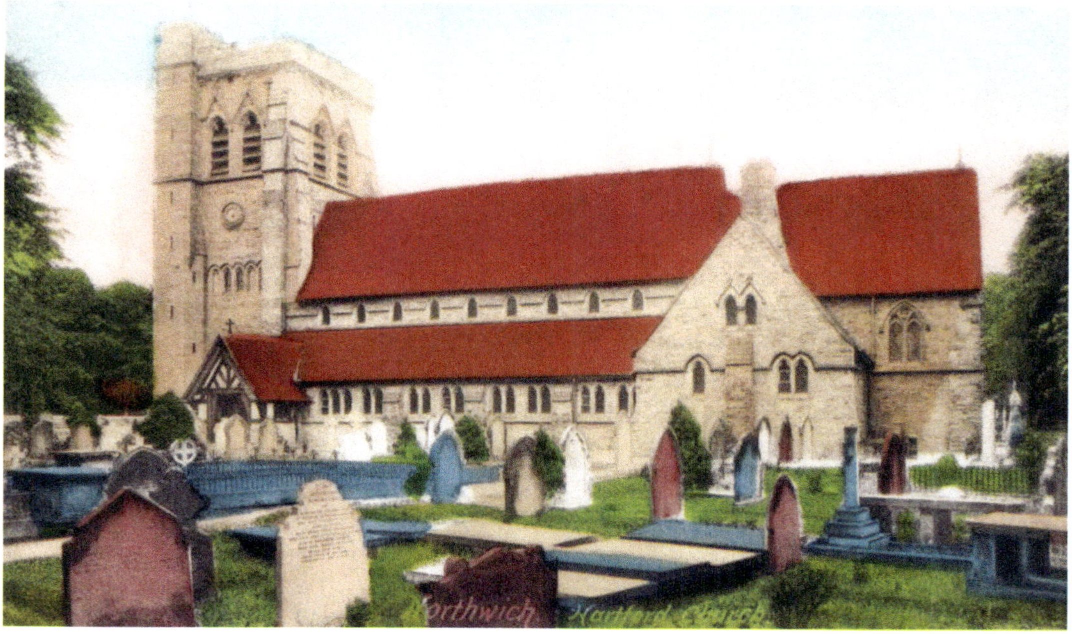

Hartford Church, Early 1900s and 2015

The older photograph enables us to take a closer look at the church of St John the Baptist at Hartford during the early part of the last century when it was quite new. A chapel of ease was built on the site in 1822 after the inhabitants had raised the cash to pay for it and it was consecrated by the Bishop of Chester. The railways soon arrived, bringing a population explosion, which meant a new church was needed. In 1873 the current building was erected on the site, and then in 1887 the tower was built to commemorate Queen Victoria's Golden Jubilee.

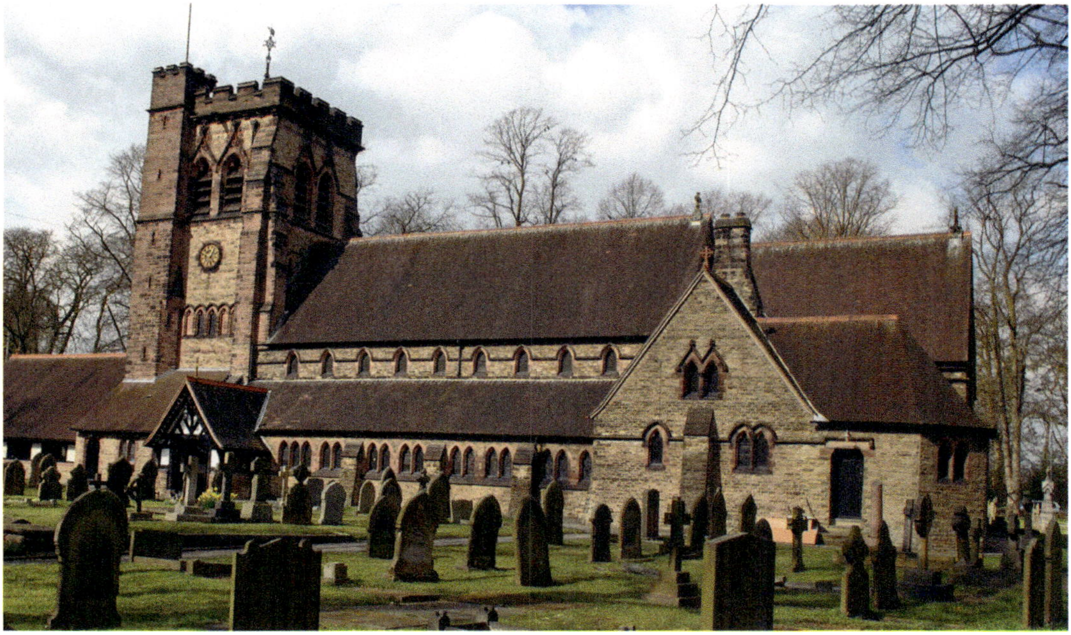

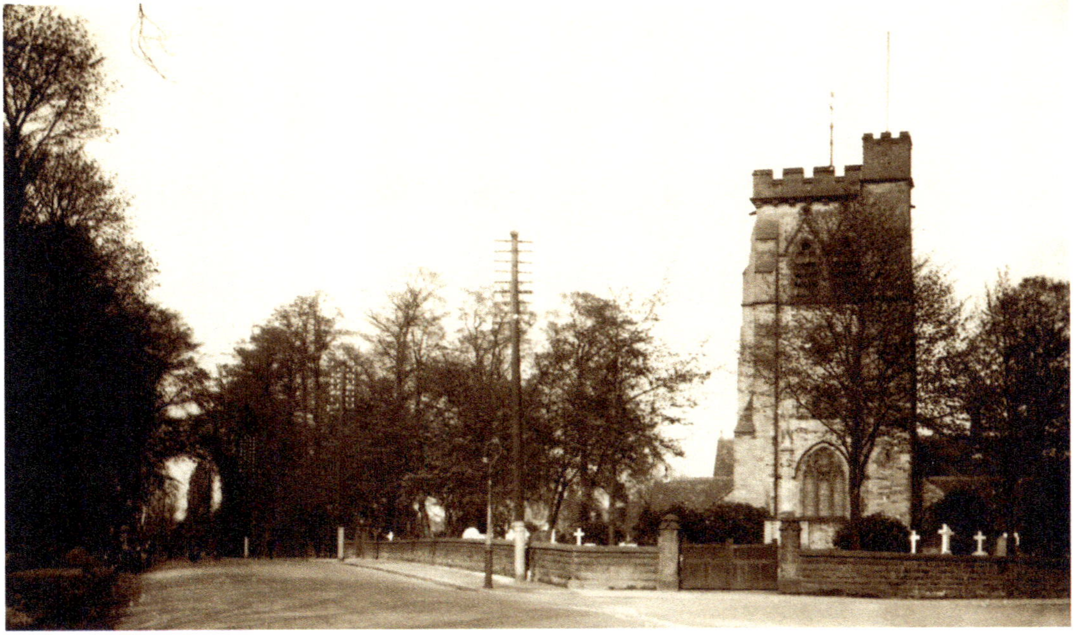

Chester Road, Hartford, Early 1900s and 2015

Another look at this part of Chester Road as it passes the church towards Northwich. Hartford had grown on the back of the London & North Eastern railway at Hartford station and the Cheshire Lines railway at Hartford and Greenbank (now just Greenbank). Large dwellings were built for merchants and North Eastern from Liverpool and Manchester who could live in leafy Cheshire away from the smoggy and crowded cities.

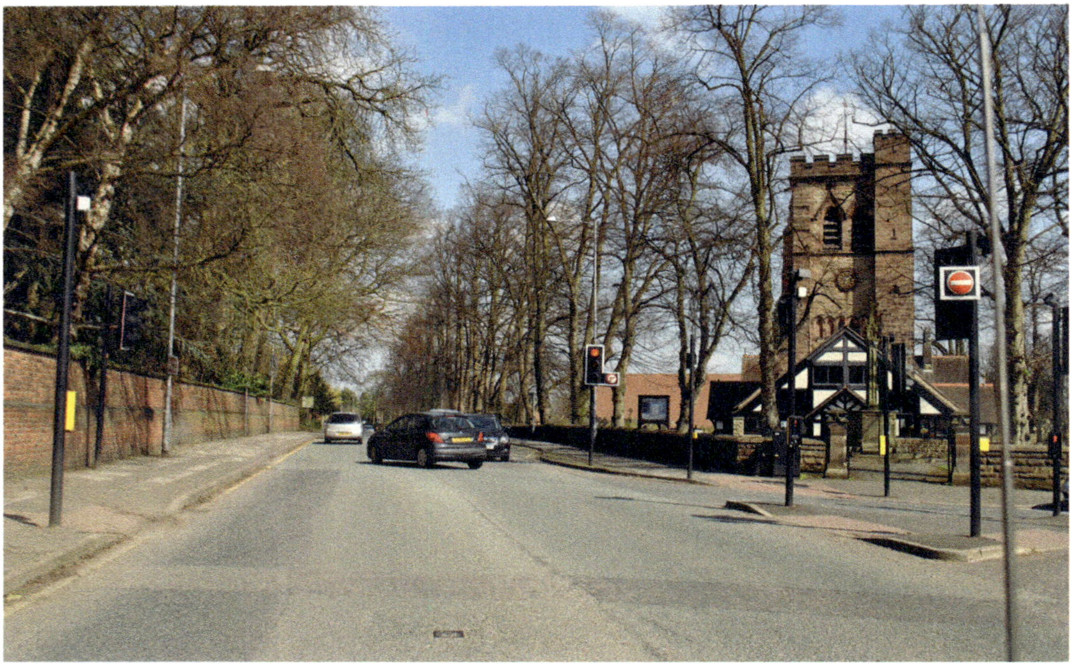

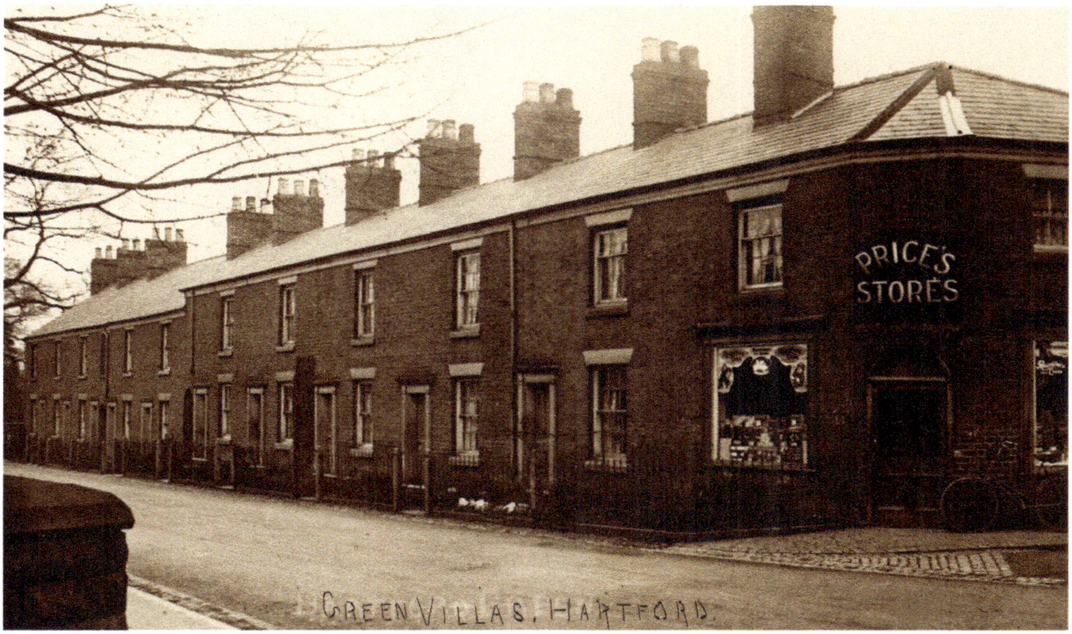

Green Villas, Hartford, 1900-1910 and 2015 with inset.
This is now a one-way street and is situated across from Hartford churchyard. As can be seen, not a lot has changed over the years. Price's general store has made way for a children's shop and the lead flashing has given way to ridge tiles on the corner. The old pedal cycle is a very early one and dates back to the late 1800s when bicycling was a popular means of travel, especially for ladies who enjoyed the freedom it gave them! The road is actually known as The Green and the houses as Green Villas, as can be seen by the inset photo of a wall plaque.

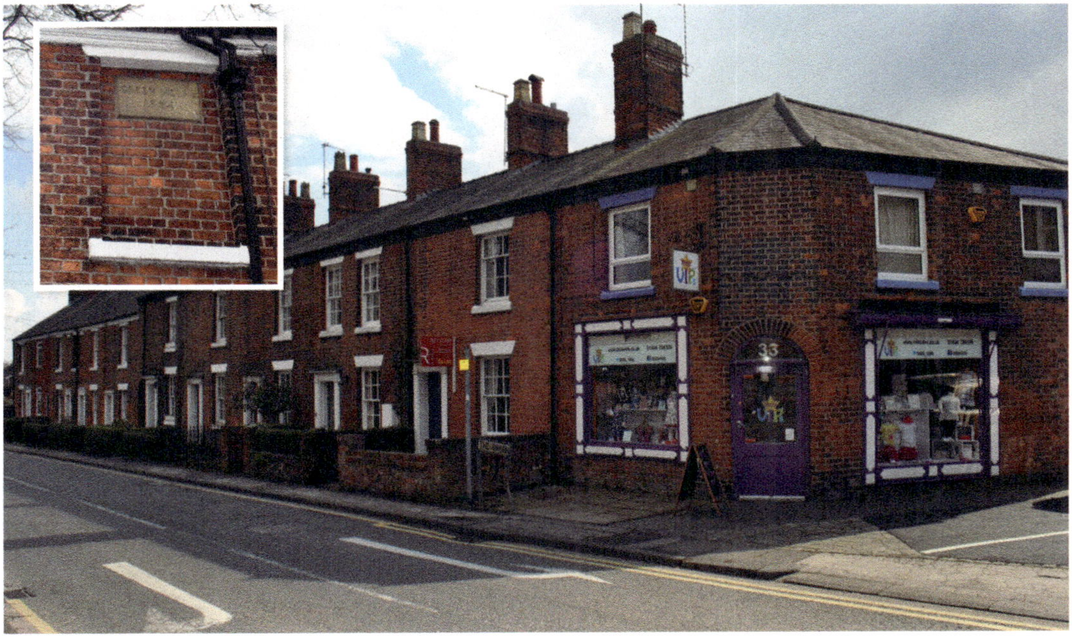

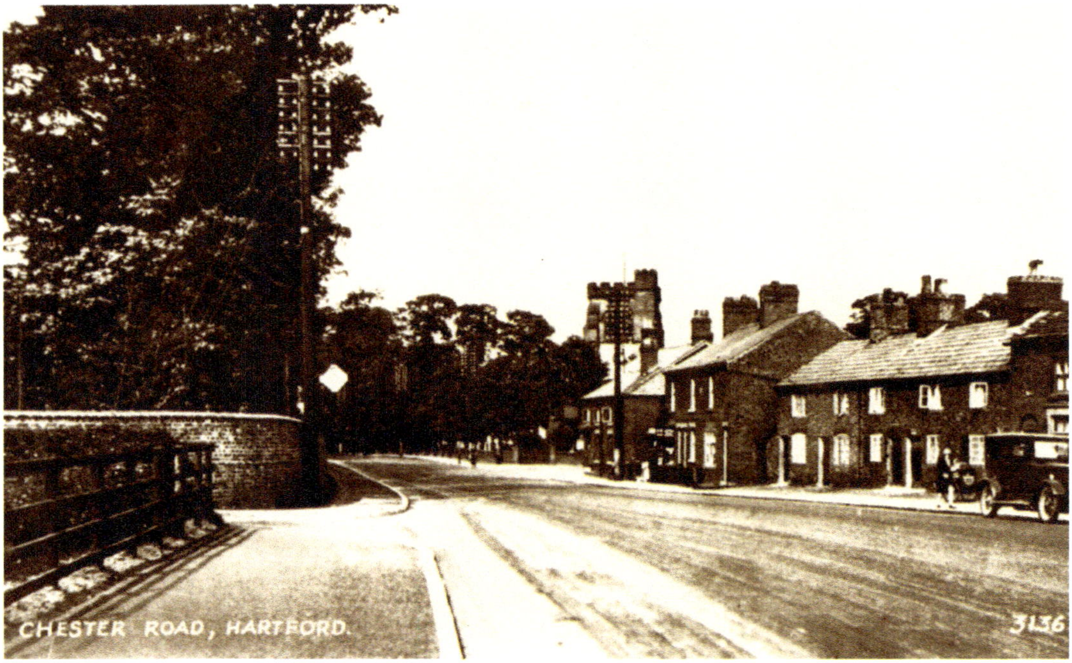

Chester Road, Hartford, 1920s and 2015

Another look at the village from further back with the Red Lion pub at the end on the right. Behind the camera in the 2015 shot, work has started on one of many large housing developments in the area, a development that not all residents of this small affluent village are comfortable with. Note the old car on the right in the old photograph.

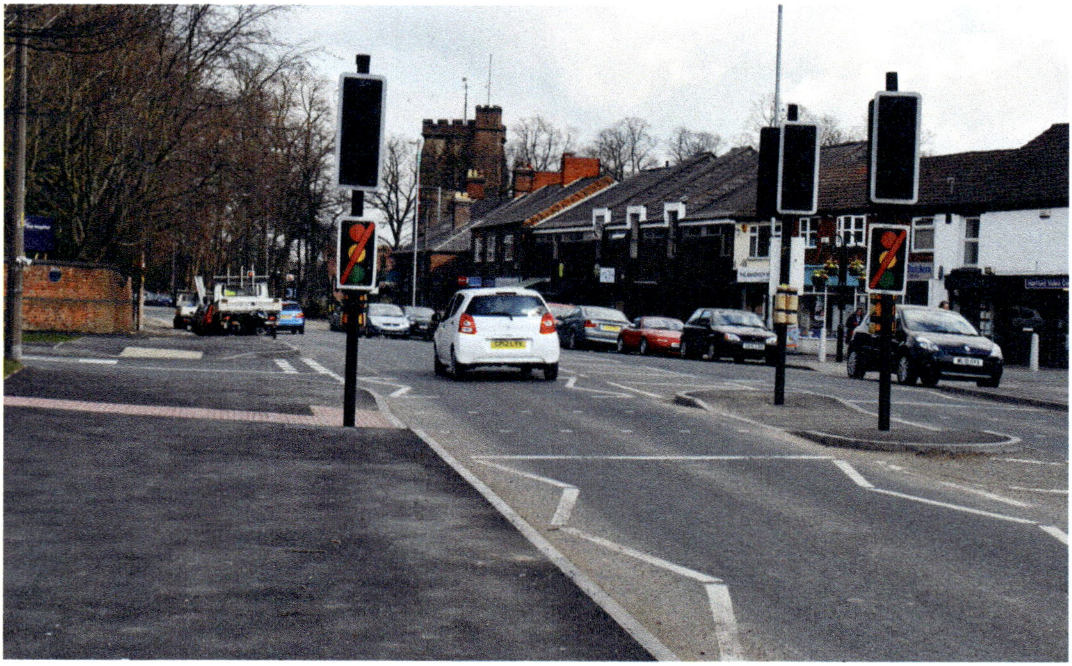

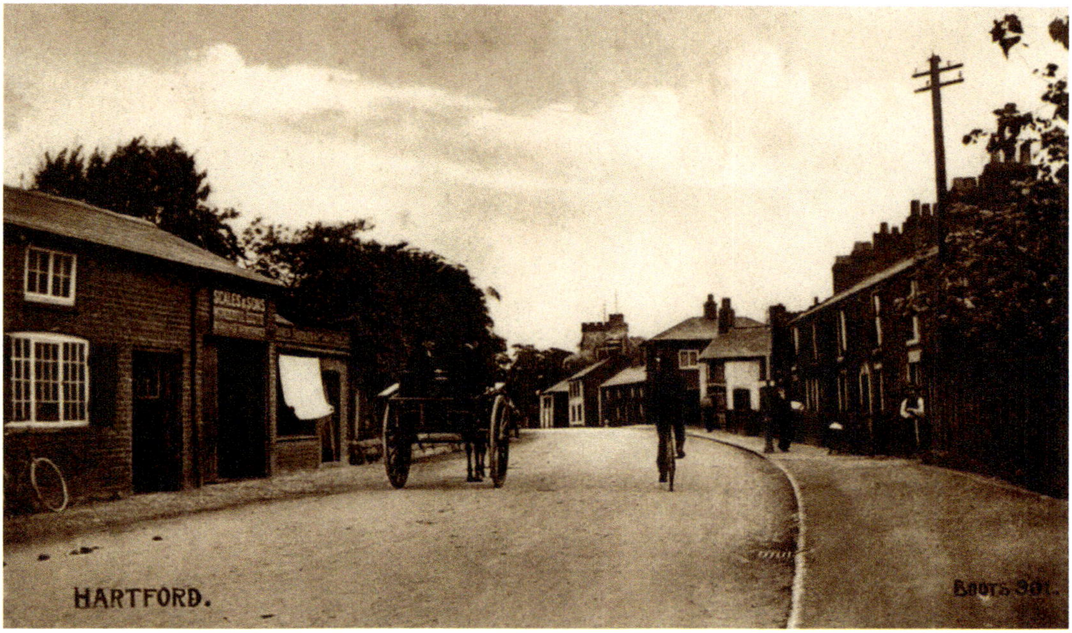

Hartford, 1915 and 2015

A last look at the village from even further back. There are one hundred years between the two photographs; in the old image, a pony and trap with a postman on his bike make up the traffic on what is now a busy road into Northwich. The premises of Scales & Sons are on the left. In the 2015 photograph, the road is wider and the shops are on the right. On the left the house building is ongoing and the road is far busier.

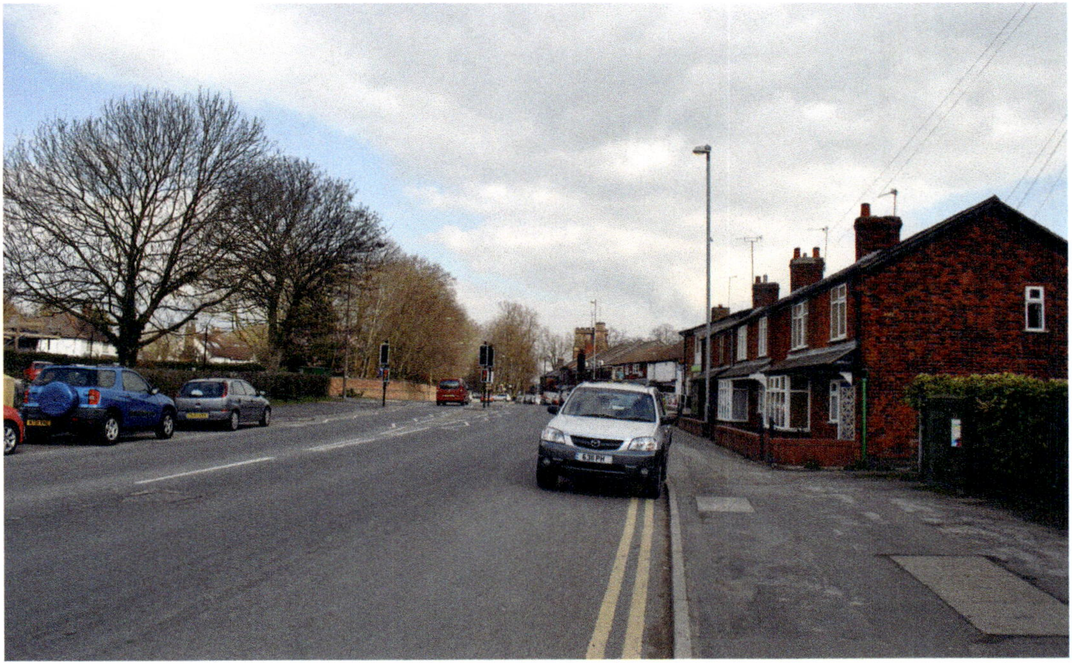

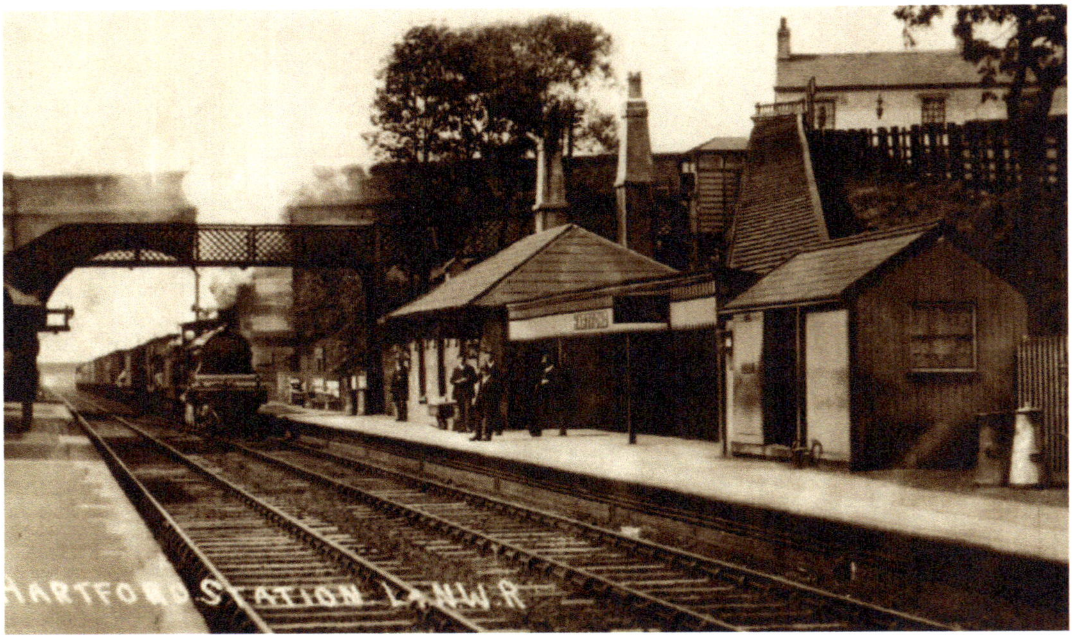

Hartford Station, 1906 and 2015

Built by the Grand Junction Railway, Hartford station was opened in September 1837. It is still a busy line with regular trains to Liverpool and Birmingham. Built in a deep cutting, the path to the main road was once covered, as can as can be seen in the old photograph from 1906. On the other side of the road is the Station Hotel; it had been a beerhouse, which was built after the station as the Hartford Station Inn. It later became the Railway Inn and then the Station Hotel. In 1971 it was renamed The Coachman and reopened in early 2015 after extensive refurbishment.

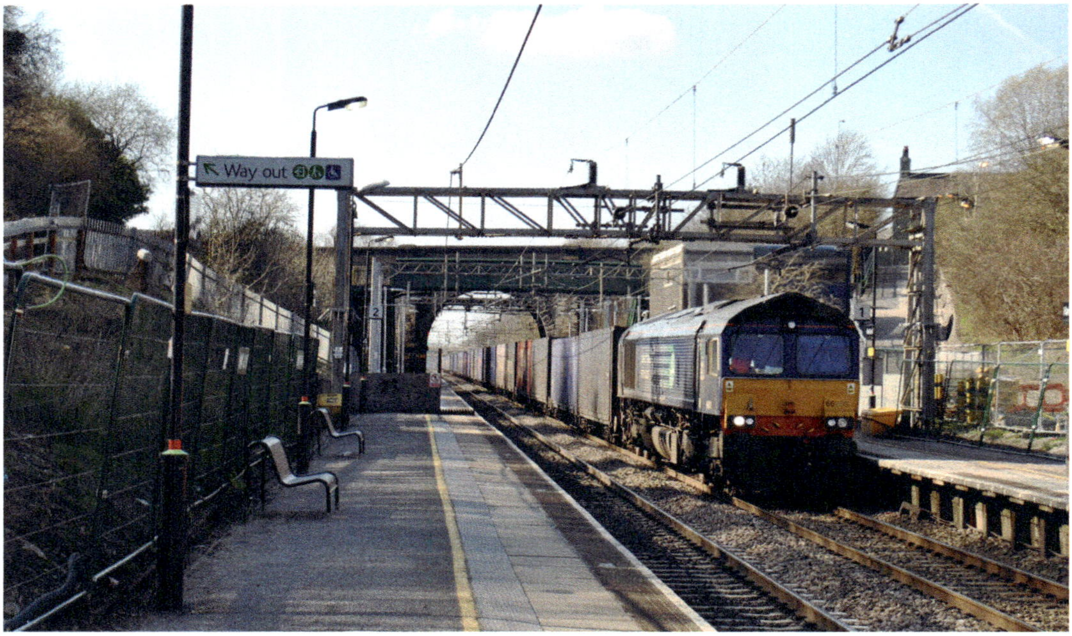

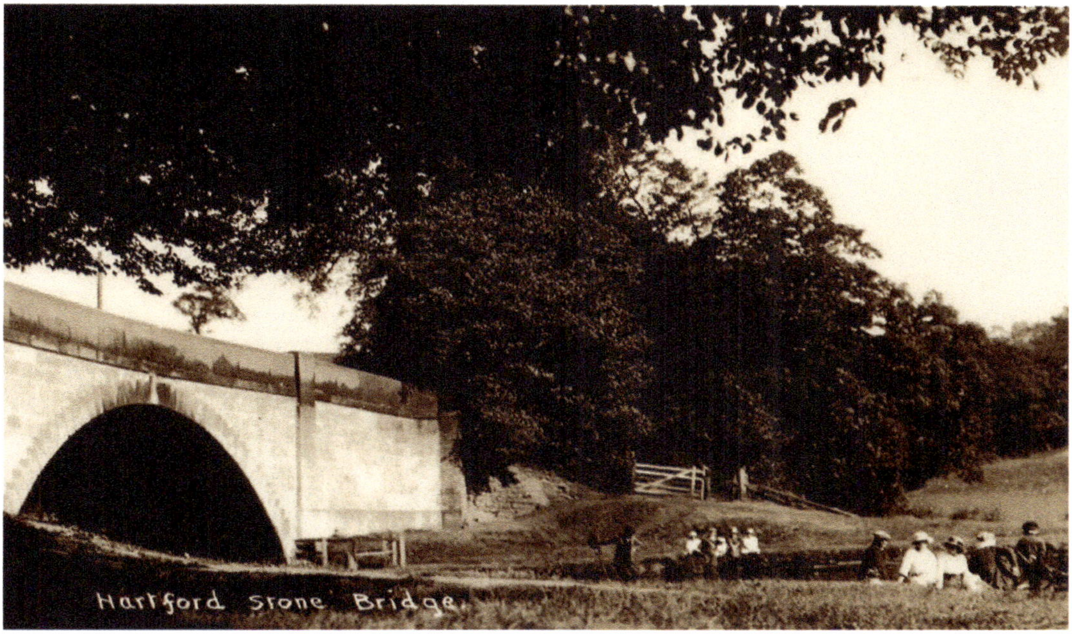

Hartford Stone Bridge, 1920
Looking at the bridge from the banks of the River Weaver we see how things have changed. Having been altered from a pretty stone bridge accommodating little traffic, the steel bridge opened in 1939 as Hartford Bridge; firstly with one carriageway, then another. It carried the Northwich bypass and due to the paint colour it became known as The Blue Bridge. The narrow stone bridge had existed there for many years and can be seen in the old photograph and more clearly in the next set.

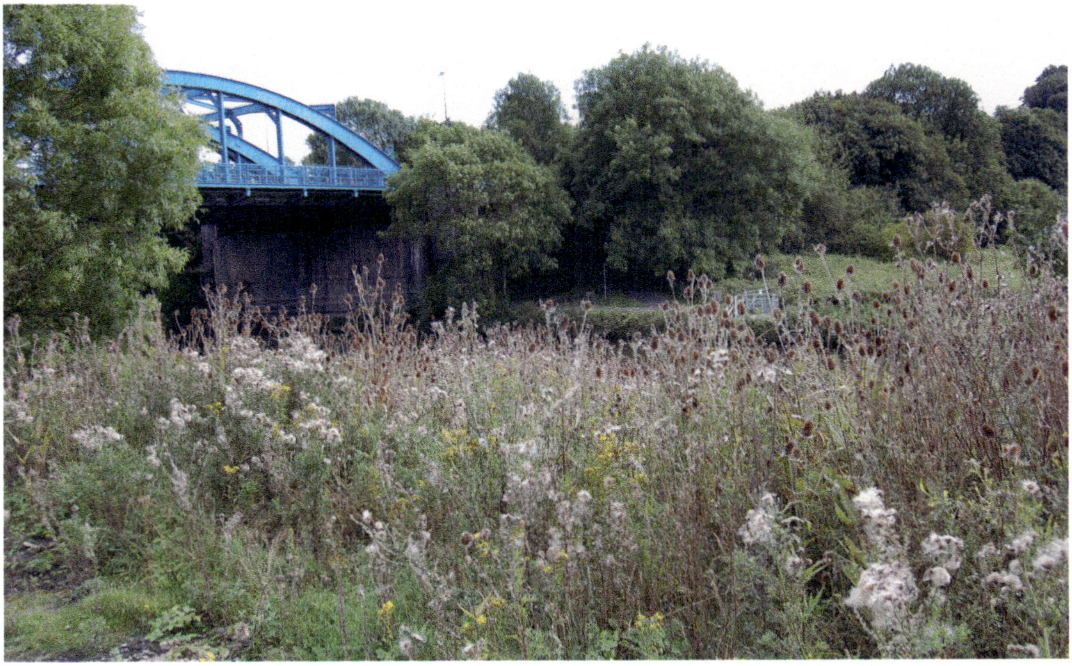

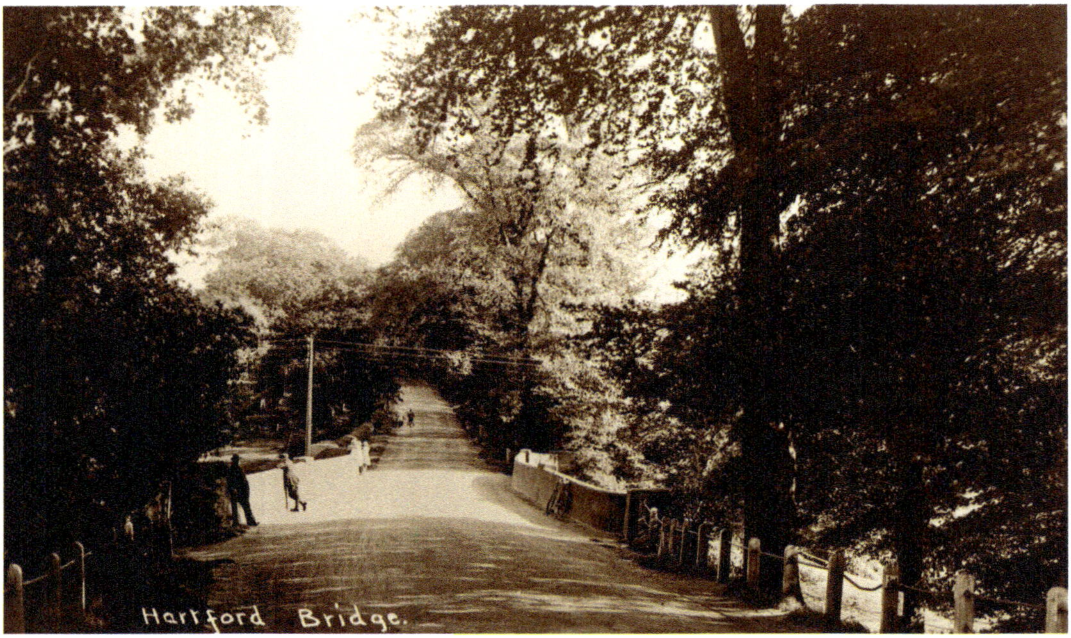

Hartford Bridge, 1900 and 2015

Northwich bypass, or the A556, was built during the 1930s and 1950s; this was a period of building in a similar manner to that undertaken in Germany at the instigation of Adolf Hitler. He provided work for the many unemployed by building autobahns that ran straight and true through Germany. This impressive road, which included a cycle track, ran from Manchester to Chester and is now dual carriageway for a lot of the way.

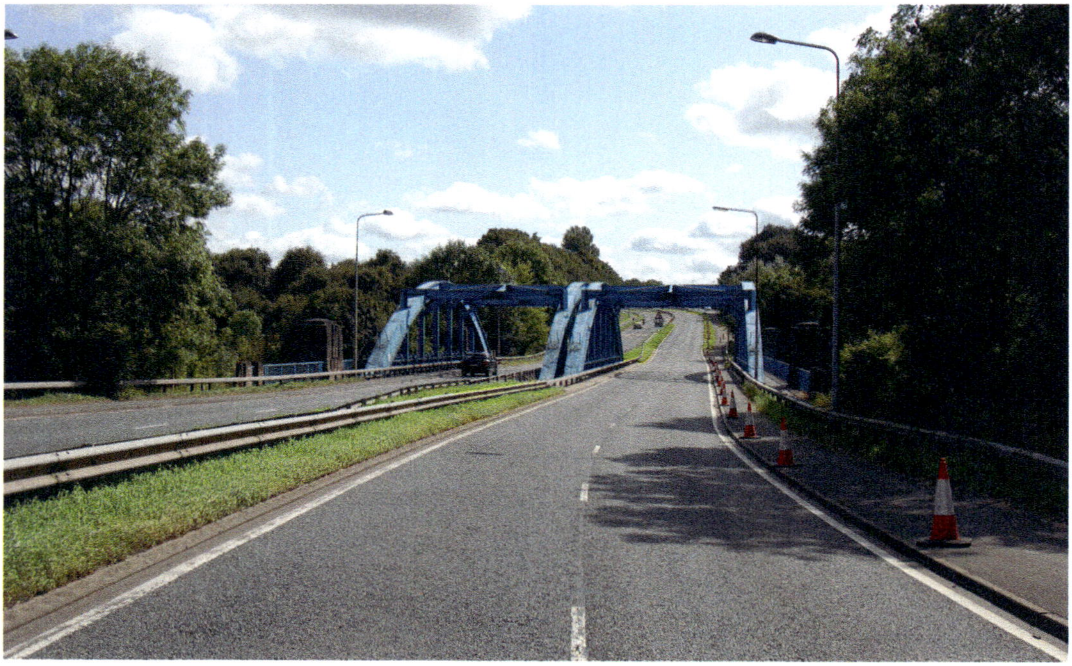

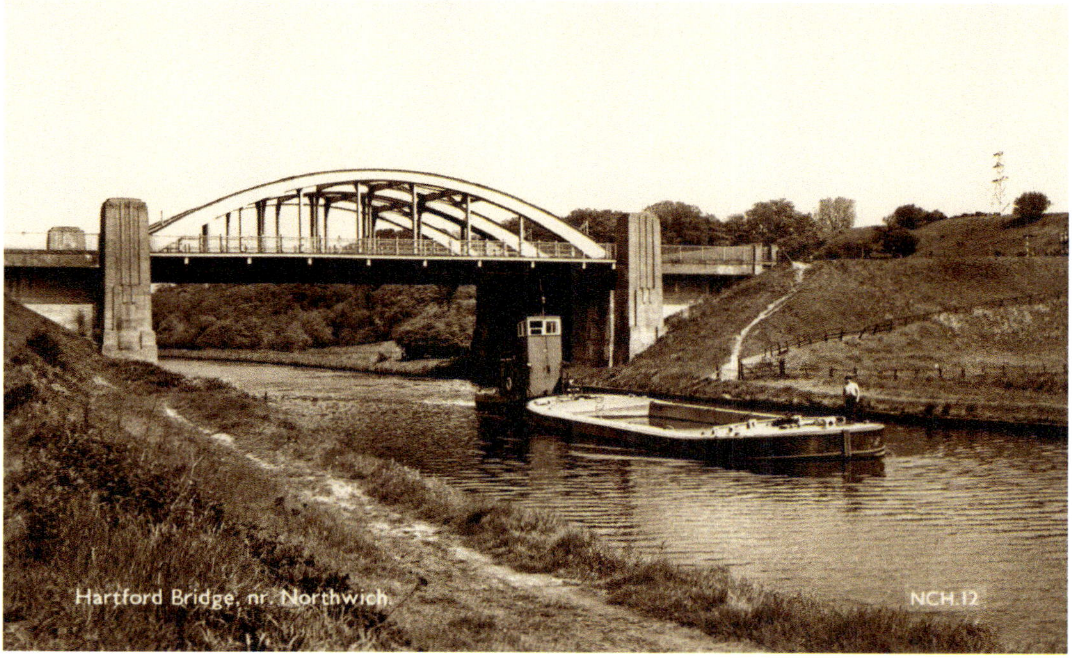

River Weaver, Hartford, 1950s and 2015
A last look at the Blue Bridge over the River Weaver from another angle as a river tug pushes through a dumb barge probably filled with the results of dredging. There is now a very pleasant walking or cycling path that runs alongside the river to Northwich and Winsford.

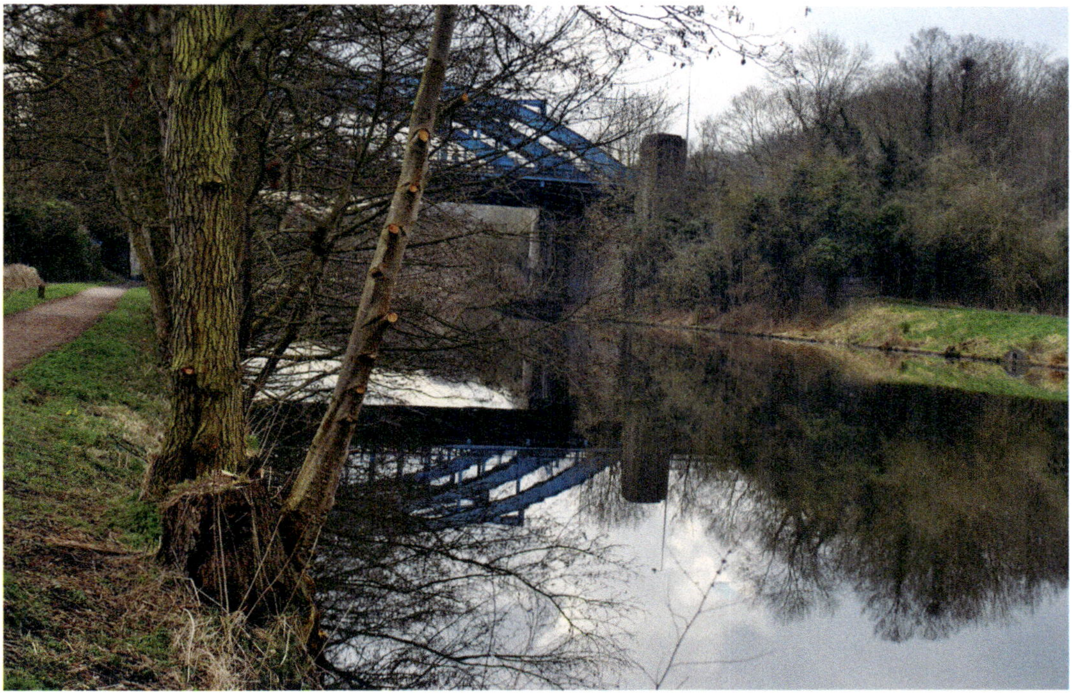

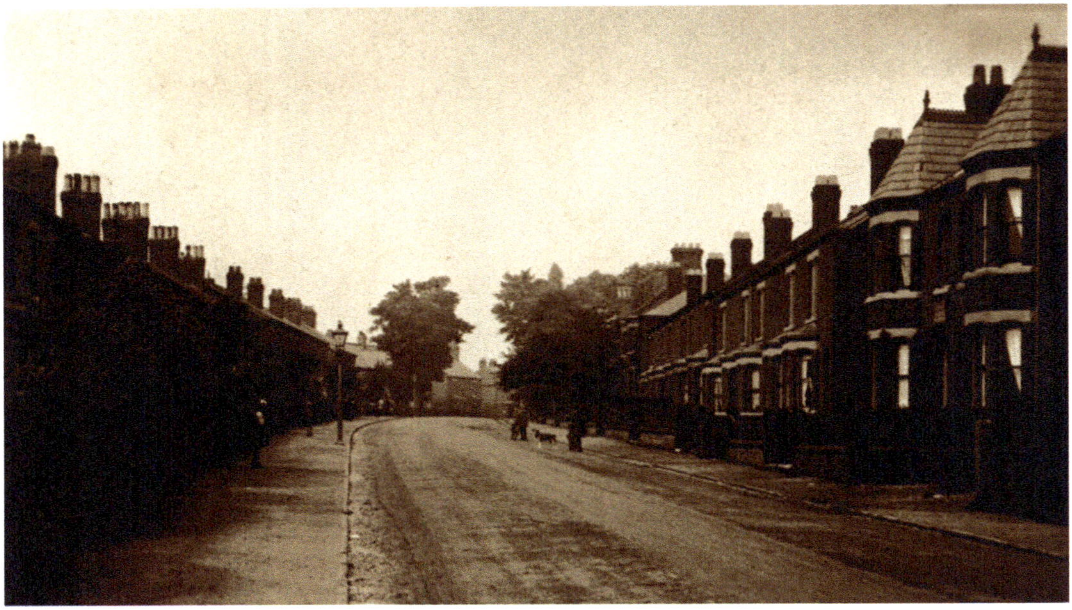

Leftwich Green, 1895 and 2015

Through the centuries, the lords of the manor were the Leftwich family who lived at Leftwich Hall. Little is known about the earliest hall, except that it was demolished and replaced in 1493. Ralph Leftwich emigrated to what was then the New World and the Leftwich family went from strength to strength in the United States. In the two photographs we are on London Road looking towards Northwich. Once again little has changed in the intervening hundred plus years. The two bay-windowed houses are in the foreground. Leftwich Green was expanded greatly after the war with the building of a large council estate. The area is better known as simply Leftwich and once covered a wide area from Davenham church to Northwich.

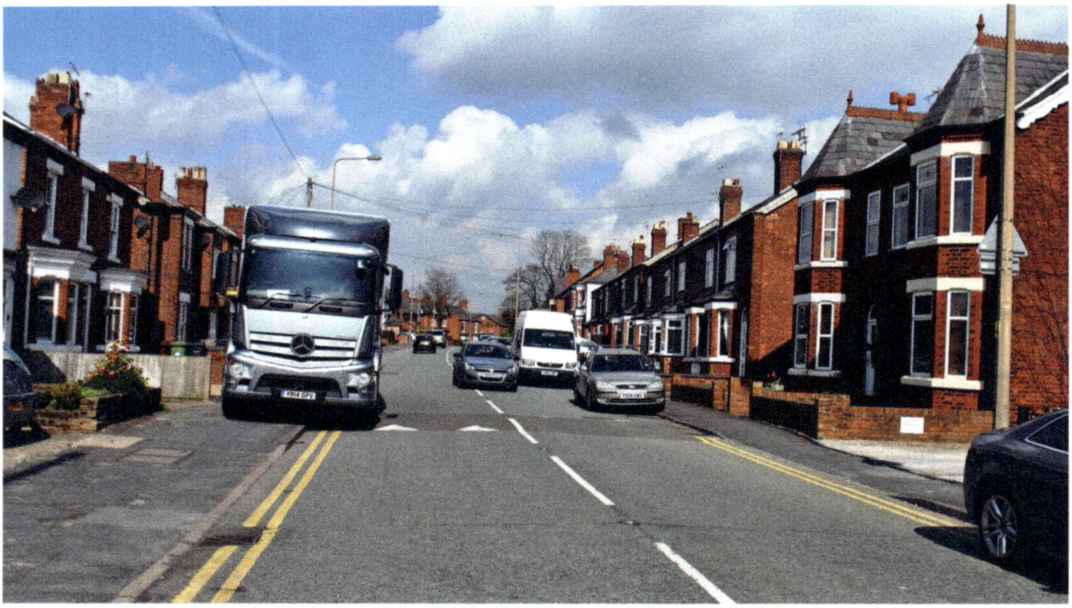

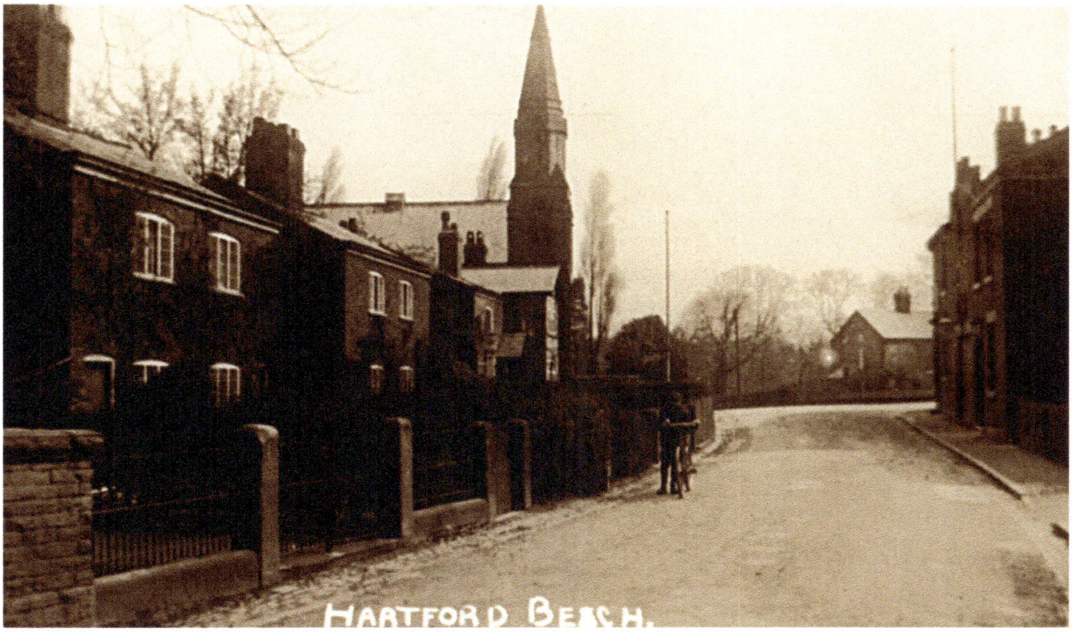

Beach Road, Hartford, 1910 and 2015

Thomas Horatio Marshall Esq. once lived at a house near here called Hartford Beach, 'a handsome residence' according to White's directory of 1860. It was built in 1802 and still exists having been split into two houses. Beach Road is an unusual road name for landlocked Mid-Cheshire. The Marshall families were members of Cheshire's Landed Gentry, local benefactors and salt mine proprietors. The name Marshall is now prevalent throughout the district.

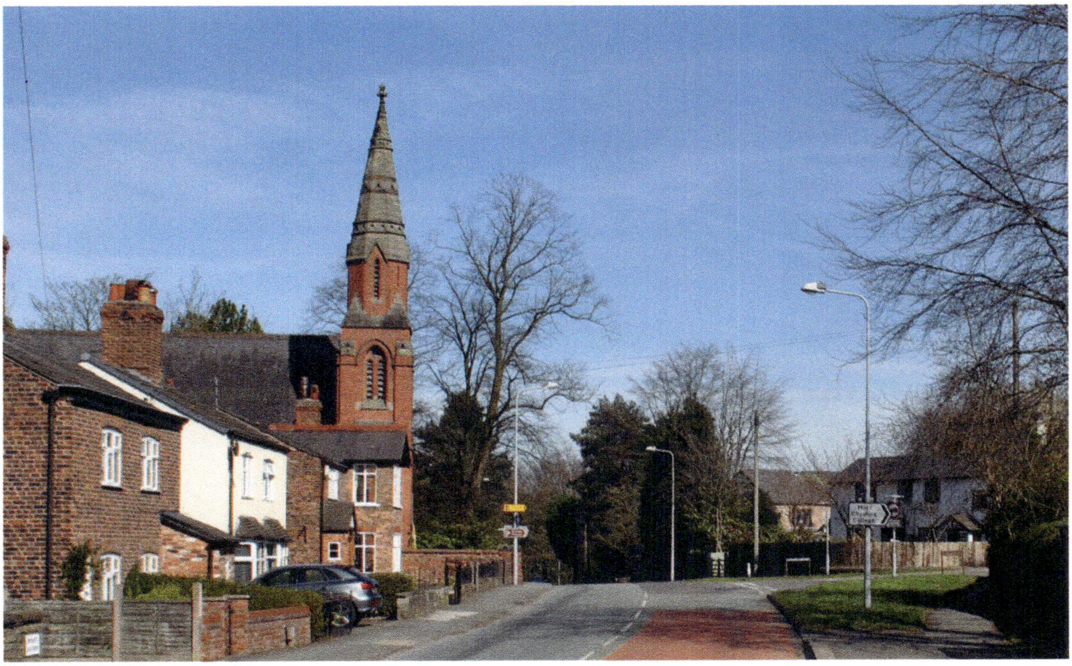

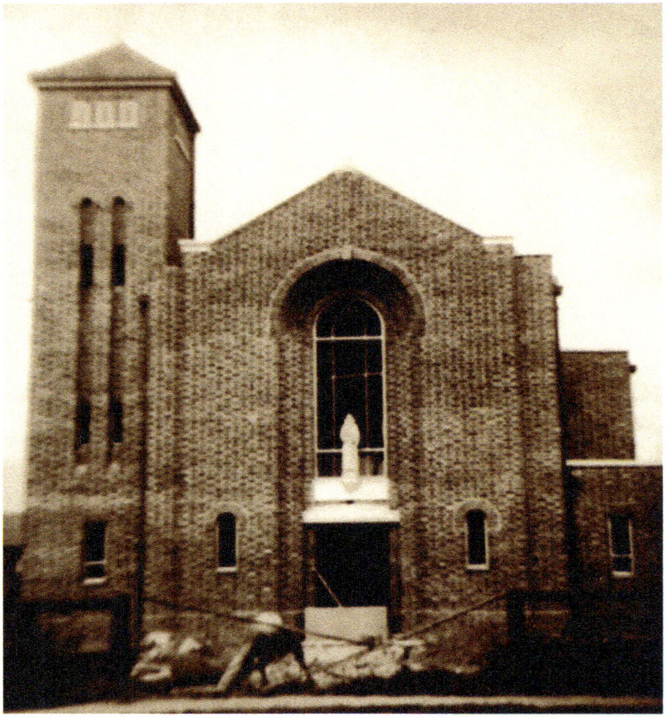

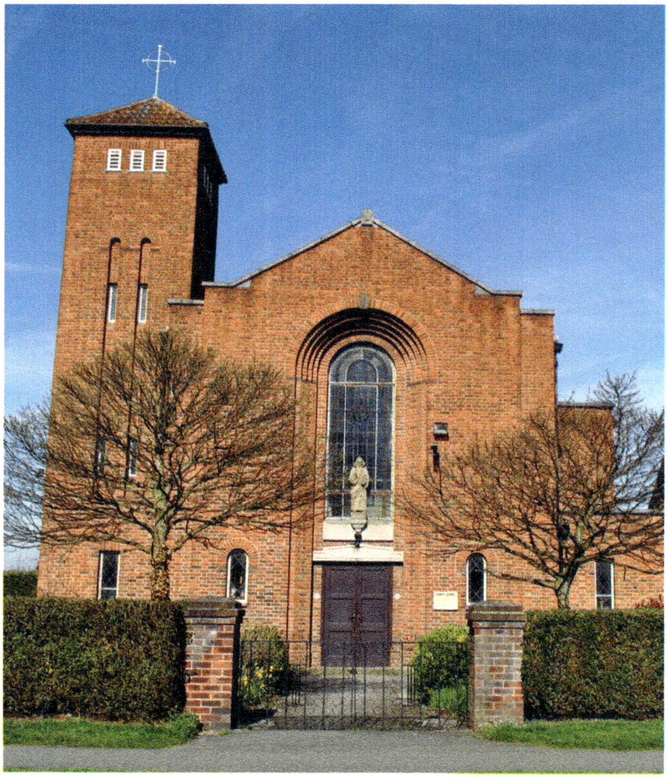

St Bedes Catholic Church, Weaverham, early 1950s and 2015

After the Second World War the population of Weaverham exploded with people from Liverpool and Manchester moving to the village, mainly to work at the ICI works. Many Catholics were included in this influx and it was time to build a church for them in Weaverham and a smaller one in Barnton called Our Lady of Fatima. Fr Leo Holleron arrived and in 1950 the parish was formed with the church and presbytery opening a few years later. The old photo here was taken when the church was being built and the 2015 shot shows the church as it is today.

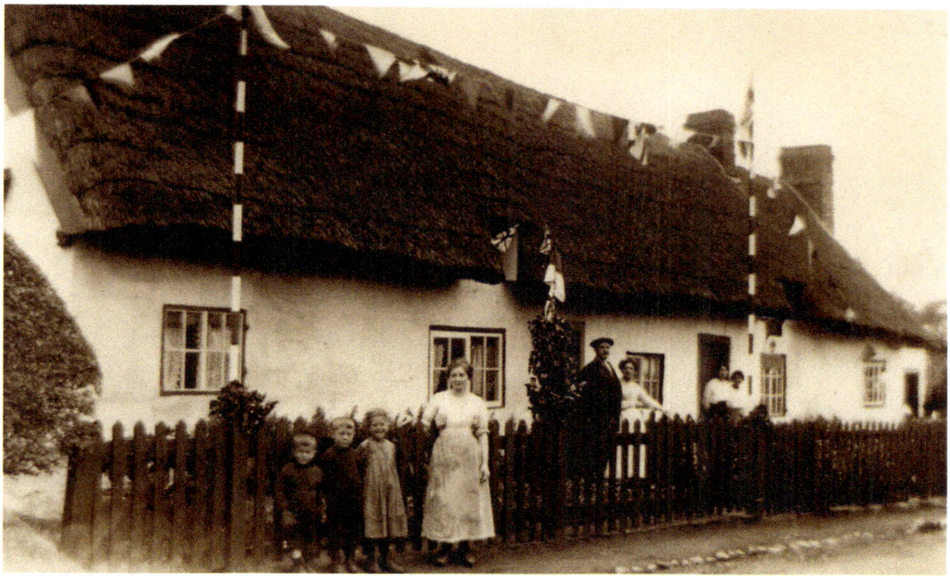

Old Cottage, Forest Street, Weaverham, 1920s and 1919

We will now look at an interesting series of photographs that illustrate the life of an ancient Weaverham cottage. It is believed that this cottage existed from between 1590 and 1630 and is on the first map of Weaverham dated 1660. Until 1870 the building housed four dwellings, probably built for farm workers and in that year it was converted to two. In these two photographs we see the cottage in 1919 taken on Peace Day, when the village celebrated what was then thought to be a lasting peace, after the horrors of the First World War. In the photograph, the extended Johnson family can be seen standing proudly beneath the bunting. Little did they know that there would not be a lasting peace and in the next conflagration just twenty years later, the fabric of the cottage would suffer! In the 1920s a simple view looking towards the old grammar school.

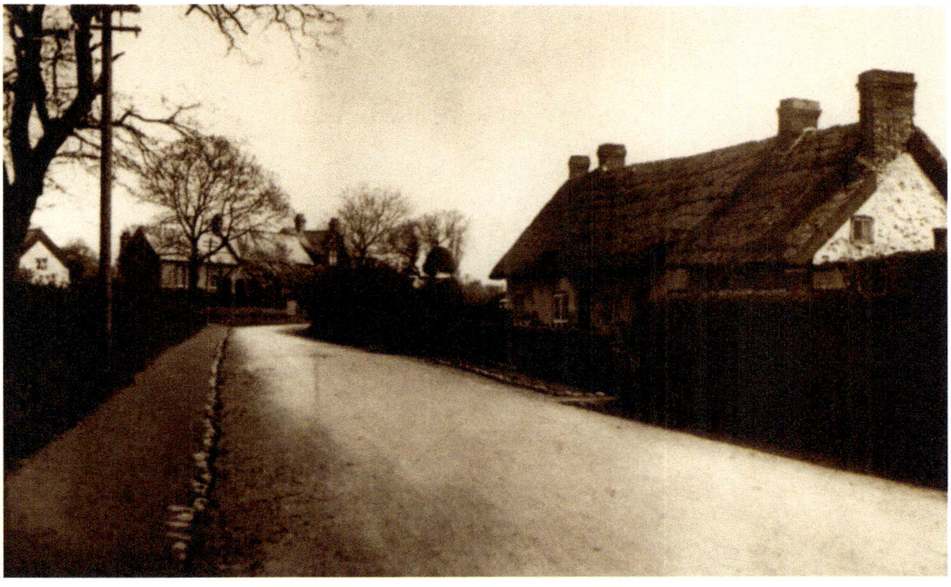

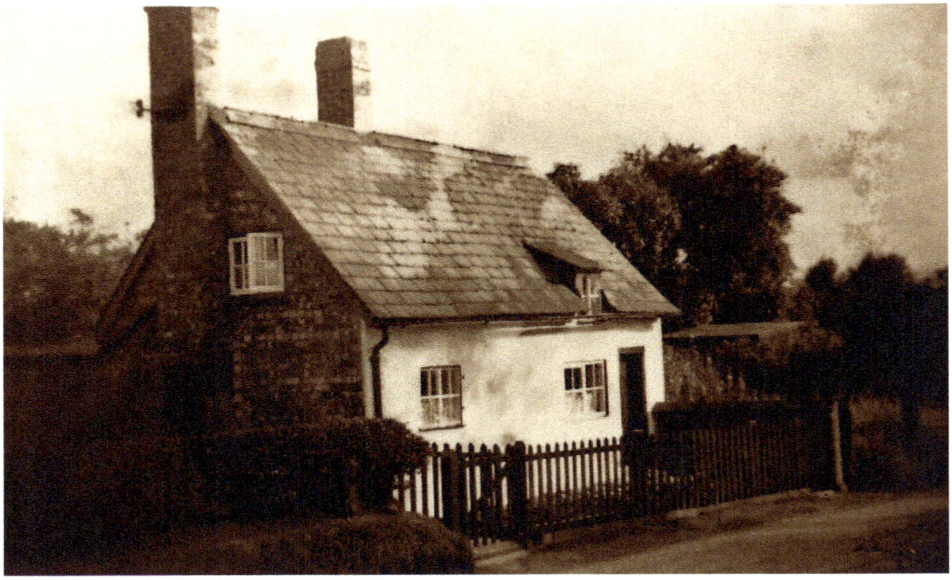

Weaverham Cottage, 1950s and 2015

The building is smaller now and the war is over. In the course of that war cousins lived in the cottage and took in children evacuated from Liverpool. The children managed to set fire to the thatched roof causing damage and then the Germans made it worse! They were aiming to blow up the railway viaduct at Dutton in 1940 when a landmine was inadvertently dropped on Nook Farm nearby. That was in the area that now houses the roundabout on the Weaverham bypass. The end of the cottage was so badly damaged that it had to be demolished. Hence the sad building in the old photo, which had to be refurbished, rebuilt and extended at the rear. The very pretty cottage in the modern photographs is the result, and at the time of writing it is for sale.

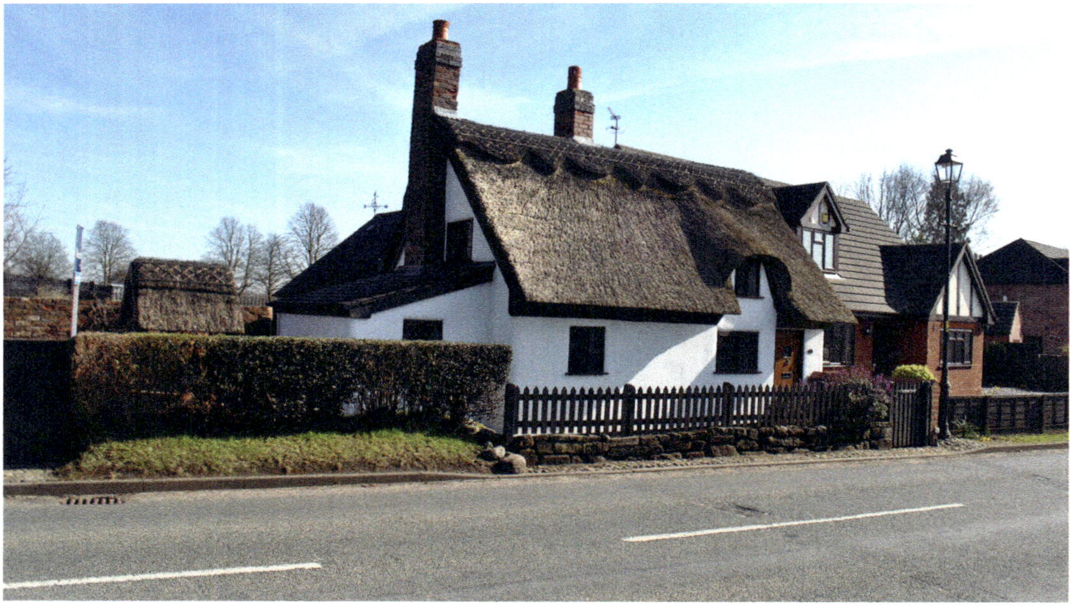

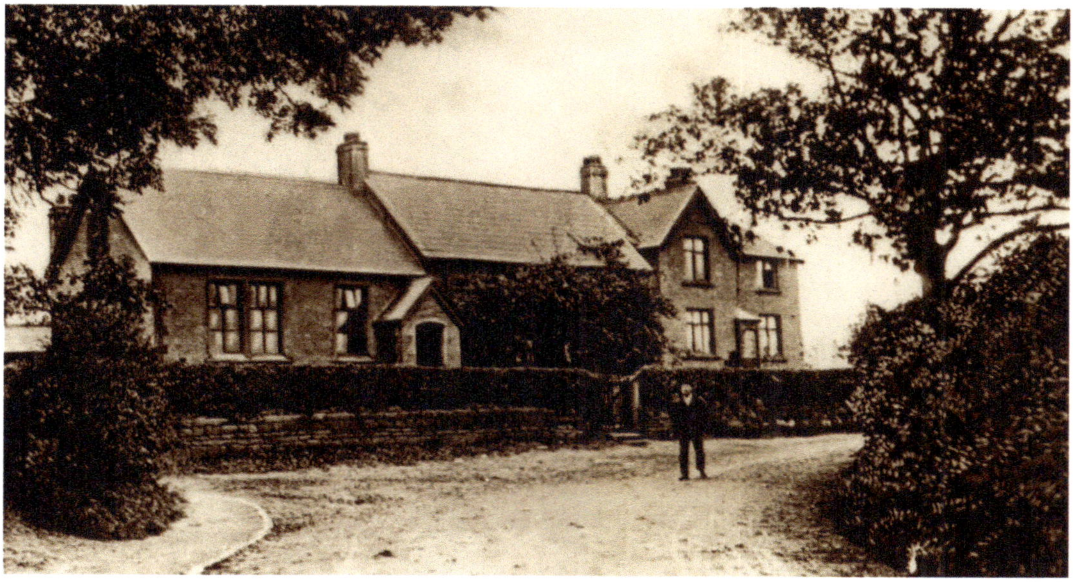

Weaverham Free Grammar School, 1905 and 2015

Just past the cottage towards Weaverham village in Forest Street is the old grammar school building, once the abbot of Vale Royal's courthouse. It was damaged by Royalists during the English Civil War and is now a dwelling house. The school was founded in 1638 but the stone building may be older. Some say that this (not Raintub Cottage) may be the oldest house in the village. For two hundred years prior to the Dissolution, the abbots of Vale Royal ruled Weaverham. When the building was a courthouse, offenders were taken across the road to Gibbet Hill (now the High School playing field). The school closed in 1916 having been a grammar school for hundreds of years, catering for the children of farmers in the area. A bit further on is a house that was once Weaverham police station.

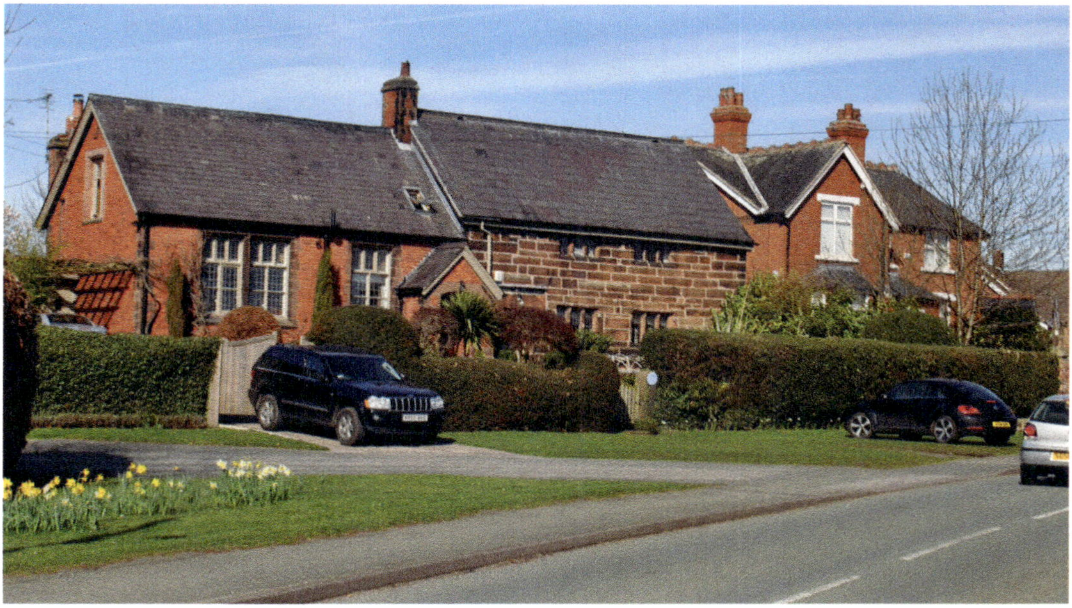

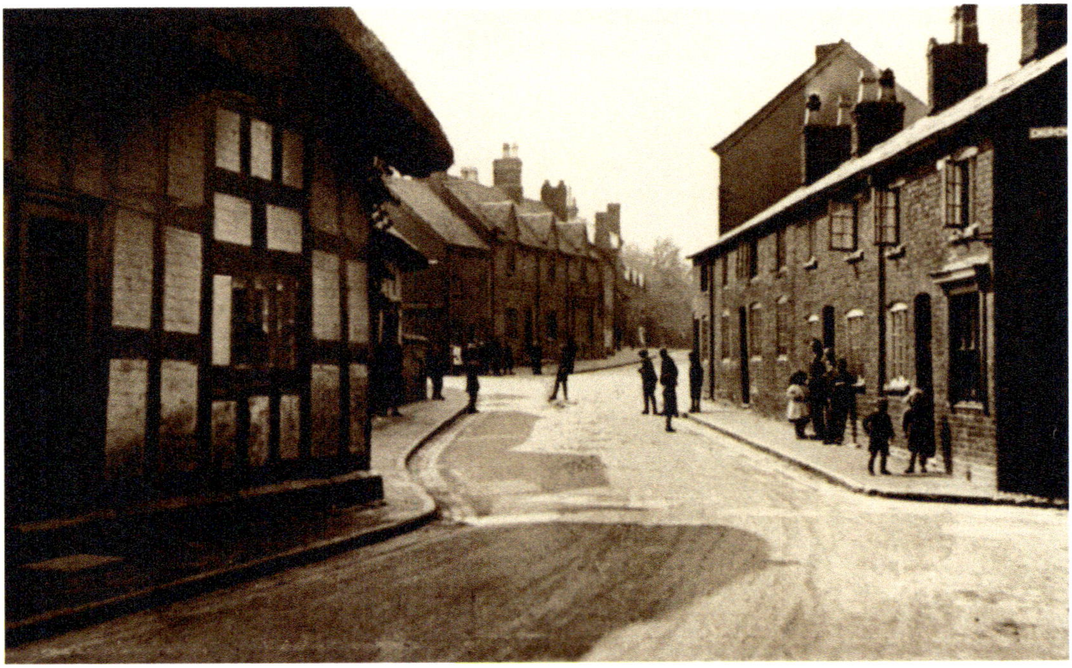

High Street, 1900 and 2015

In this, the first of the photographs of Weaverham High Street, we look into the old village from the Northwich direction and see people walking around in the roadway. In the 2015 photo the row of cottages on the right has gone, leaving open land to the Wheatsheaf pub. Other than this, there is little in the way of change over the intervening years.

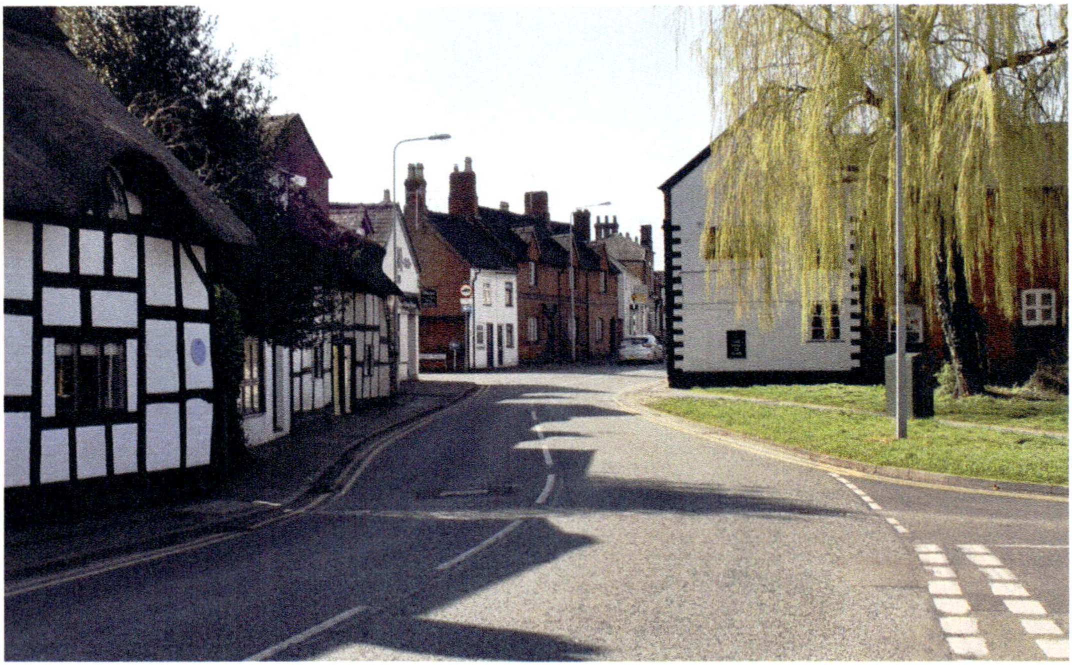

Weaverham fire, 1950s and 2015

The old photo of the fire was given to me some time ago because one of the children shown is me! I don't know which one I am, but I was there watching the firemen fighting the fire in the thatched roof. The building was next door to the Wheatsheaf and housed a cabinet maker's business, Mr J. Burns being the proprietor. It is now two houses and has been beautifully restored. The building on the extreme left is 14-16 High Street, also two houses; it was once the Rifleman pub.

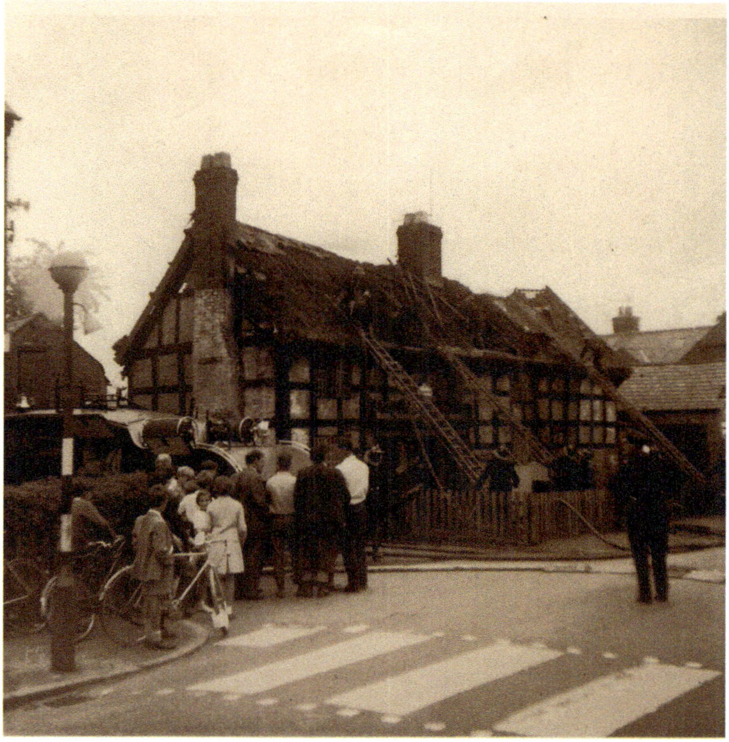

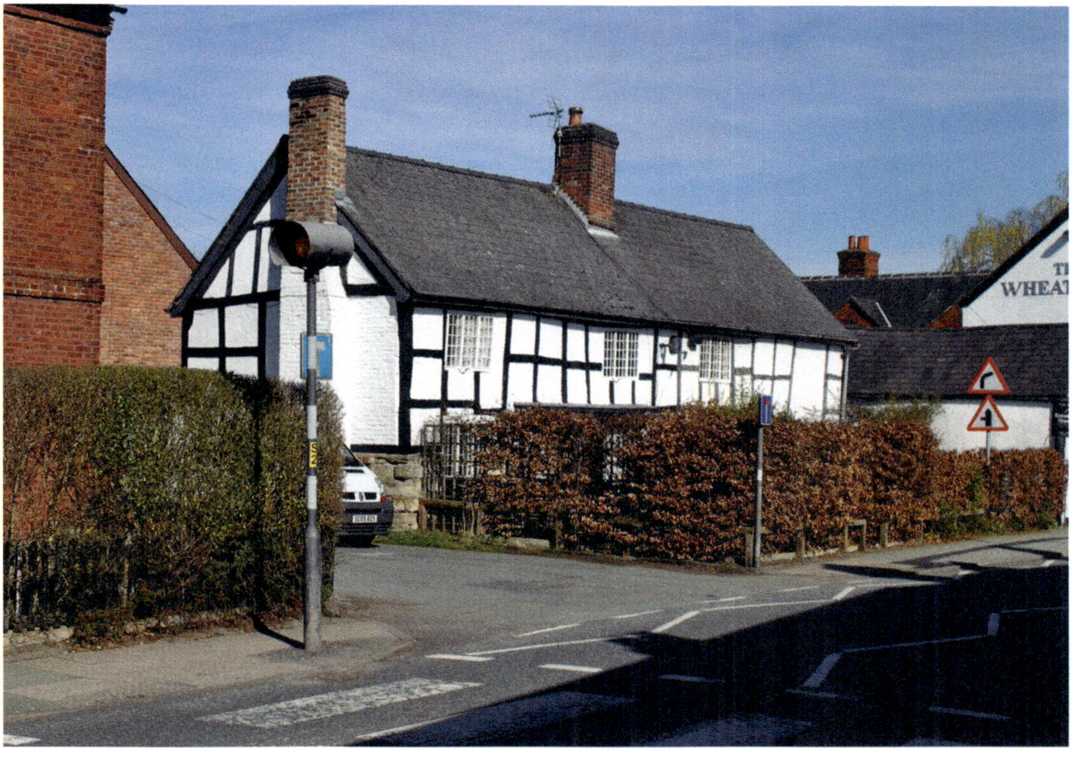

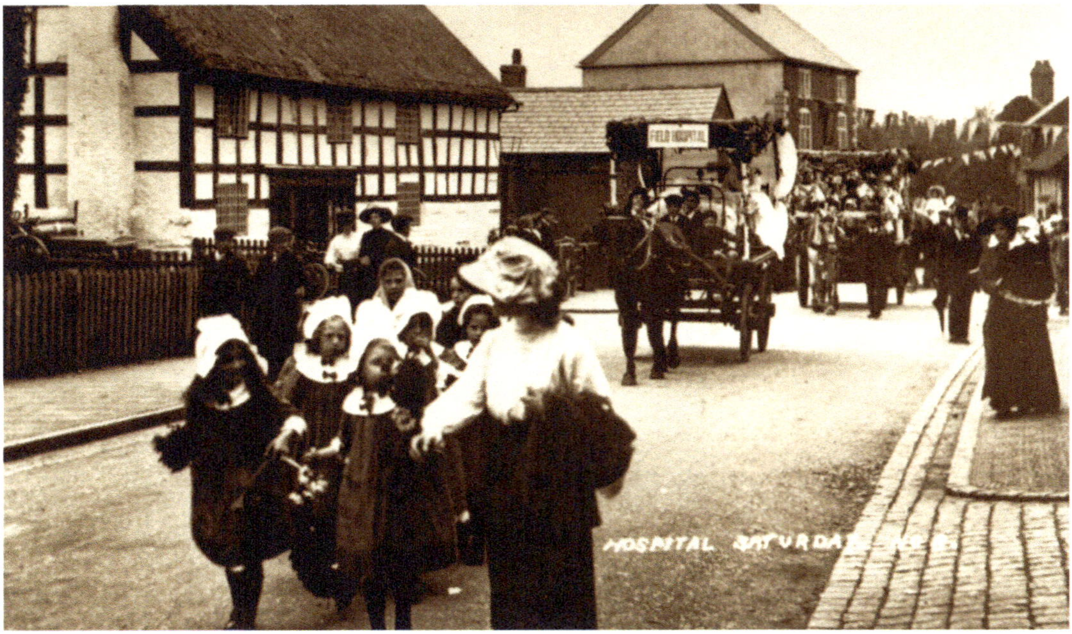

Hospital Saturday procession, 1910–1920 and 2015

Another look at the old black-and-white building. The old photograph will have been taken in the early 1900s when the building housed William Phipps, painter and plumber. The procession is in aid of Northwich Infirmary and is titled Hospital Saturday. This dates the photograph from before 1927 when it became known as the Weaverham Rose Festival, later Rose Fête. The first float depicts a Field Hospital from the first war. What a pretty picture the modern one is with the gleaming white paint and exposed beams.

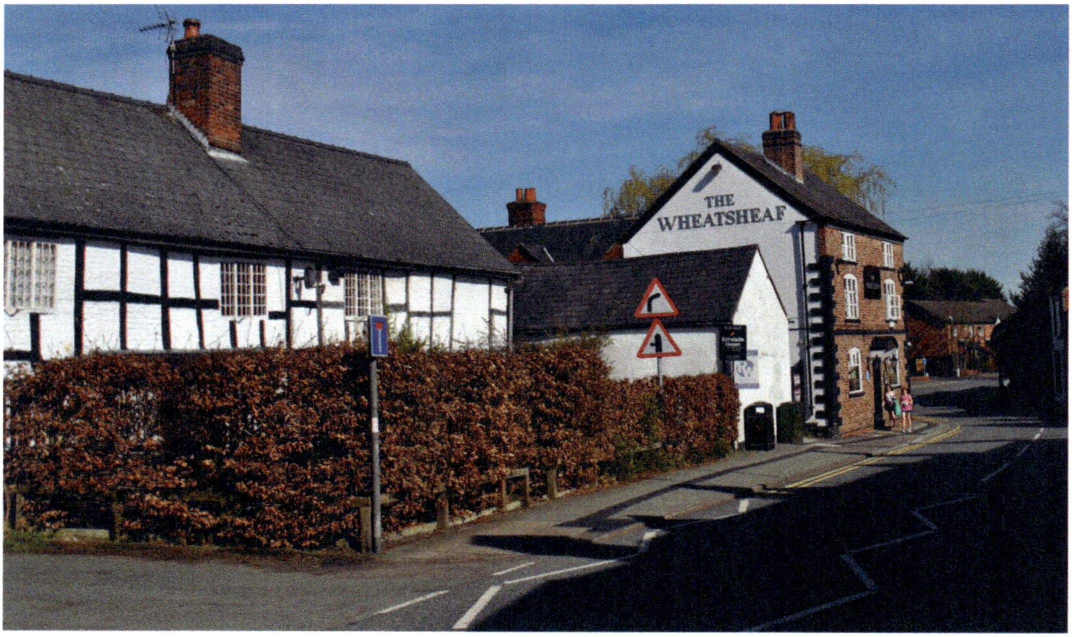

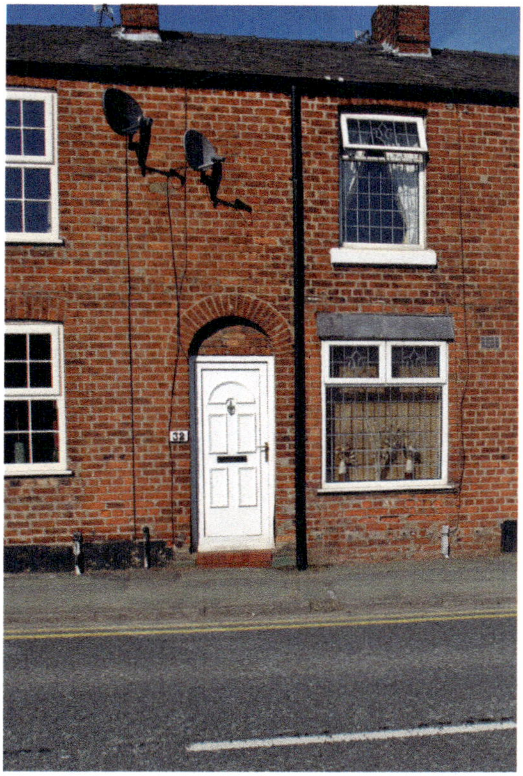

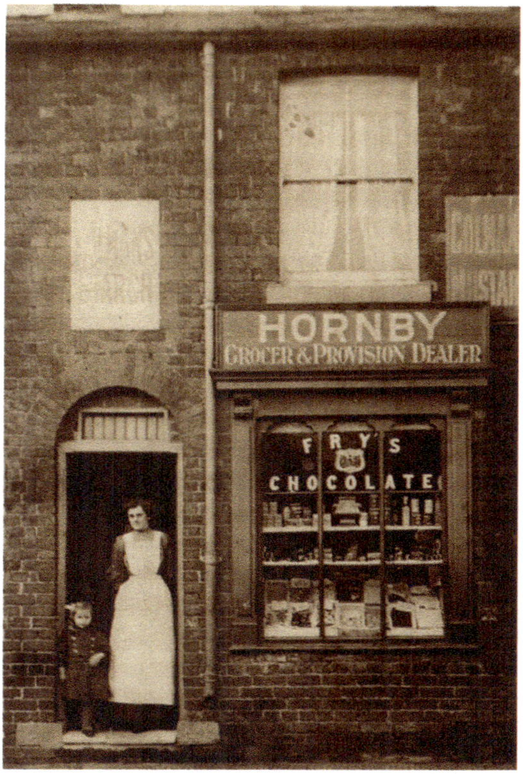

Grandma Hornby, 1920s and 2015

The chairman of the Weaverham Historical Society is Mike Hornby. Mike's family has lived in the village for generations, and the lady in the photograph is his grandmother. The shop was situated at No. 32 High Street and owned by Bill Hornby; by 1928 they had relocated to a larger shop on the other side of the High Street at No. 21.

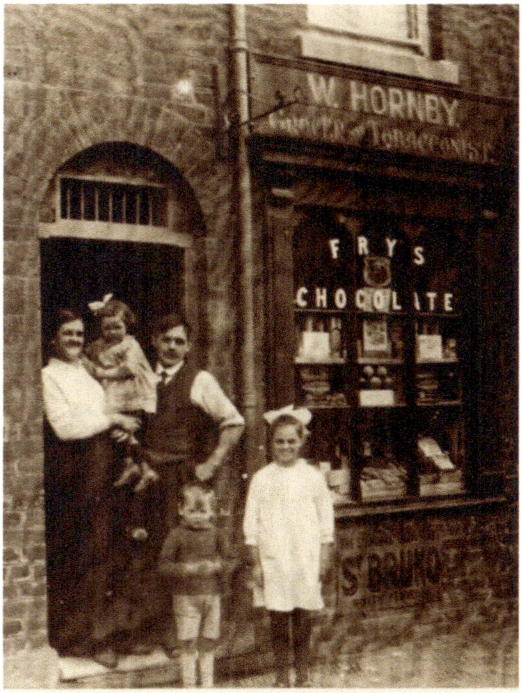

Hornby family and shop, High Street

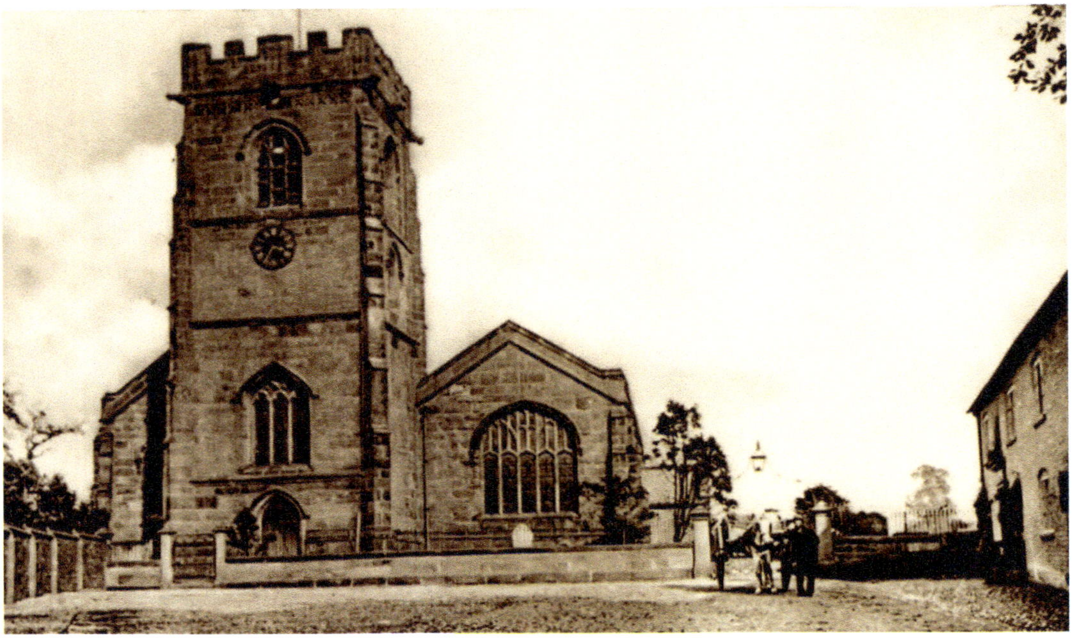

Weaverham church, 1903 and 2015

The parish church of St Mary the Virgin is situated at the end of Church Street and dates to the fifteenth and sixteenth centuries. The building on the right in the old photograph is the Ring o' Bells pub, as it was named in the early 1800s. It then became Church Stile and Church Gates before reverting to the Ring o' Bells. In 1924 the licence was removed and a new and larger Ring o' Bells was built in the village. The old pub building was demolished to make way for the car park.

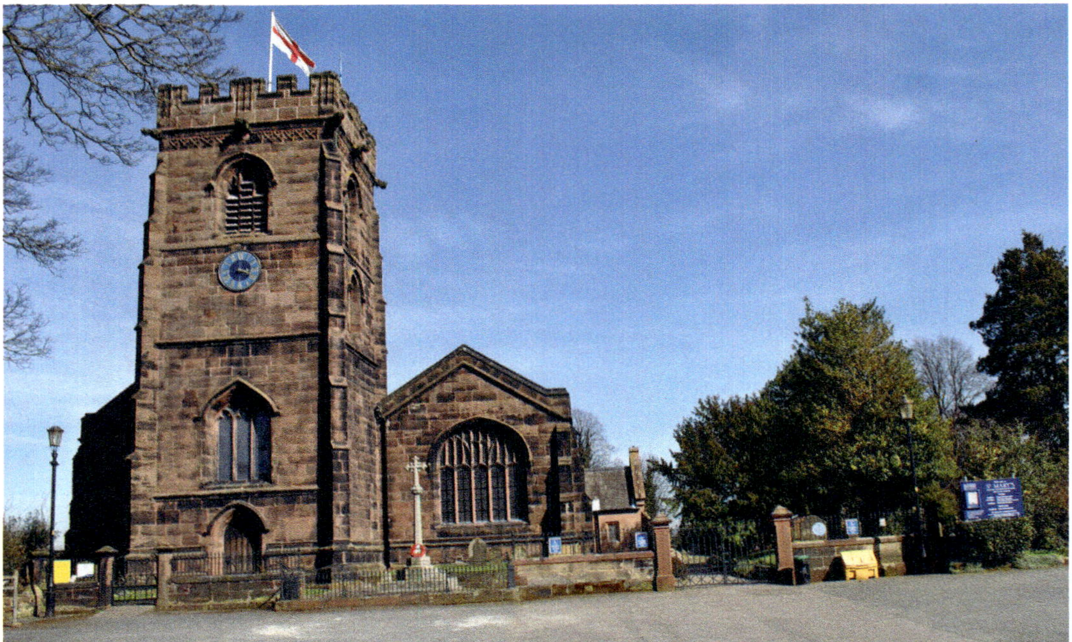

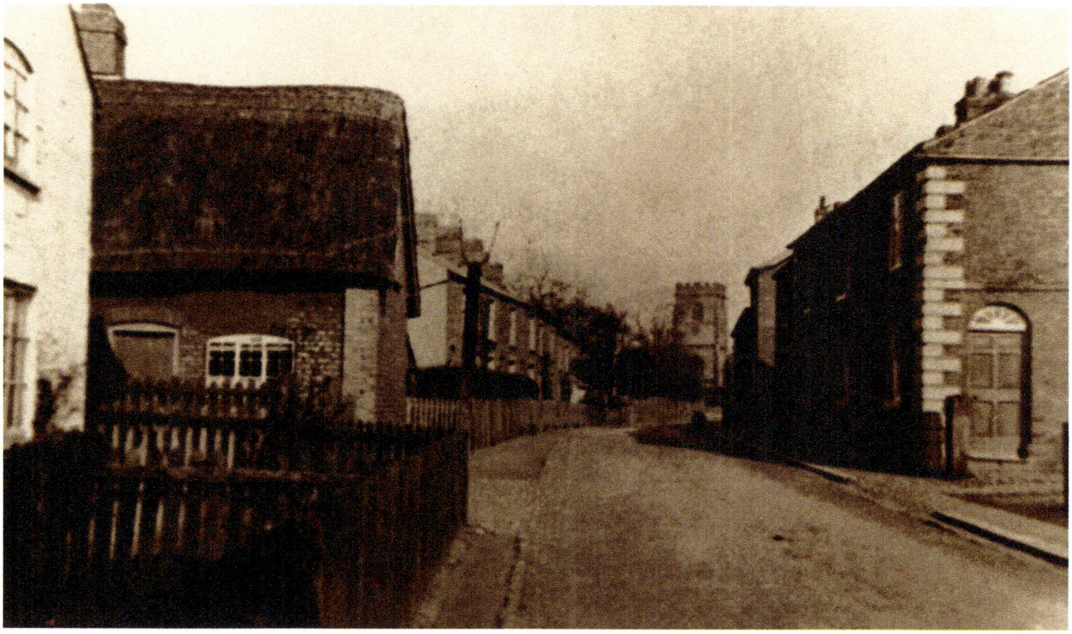

Raintub Cottage, Undated and 2015

Located in Church Street, Raintub Cottage dates from around the time of Henry VIII. When under renovation in the 1980s a wall painting was discovered on the wattle-and-daub wall beneath layers of plaster. It depicted the branches of a yew tree and would have been painted both for decoration and to fend off evil spirits as the yew was indigestible and sometimes fatal if eaten. It was considered effective against demons. Said to be the oldest house in Weaverham, this is now disputed as the old grammar school, now a house, may be older.

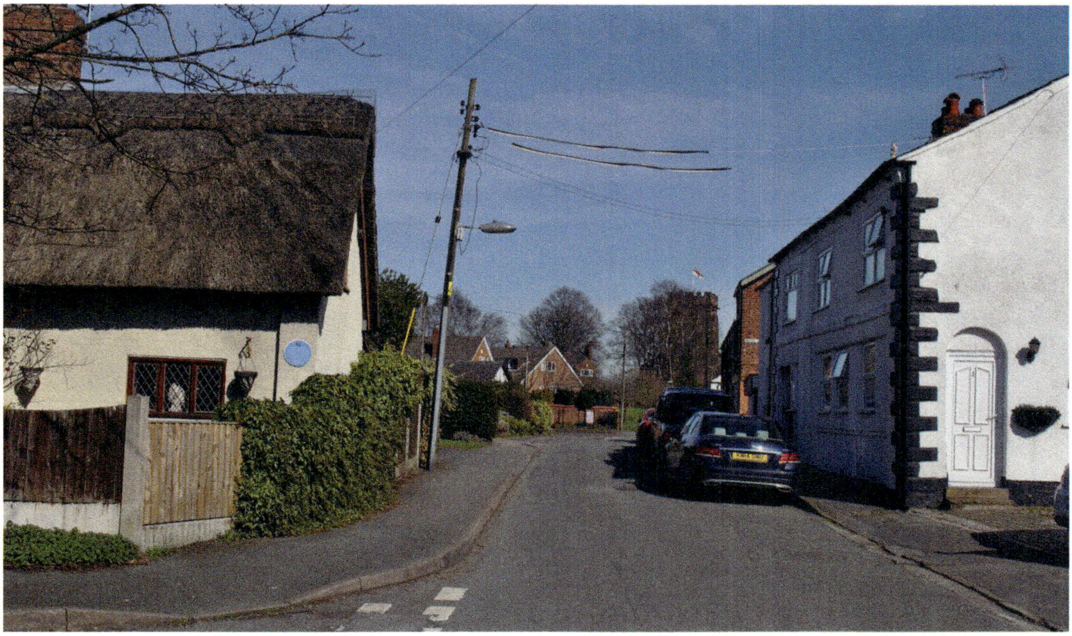

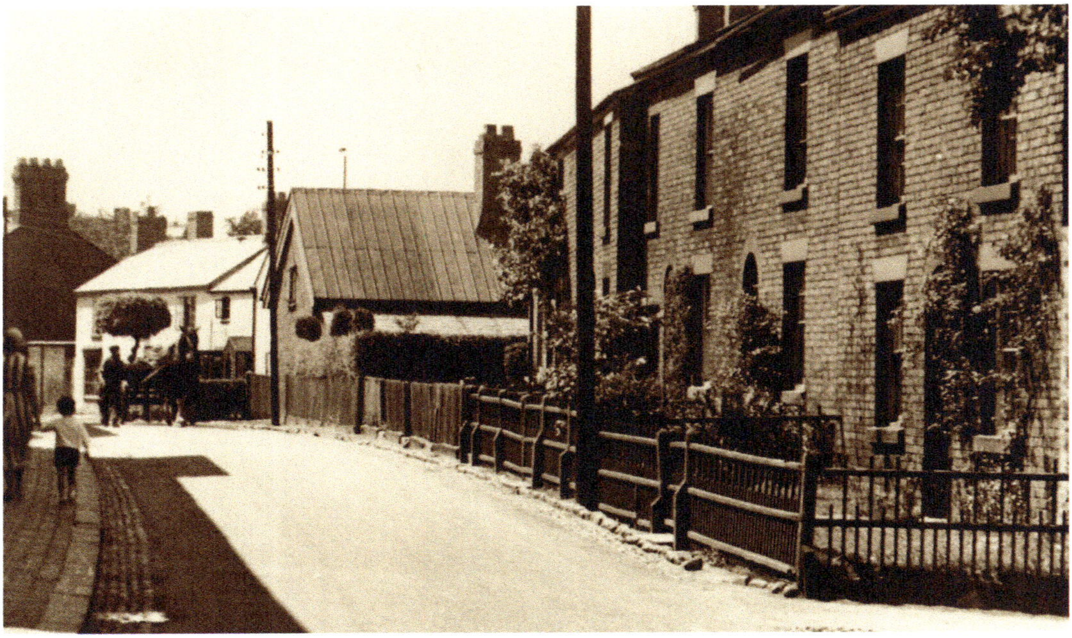

Church Street, 1920s and 2015

Another view of Raintub Cottage, this time from the opposite direction, in this old photograph the cottage has a corrugated iron or asbestos roof. As a child in Weaverham, I remember that the old lady who lived in the cottage would sell groceries from the kitchen door when the shop over the road was closed. There is a coffin hole in the half loft ceiling as a coffin would be too large to bring down the narrow staircase. Note the horse and dray plodding towards the camera in the old photograph.

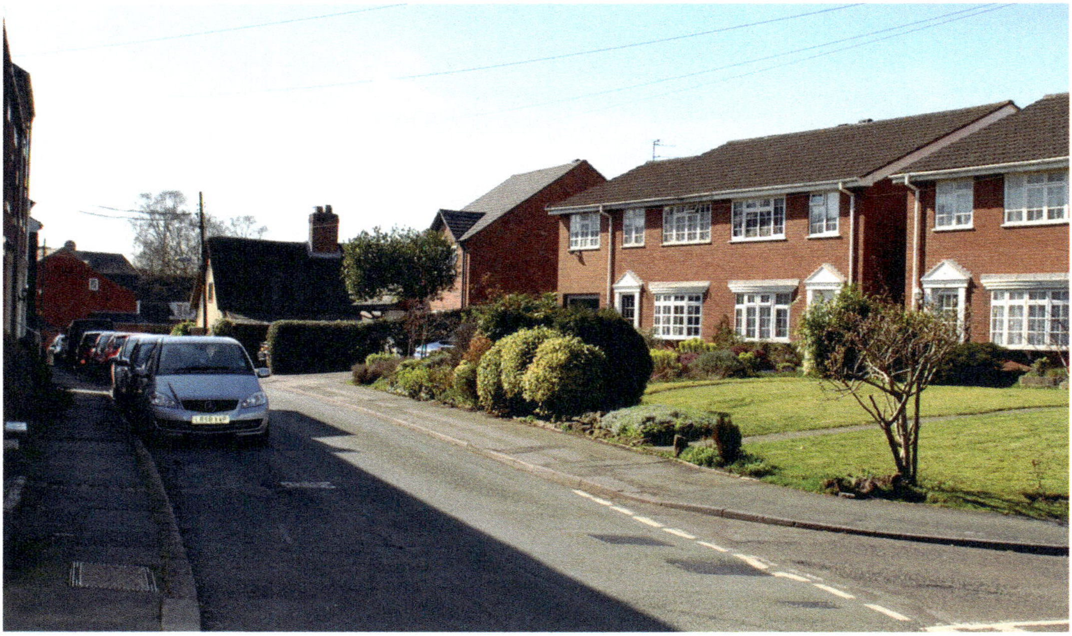

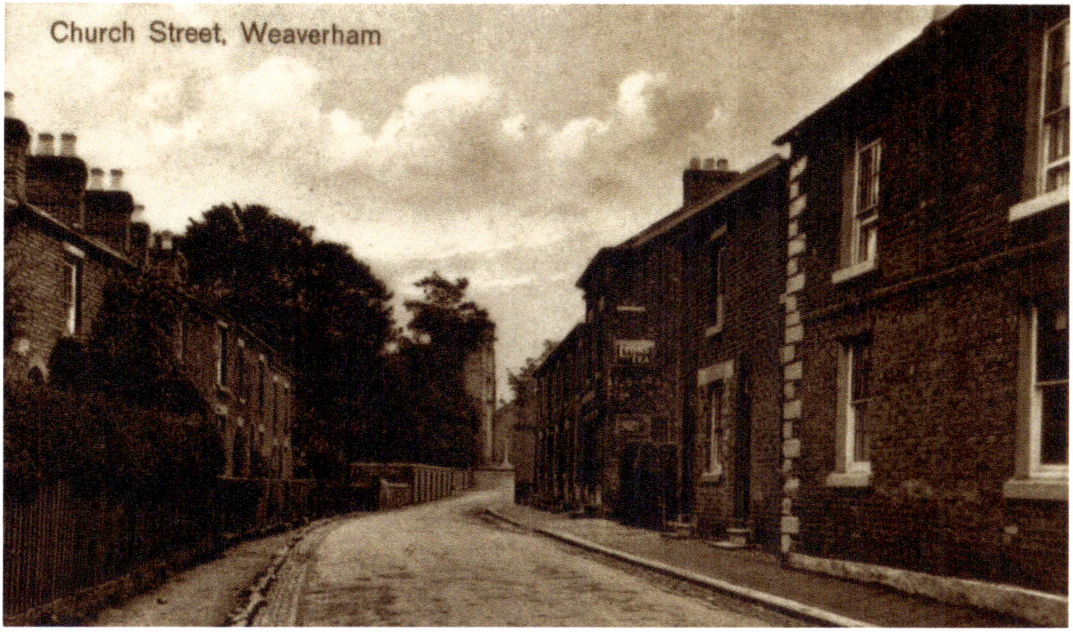

Church Street, 1900s and 2015

A last look at Church Street, looking towards the church with the now demolished terraced cottages on the right; these cottages have been replaced with modern houses. The vicarage wall can be seen on the left and is at the junction with Well Lane. Small lanes ran off this street such as Moss Street on the right and Woodward Street opposite Raintub Cottage. They are still cobbled and simply ooze historical ambience.

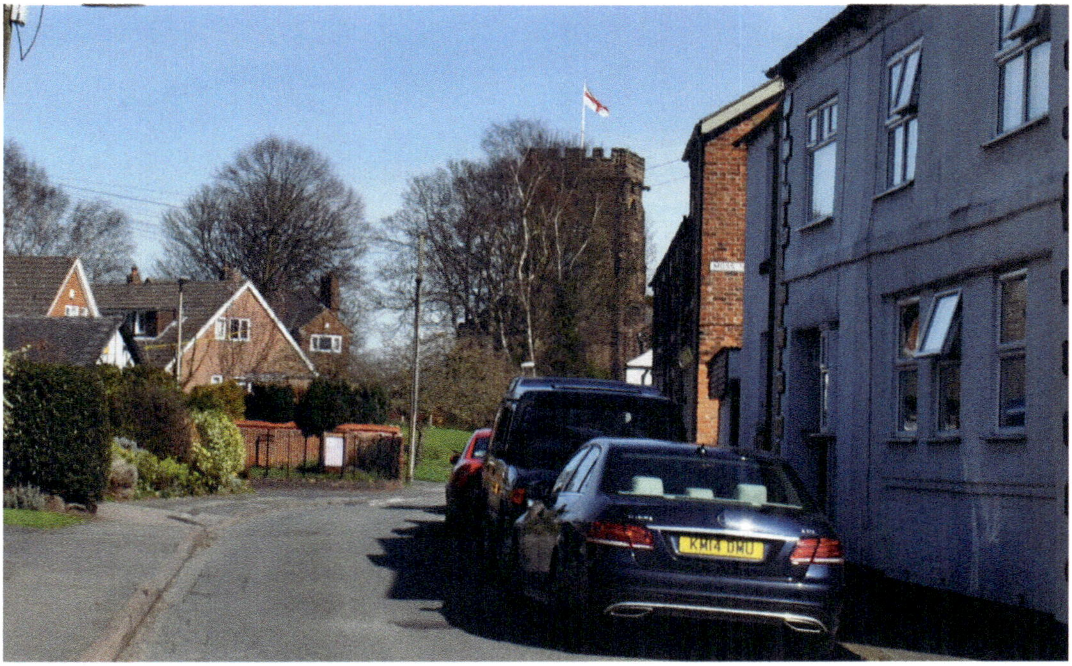

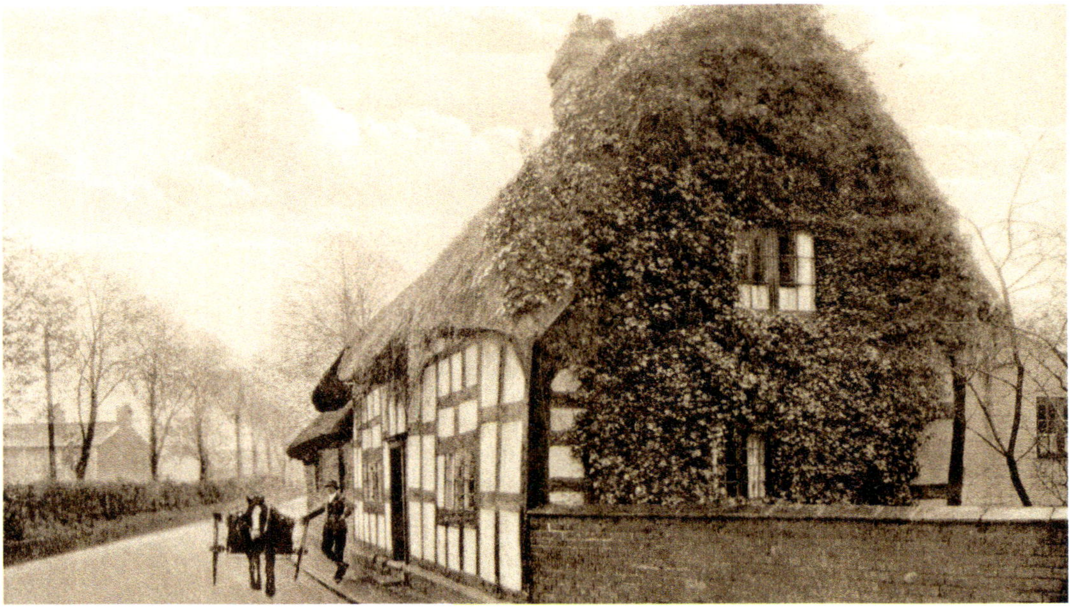

Northwich Road, 1890 and 2015

The main road through Weaverham before the coming of the bypass in the 1990s. The view looks back towards Northwich with the ancient Poplar Cottage on the right. This is an excellent example of domestic Tudor architecture, having been built in the fifteenth century. There is a 'birth chamber' – a small room on the lower floor. Tradition has it that if a baby is carried upstairs after birth it will continue to go up in life! For over one hundred years, it was the home of the Bebbington family who were cabinet makers and wood carvers. The last in the line was Cyril Stockton, a cabinet maker and undertaker.

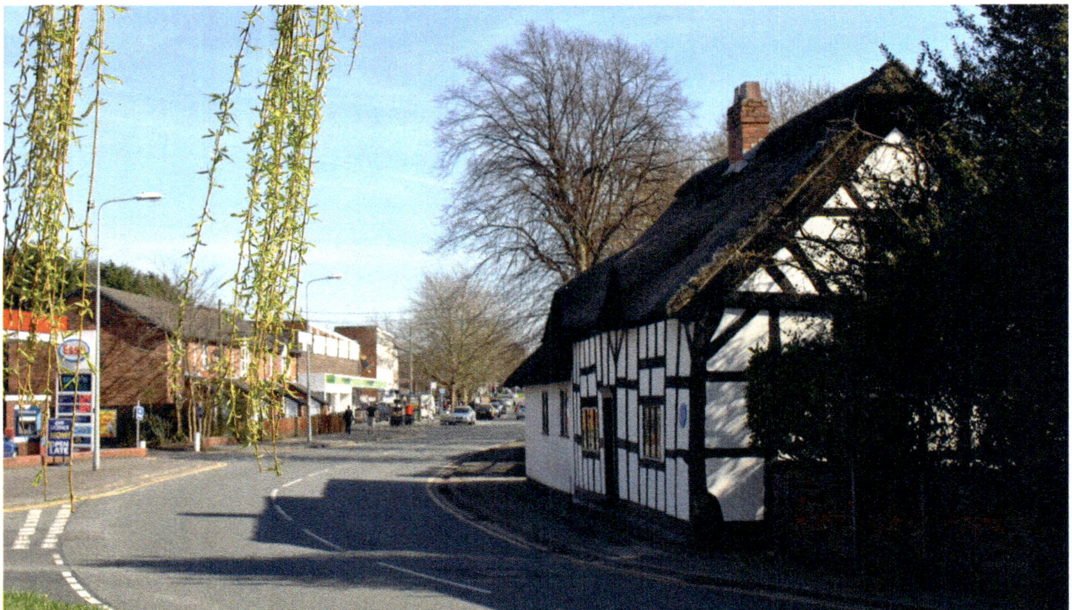

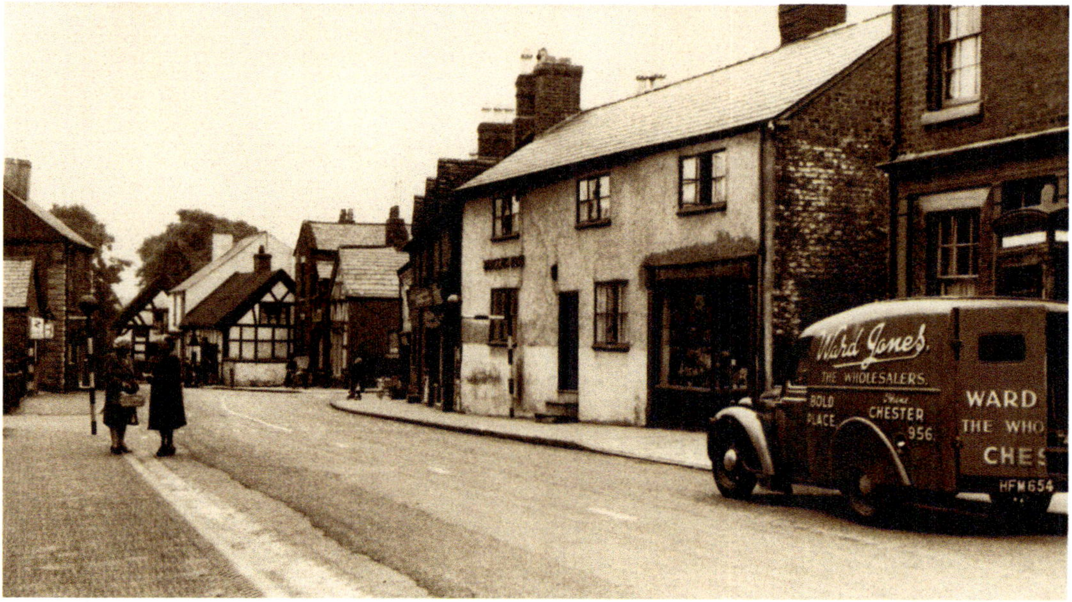

Weaverham High Street, 1950s and 2015

This photo is filled with 1950s period charm.The ladies chat quite comfortably on the road and the road signs near the Wheatsheaf are black and white and filled with cat's eyes! Chapels Wine Bar on the right is a shop with a delivery van. The Belisha beacons outside Barclays Bank stand alone with no zigzags or black-and-white crossing and the 2015 photo shows that the shop next to the bank has gone. The narrow cobbled entry in front of the van is believed to have led to the Abbot's prison from the aforementioned grammar school, which was the court. This prison was owned by the monks of Vale Royal who ruled Weaverham in a most unpleasant and ruthless manner.

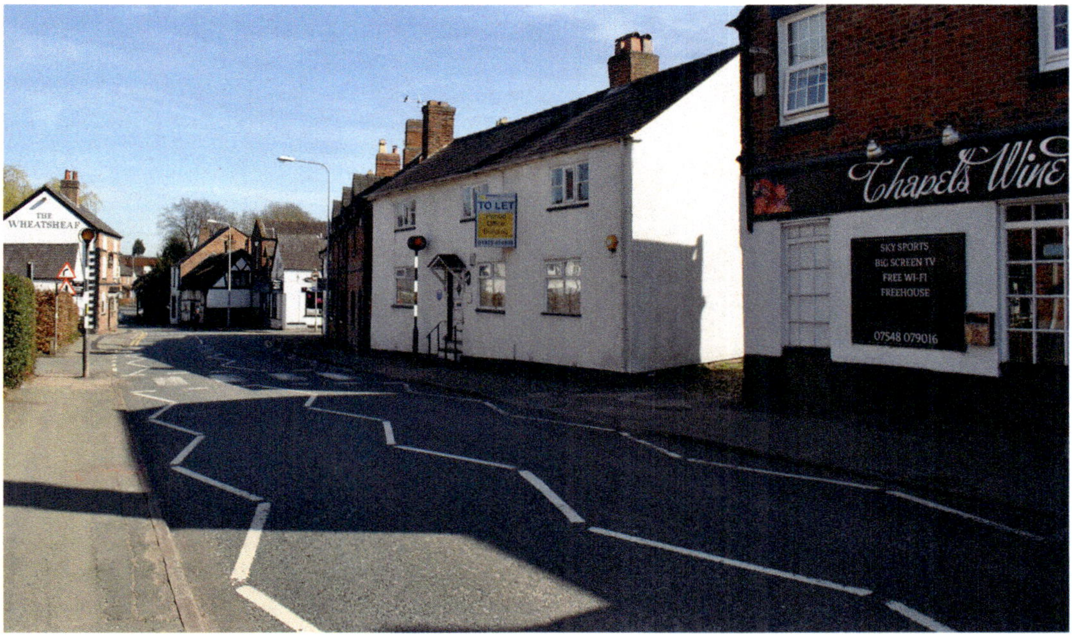

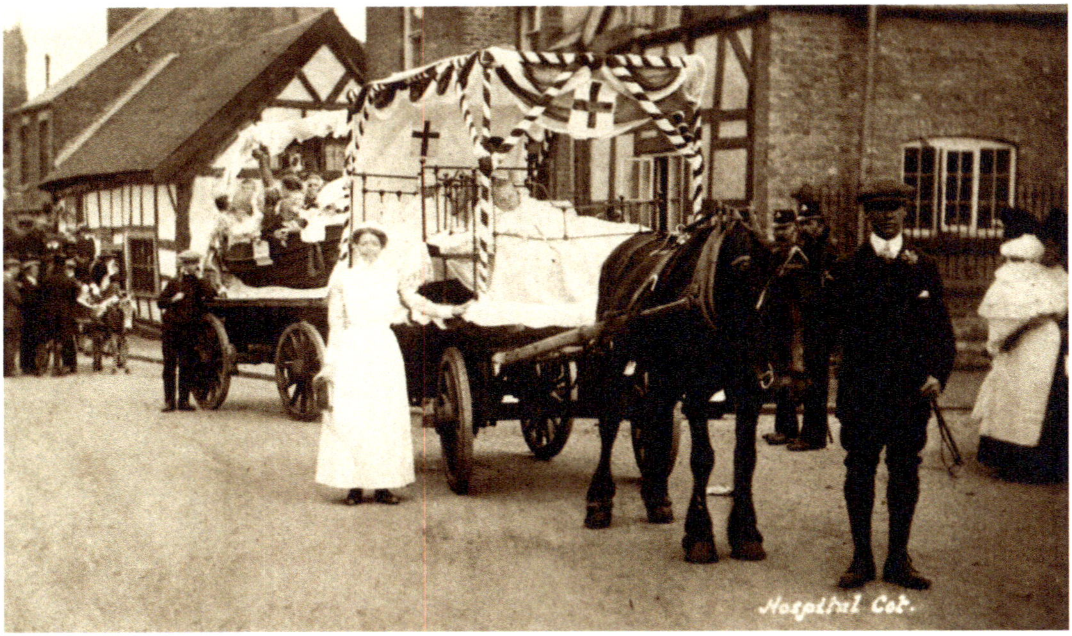

Hospital Festival, 1915–1920 and 2015
More now of the Hospital Saturday procession, this one dating from around the end of the First World War, the building at the Forest Street junction has now gone and railings have been erected. The first procession float depicts children in beds with a red cross behind them and the second children in a rowing boat, while two policemen in their shako helmets look on, possibly one being the local bobby Sgt Ellwood. In the modern photograph big changes have taken place and the old Star Inn is now two shops.

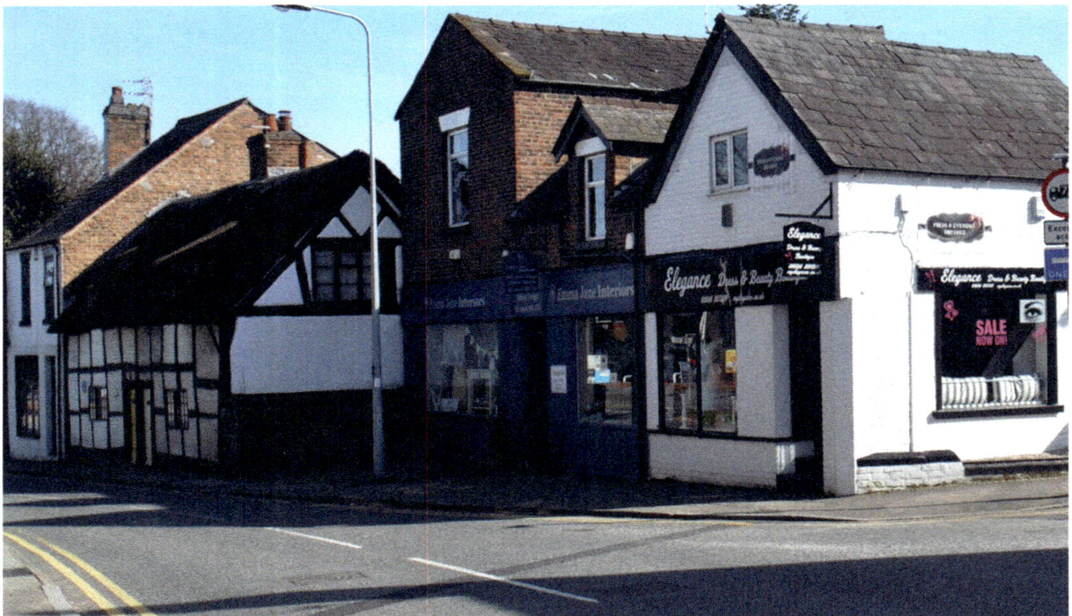

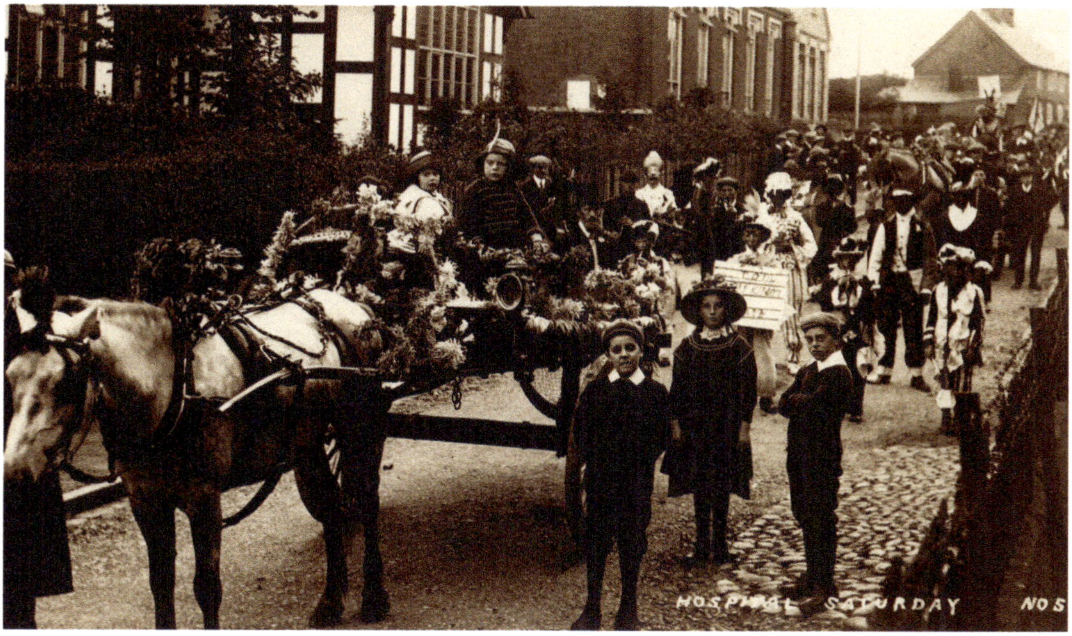

Forest Street, 1912 and 2015

A final look at the Hospital Saturday procession, this time in Forest Street.The banner carried by the lad with the penny whistle seems to say 'The Tom Wilkinson Band'. The black-and-white building is the Barrymore Institute, built on the site of an old cottage in 1907. The procession left from the Hanging Gate, paraded around the village and returned there for festivities, games and a pint or two in the field opposite.

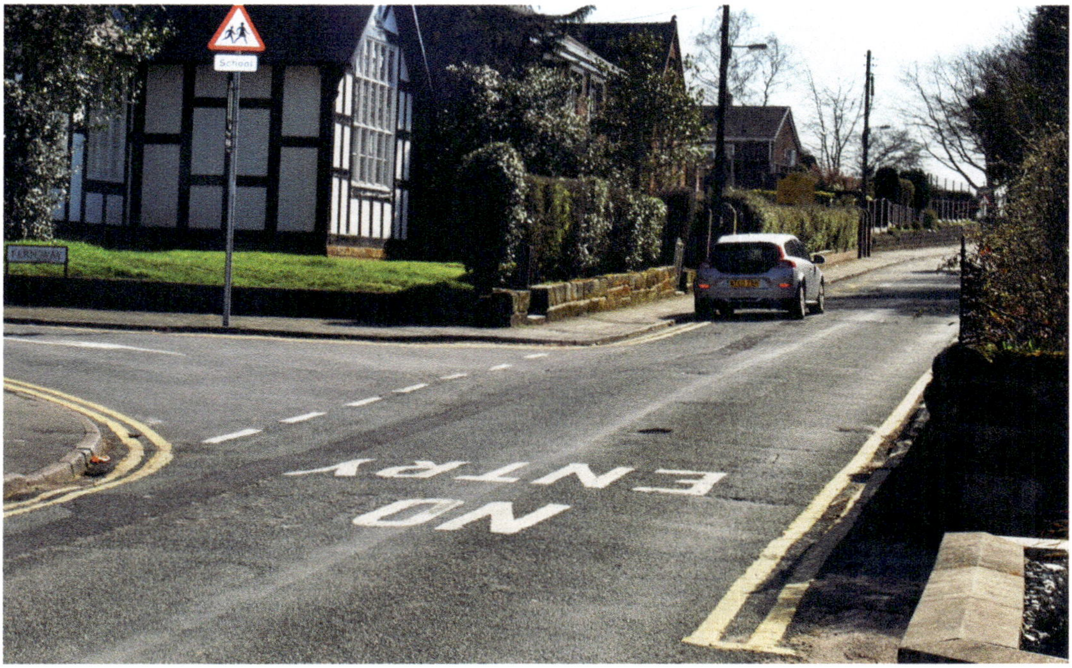

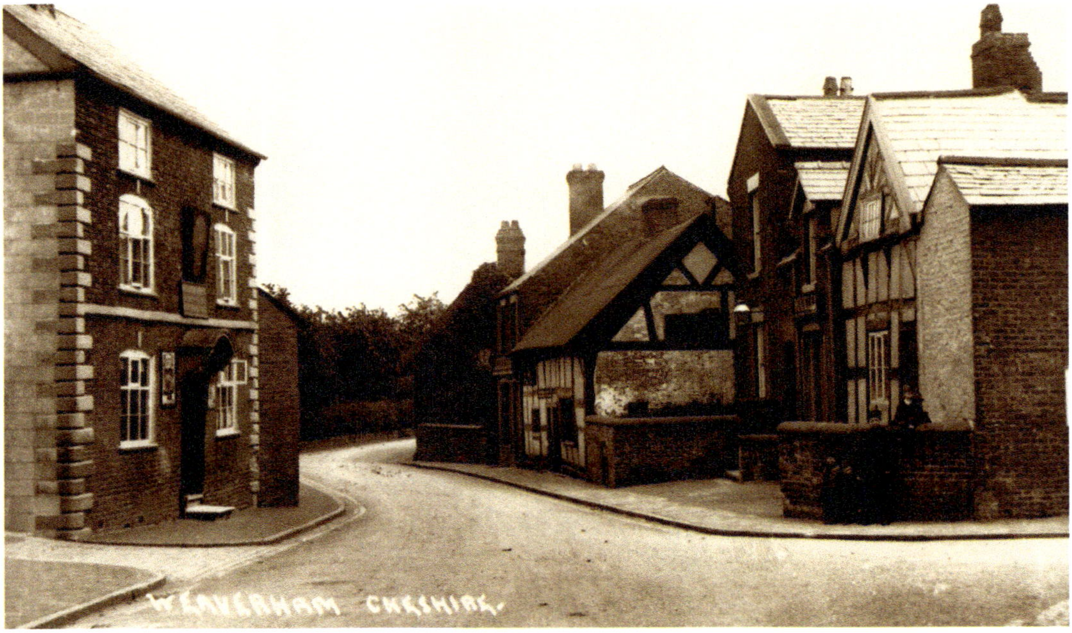

The Star Inn, 1900s and 2015

The building on the right was the pub known as the Star Inn; it had been a pub since the 1700s. It was acquired by Greenall's in 1872 and compulsorily closed in 1908 when it was sold to W. C. Buckley and opened as a clog maker and later a shoe and clothes shop. The Star Inn was the meeting place for the Weaverham Virgins' Club who on occasions became a little rowdy. Don't get the wrong idea here. They acquired that name from St Mary the Virgin church to which they belonged, not their abstinence from the pleasures of the flesh!

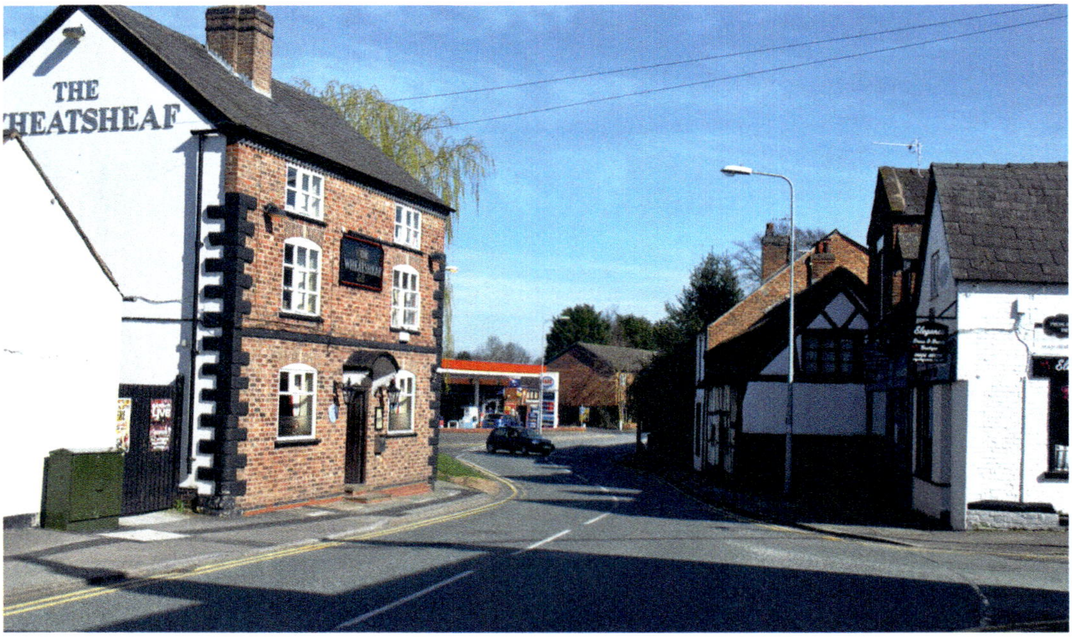

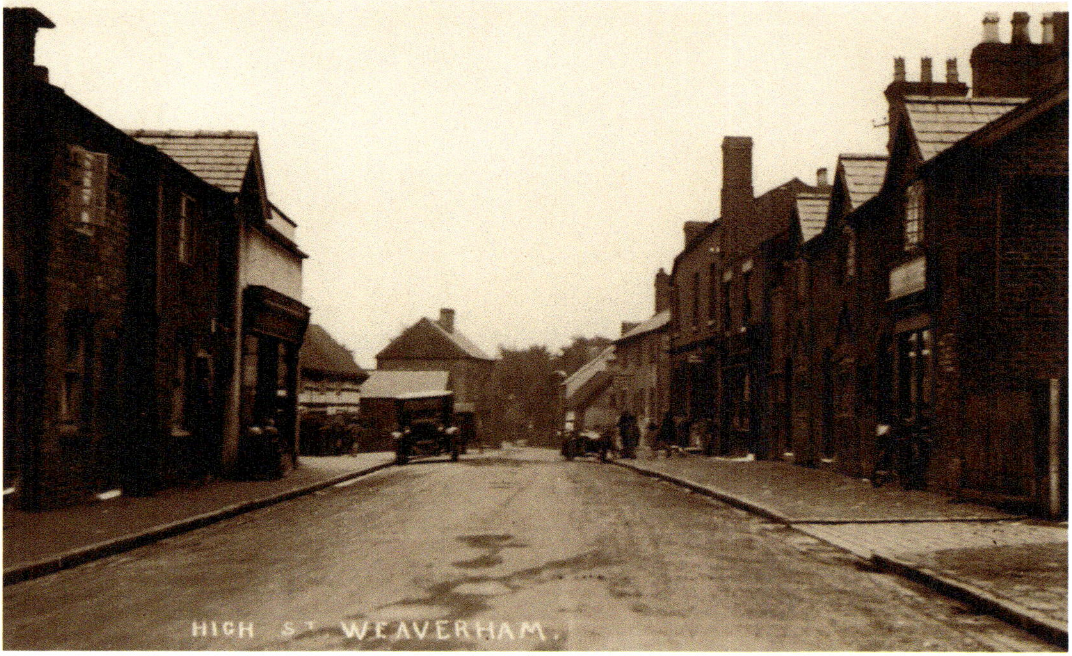

Weaverham High Street, 1910–1920 and 2015
Travelling backwards and forwards through time we have reached the time of First World War. The traffic consists of a petrol van, a horse van and a motorcycle and sidecar. Building wise, there is very little change over the years. Weaverham is a very pretty and ancient village with many interesting features.

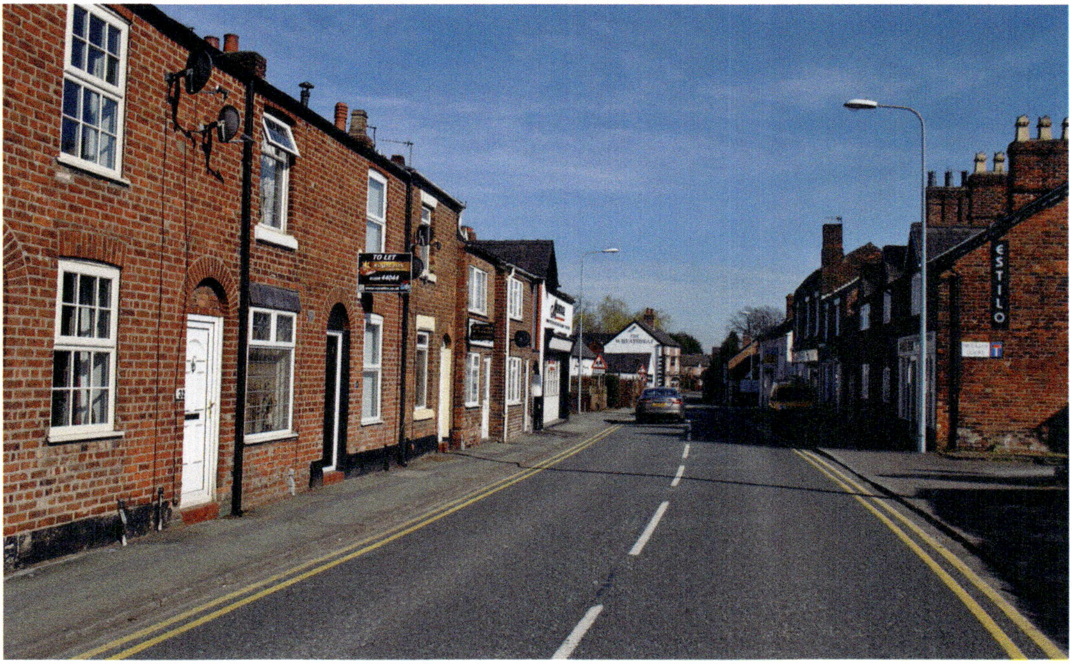

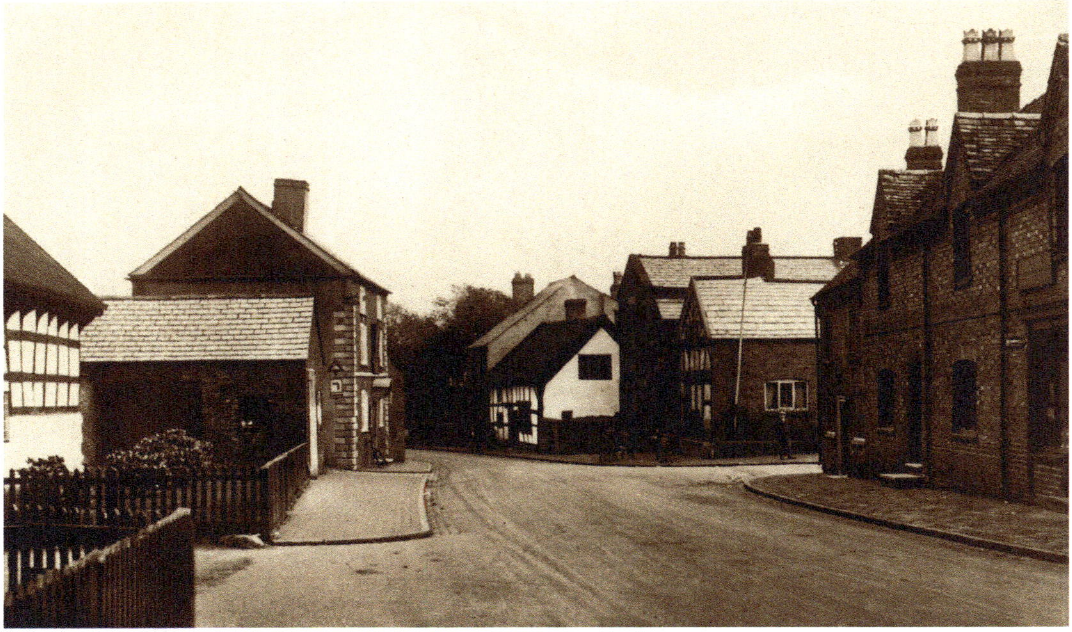

Weaverham High Street, 1930s and 2015

A last look back at Weaverham village and the old Wheatsheaf pub, which dates back to 1822 as a pub and probably further back to the 1700s. This has been a very popular pub over the years, in which the village elders ruminated over glasses of ale in the Knowledge Room, a bar room at the front of the building. One notable elder was 'Sergeant' George Allen who went to the First World War with the local territorials as a sergeant and retained the title for the rest of his long life. Note the very early left turn sign.

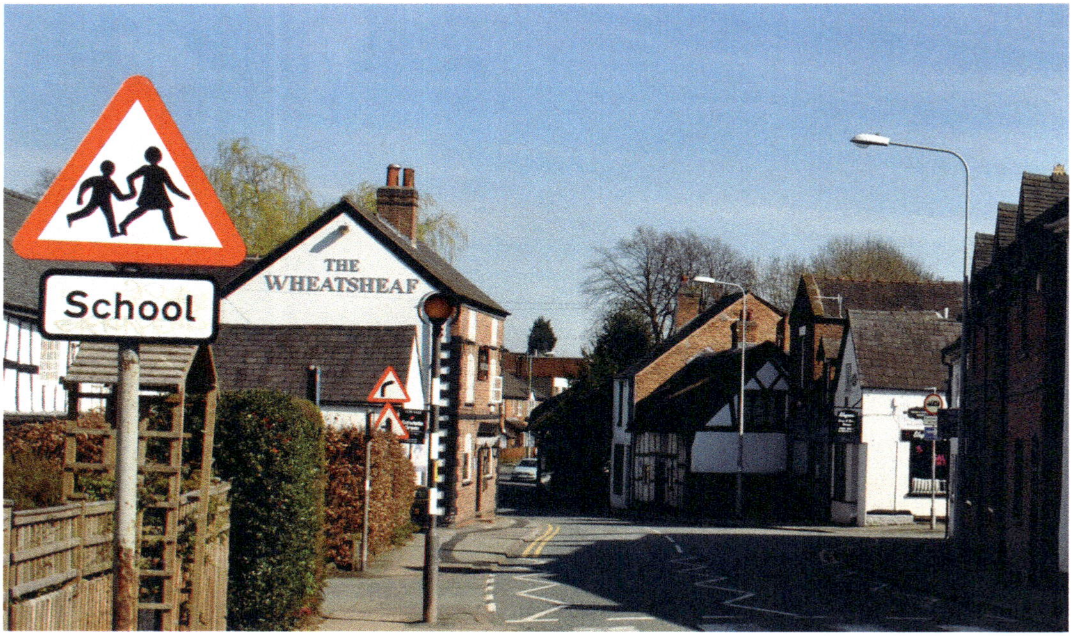

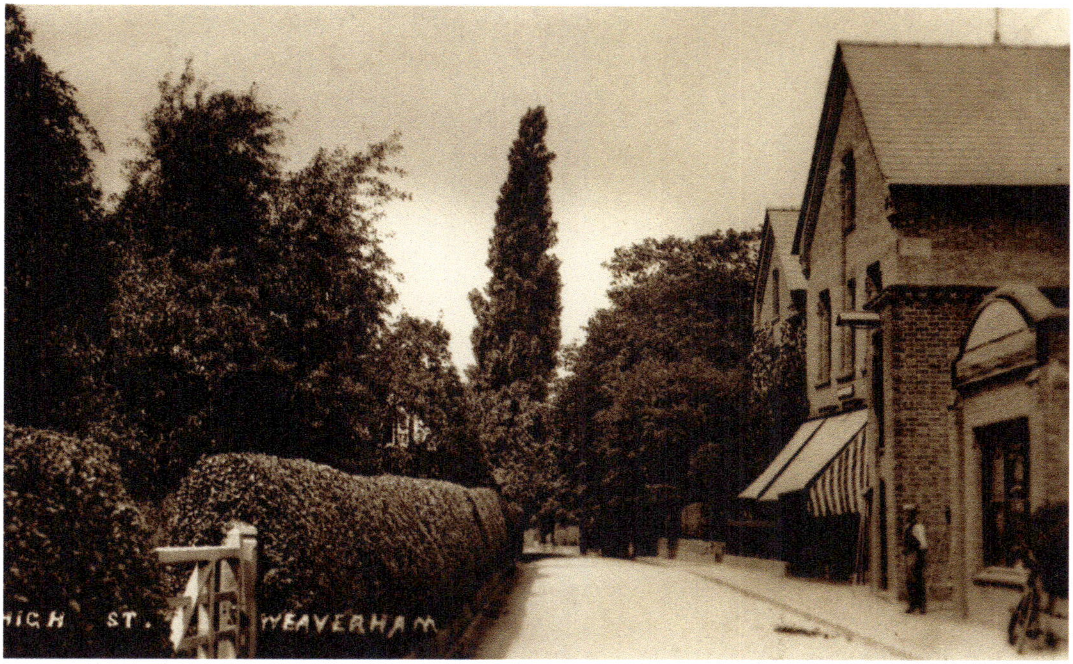

Weaverham High Street, 1900 and 2015
During the 1800s, the large house and shop on the right was the business of Mr Benjamin and Mr William Burgess who traded as Burgess Brothers. At the time, this long-standing company traded in saddlery, drapery and furniture. Under different family members, it went on to become the well-known Northwich company Burgess Bros (Agricultural Engineers) Ltd.

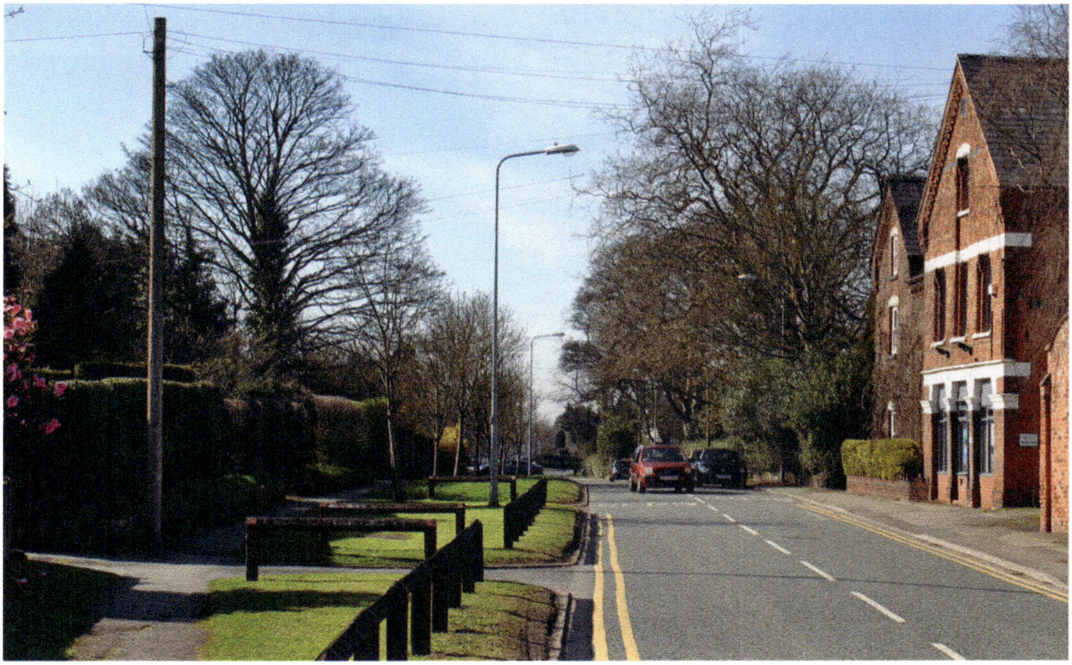

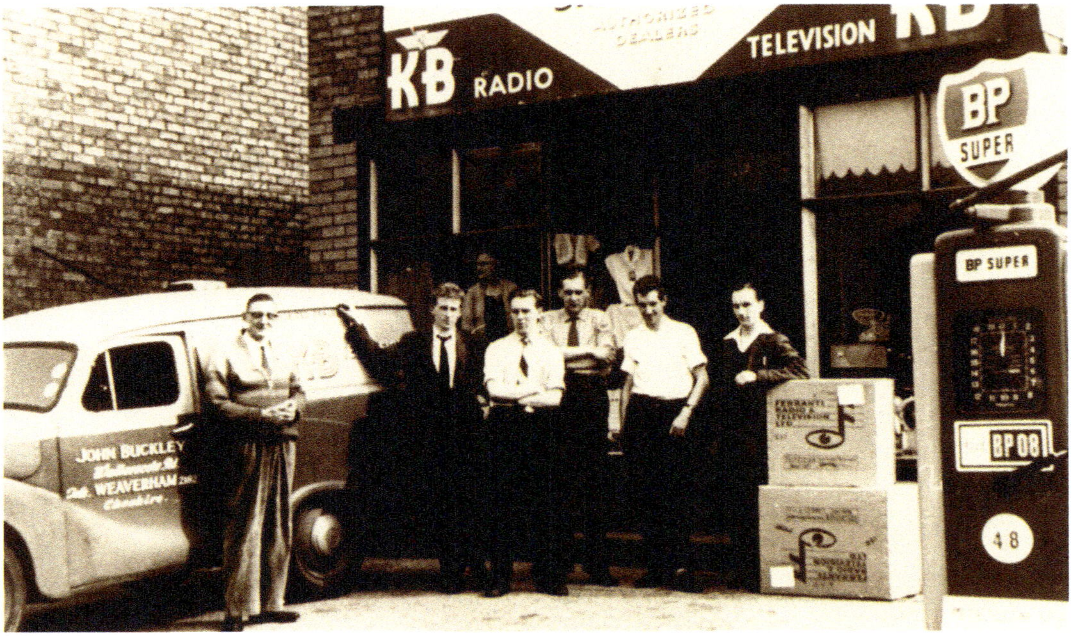

Buckley's Shop, 1950s and 2015

John Buckley had this shop in Wallerscote Road and in the early 1950s branched out as an electrical retailer. Televisions had started to appear and he took advantage of this, but it would perhaps have been advisable to keep the new TV the right way up in its box as the valves were very delicate! Businesses in these post-war days made a living by having fingers in many pies; Buckley's also sold petrol and clothes.

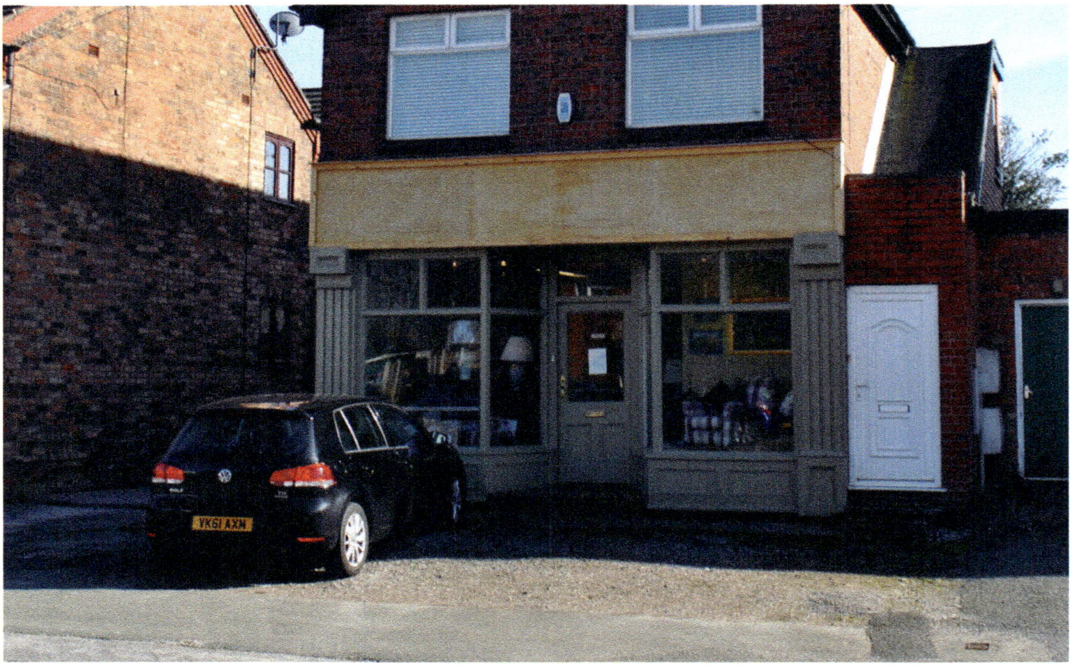

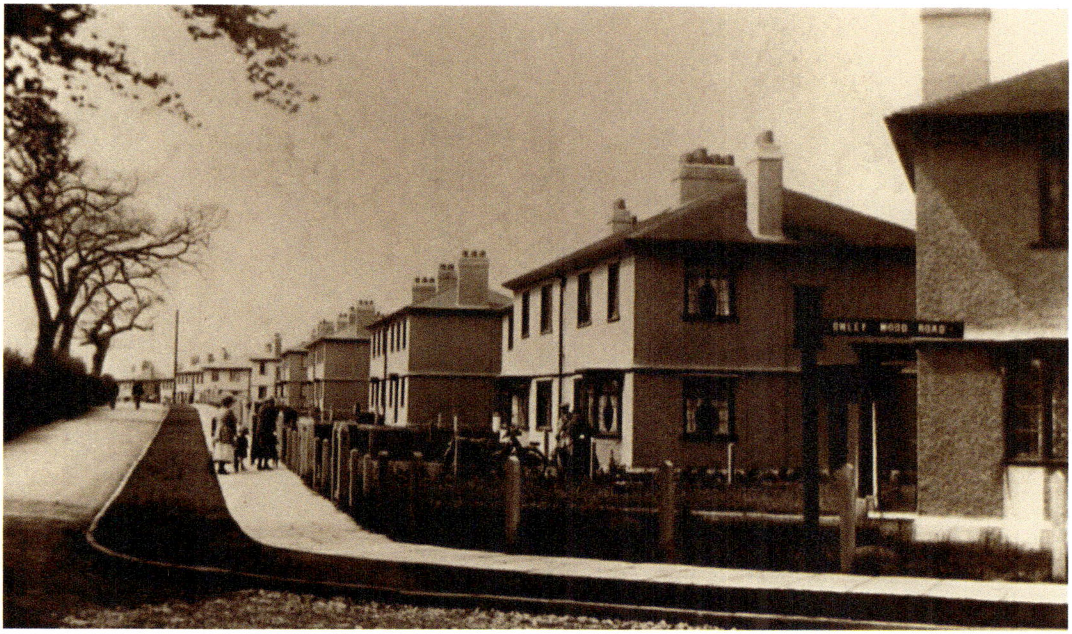

Wallerscote Road, 1935 and 2015

Until the 1920s Weaverham was a rural community of some 1,000 people, then ICI built the first of the estates for their workers in the village. Known as the Owley Wood Estate, these houses were built of light-coloured brick but, quite unusually, each house had a concrete floor upstairs. Northwich Rural District Council were also busy building houses in the area and then after the war the building of council and private estates greatly extended the village.

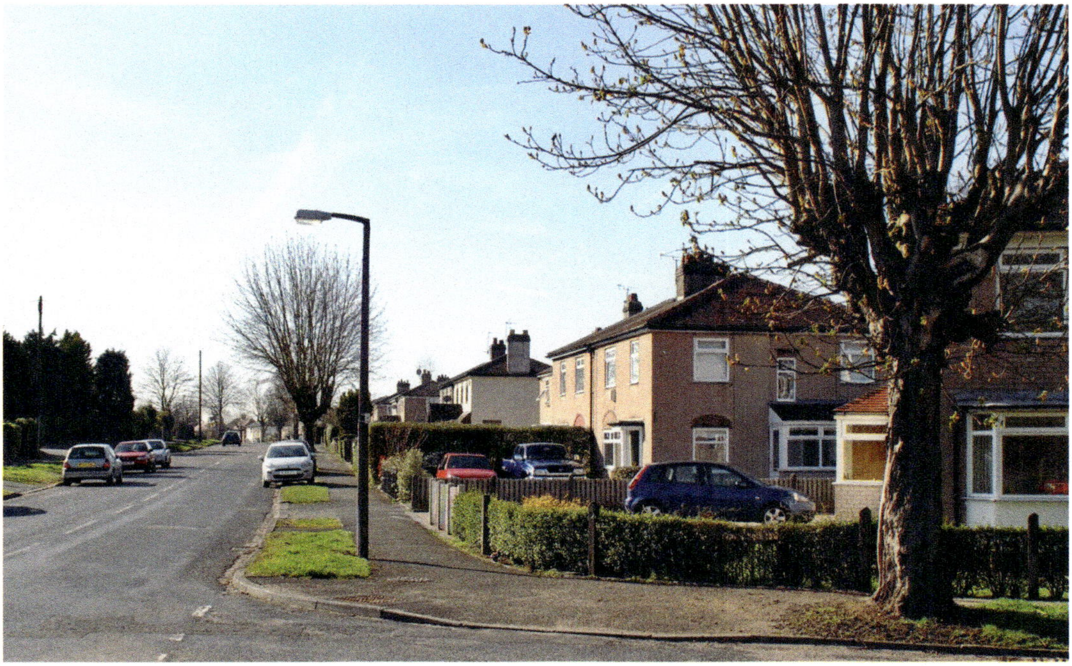

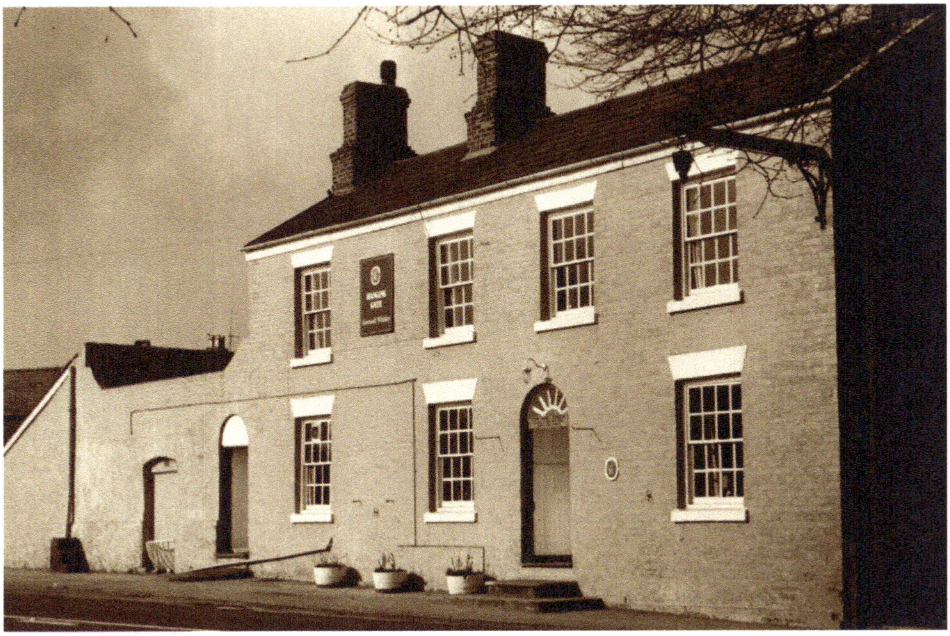

The Hanging Gate Pub, Undated and 2015

This is The Hanging Gate, an ancient pub with its actual age lost in the mists of time. Prior to 1827 it was called The Weaverham Gate then The Barrymore Arms and then simply The Gate. It was owned by Lord Barrymore until it was purchased by Greenall's in 1928. It is believed that further down the road from the pub was a toll gate as the A49 was a turnpike. The story is that when the gates were finally removed, one of them was hung from a bracket outside The Gate Inn, probably causing the change of name. It is now a gastro pub called, again, The Hanging Gate.

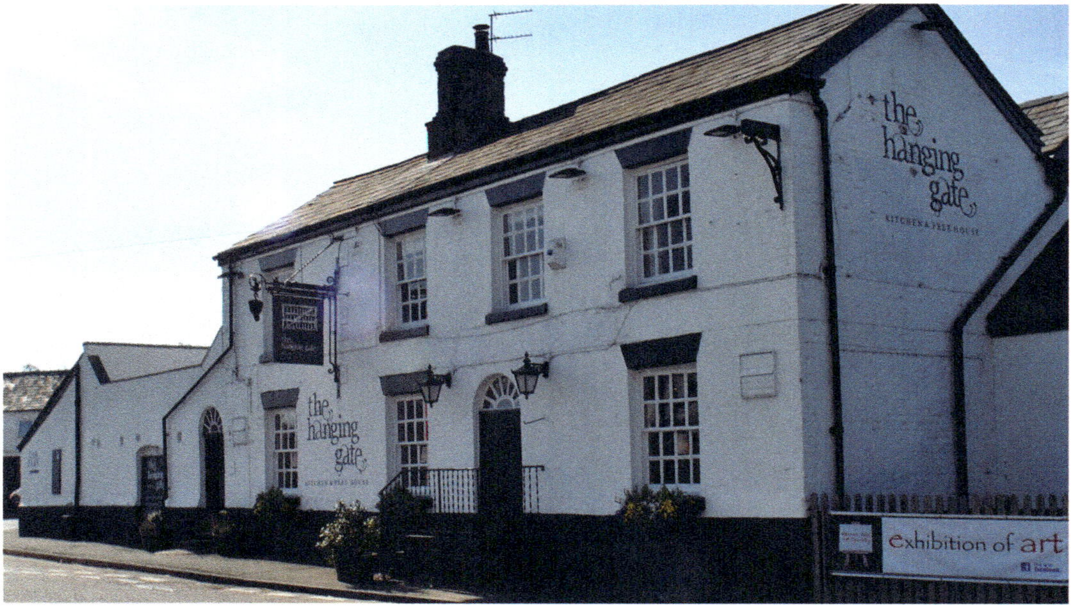

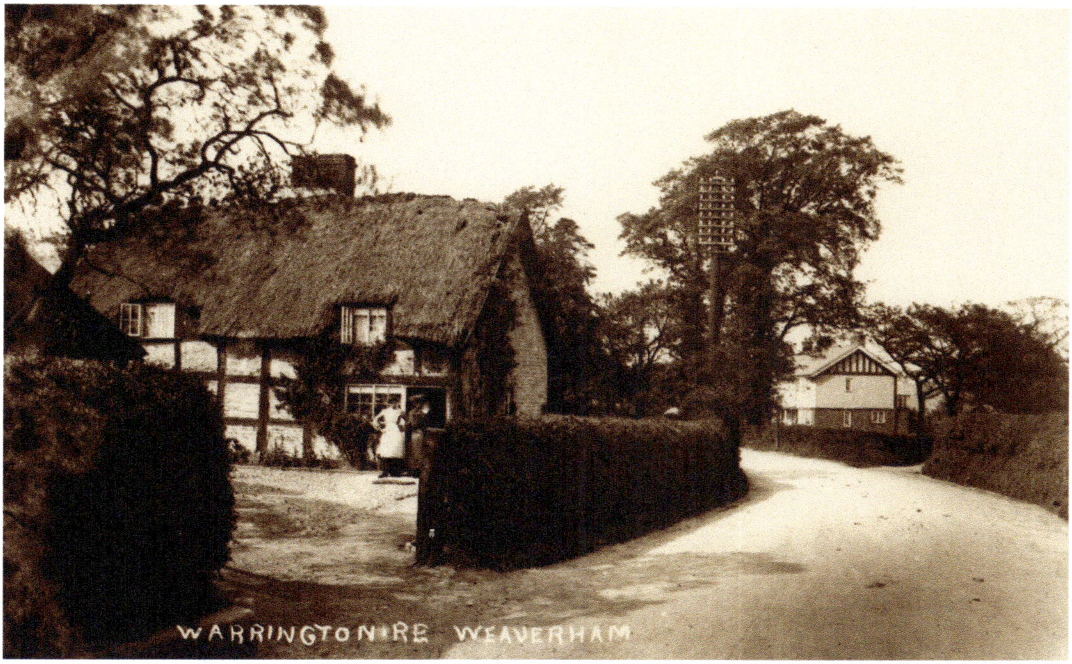

Inglenook Café, Early 1900s and 2014
This old cottage stood on Sandy Lane just past The Hanging Gate and almost opposite the entrance to Shady Brook Lane. It was called Mainwaring's Cottage, and then became the Inglenook Café, a popular haunt of cyclists in the 1920s.

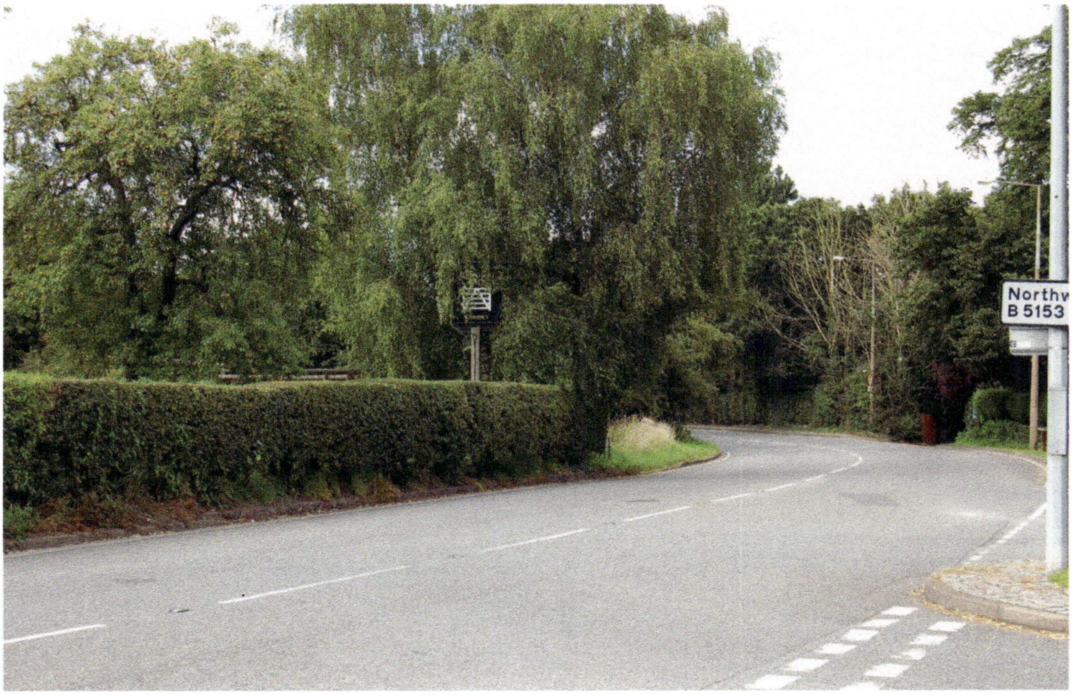

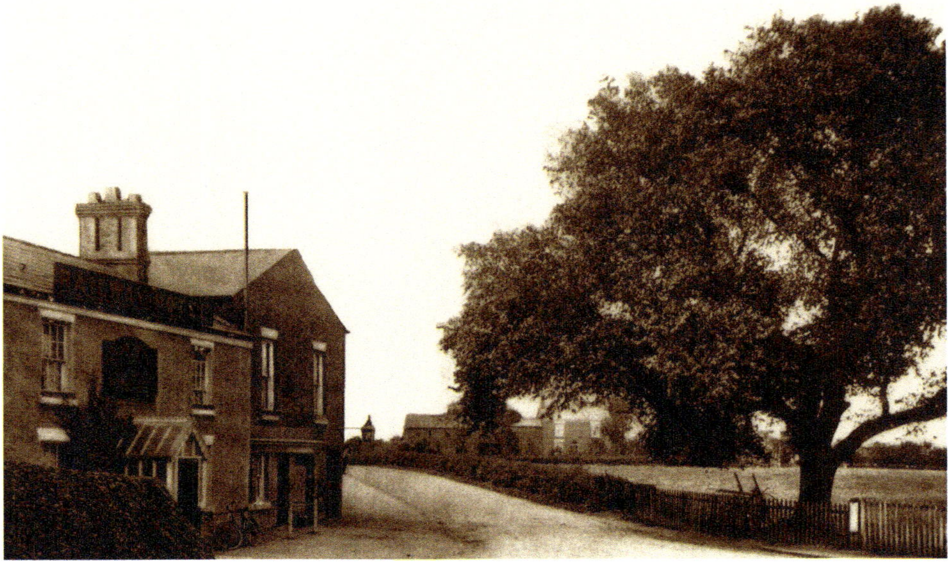

Hazel Pear, 1900 and 2015

Over the years the name Railway Hotel went out of favour and most pubs of that name saw it changed (a bit of snobbery perhaps?). At the time that Acton Bridge Railway Hotel had to be renamed, one of the commonest pears in the area was the hazel or hessle pear; there was an orchard of them at the rear of the pub, so in 1972 the pub's name was changed from The Railway Hotel to The Hazel Pear. Arthur Garner and his wife had the pub through the bleak years of the Second World War and the story goes that Mrs Garner served a double whisky to Gen. Patton as he waited with his troops to board the train at Acton Bridge. He knocked it back and asked her for another; she refused, pointing out that it was rationed. The ivory-handled pistol and the four silver stars on this most outspoken of generals did not faze this country woman!

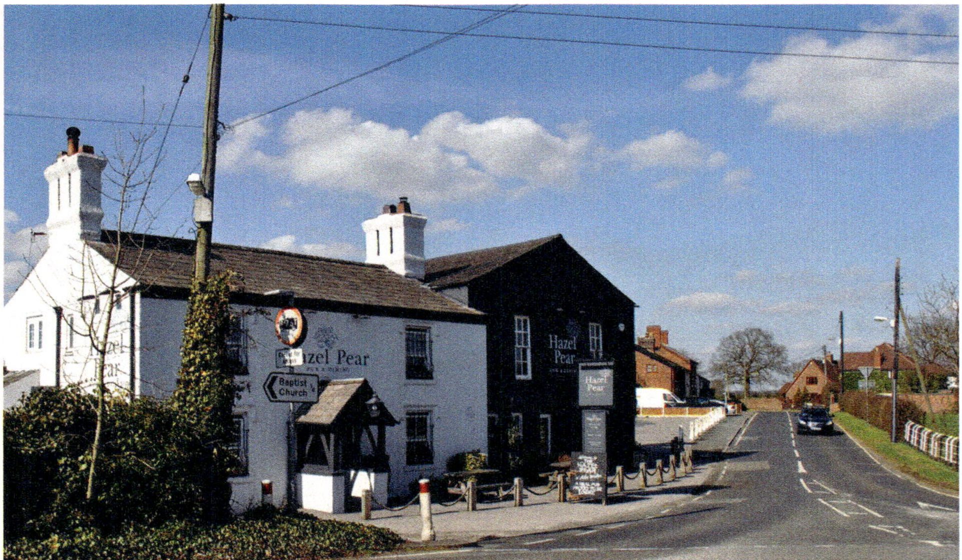

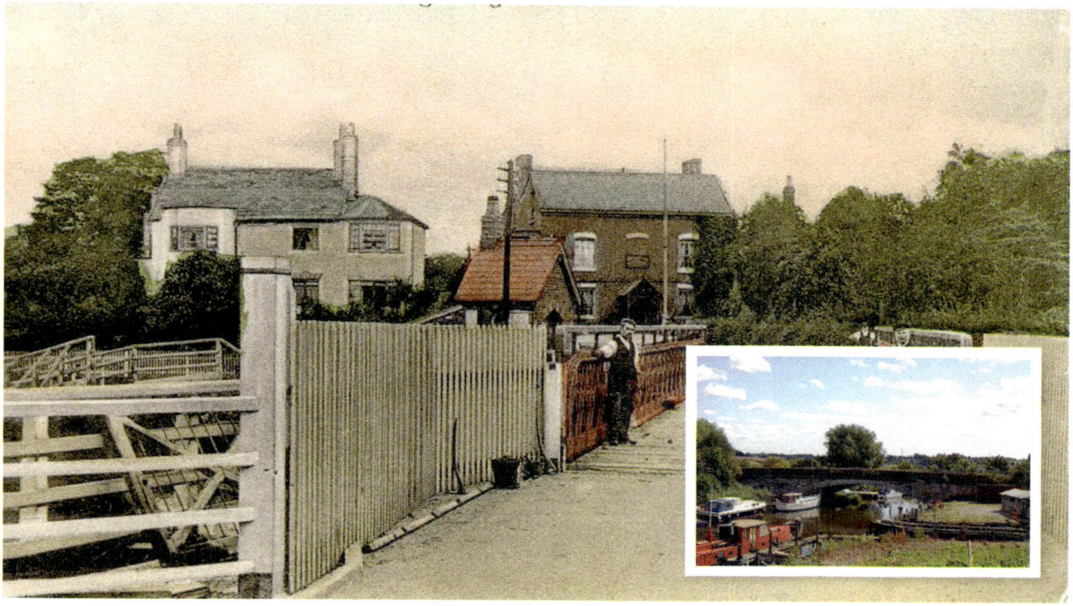

Old Acton Stone Bridge, 1895 and 2014

In 1730 a lock was constructed at Little Leigh to make the River Weaver navigable from Frodsham Bridge to Winsford. To cross the river there was a stone bridge to a small island (*inset*), then a swing bridge allowing traffic to cross and boats to pass through. As can be seen in the old photograph, the side of the bridge has been raised. This was in order to prevent horses jumping over it. The building on the right is the Leigh Arms Hotel. The stone bridge is still there but the narrow swing bridge shown in the old photograph with its location in the new was removed. The Acton Swing Bridge on the A54 was built in 1933 to replace it.

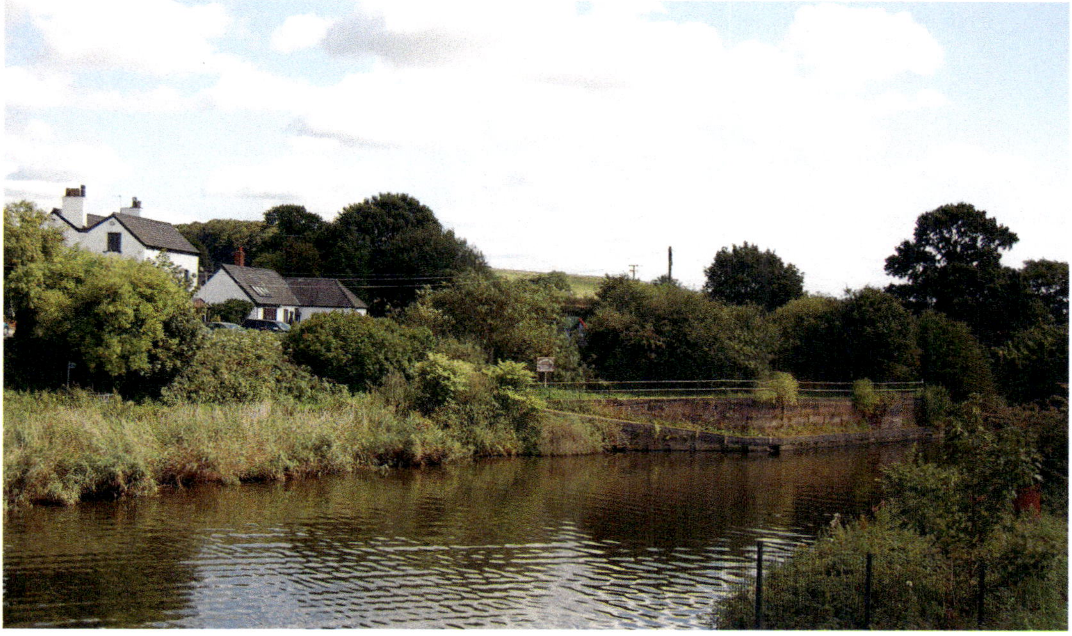

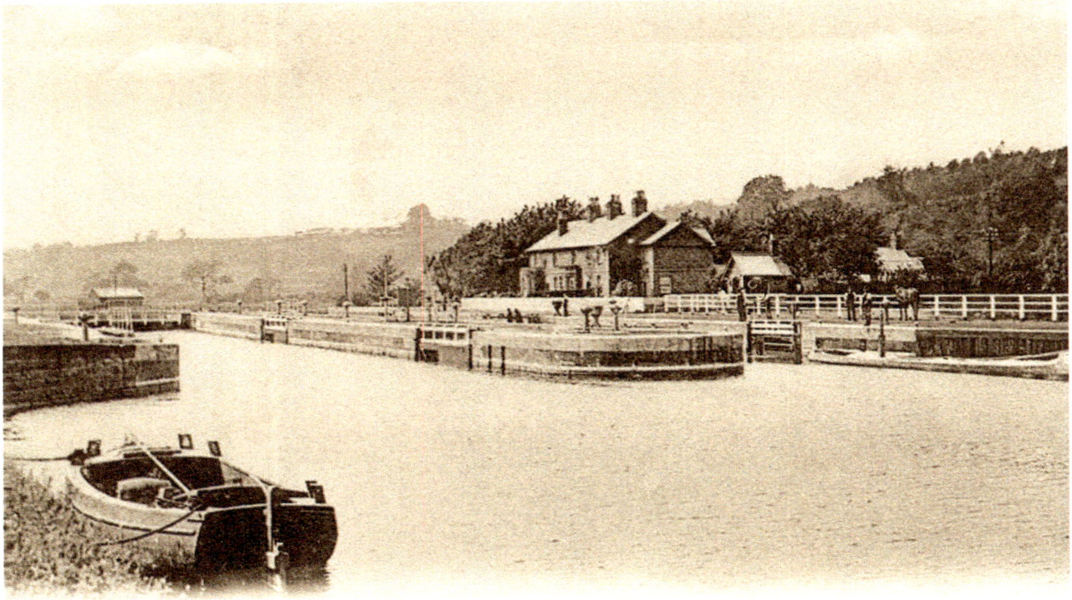

Saltersford Lock, 1800s and 2012

This large lock downstream from Acton Bridge towards Northwich has carried over the years a large number of coasters and salt flats. Now, however, it only serves the odd ocean-going ship, the main traffic consists of pleasure boats carried from the canal by the Anderton Lift. The old photo shows a well-loaded canal boat about to enter the lock as the horse stands patiently, enjoying the break perhaps. The lock keepers' cottages have large bay windows, allowing the incumbents a good look along the river.

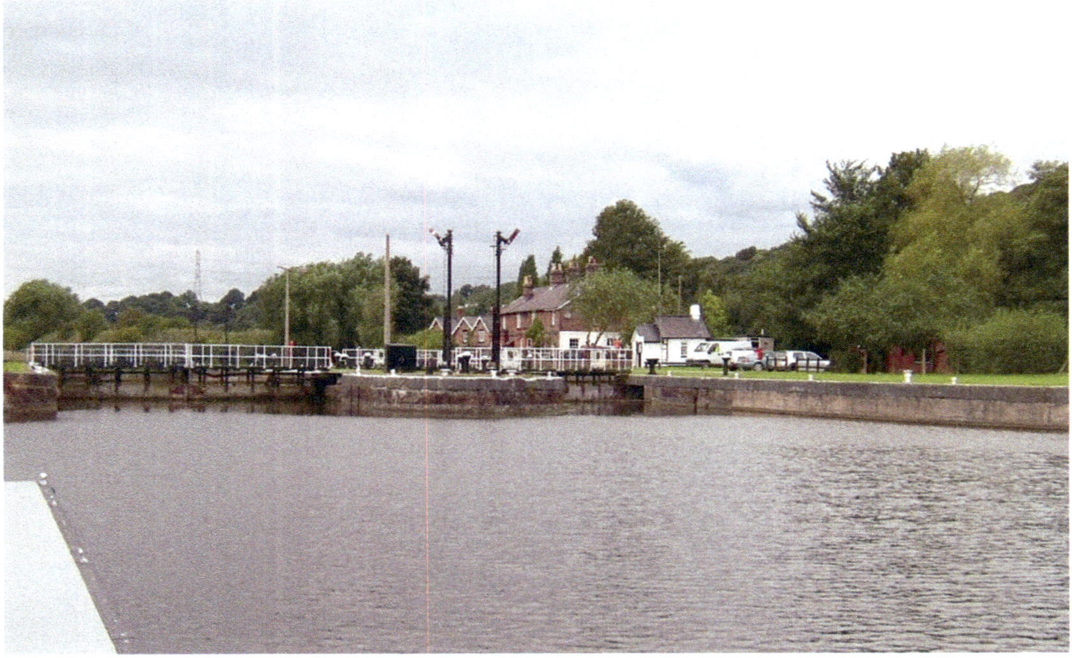

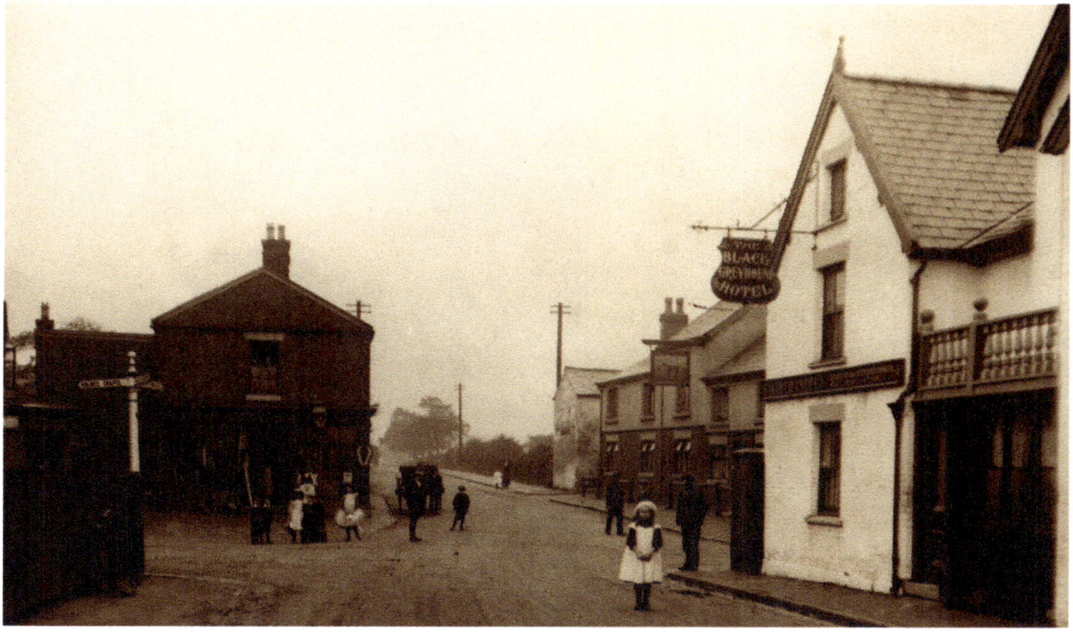

Four Lane Ends, Lostock Gralam, 1890s and 2015

In this atmospheric photograph, the Black Greyhound pub can be seen on the right and across the junction is the old Slow and Easy, named, like a lot of pubs in the area, after a horse or in this case two horses! The pub had existed since 1763 but was demolished in 1937 when a new Slow and Easy was built set back from the road. The large building on the left has gone to allow road widening and the one shown in the modern picture, now a Chinese restaurant, was behind it. The old Black Greyhound was demolished in 1937 and a replacement was built in Wincham.

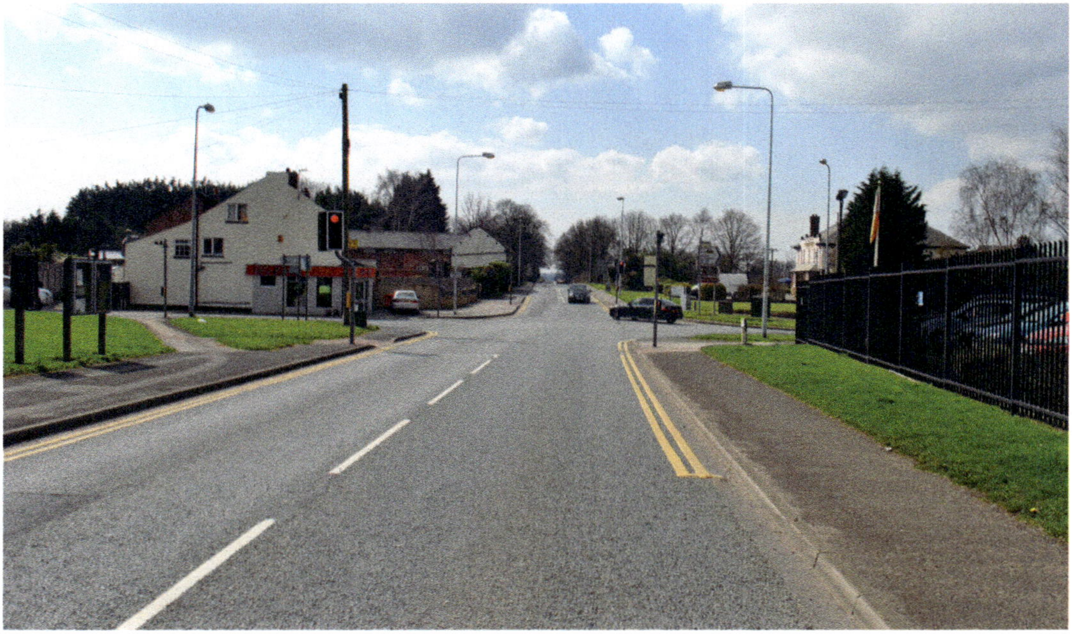

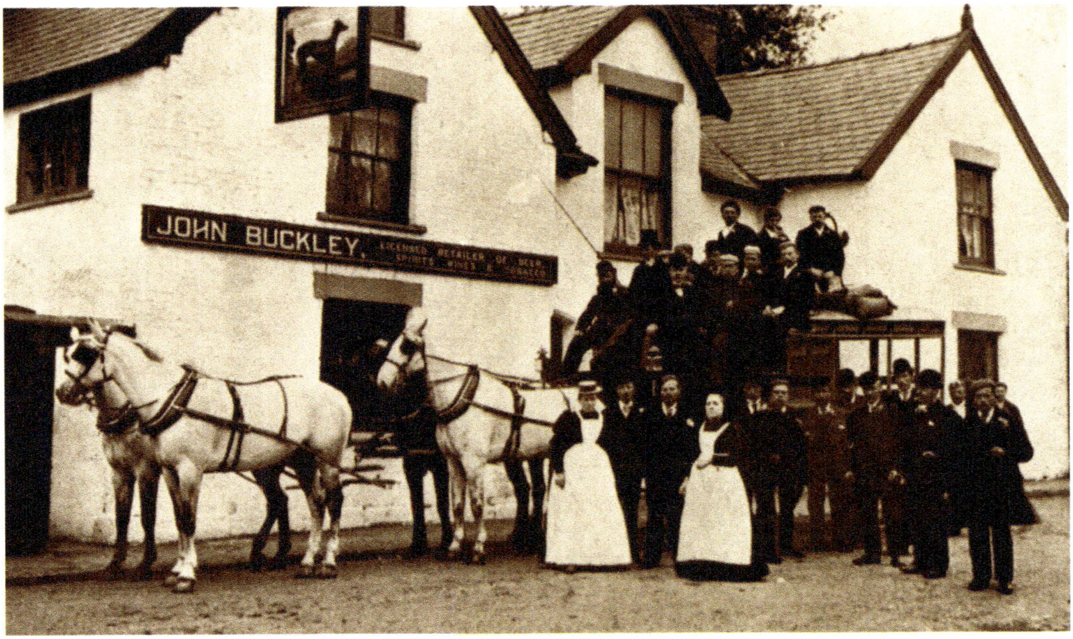

Black Greyhound, Lostock Gralam, and Wincham, 1895 and 2015
A look at the Black Greyhound at Four Lane Ends as a horse drawn coach awaits passengers. The name of the licensee is John Buckley who held the licence from 1888 to 1900. Later the pub would be demolished and the land is now a car sales premises. This is the first 'Then and Now' photo that is not really correct as the new Black Greyhound built in 1938 is about 2 miles away at the Wincham crossroads. It is this building that is in the 2015 photo; note the similarities in the old and new buildings. The new one is now semi-derelict and for sale.

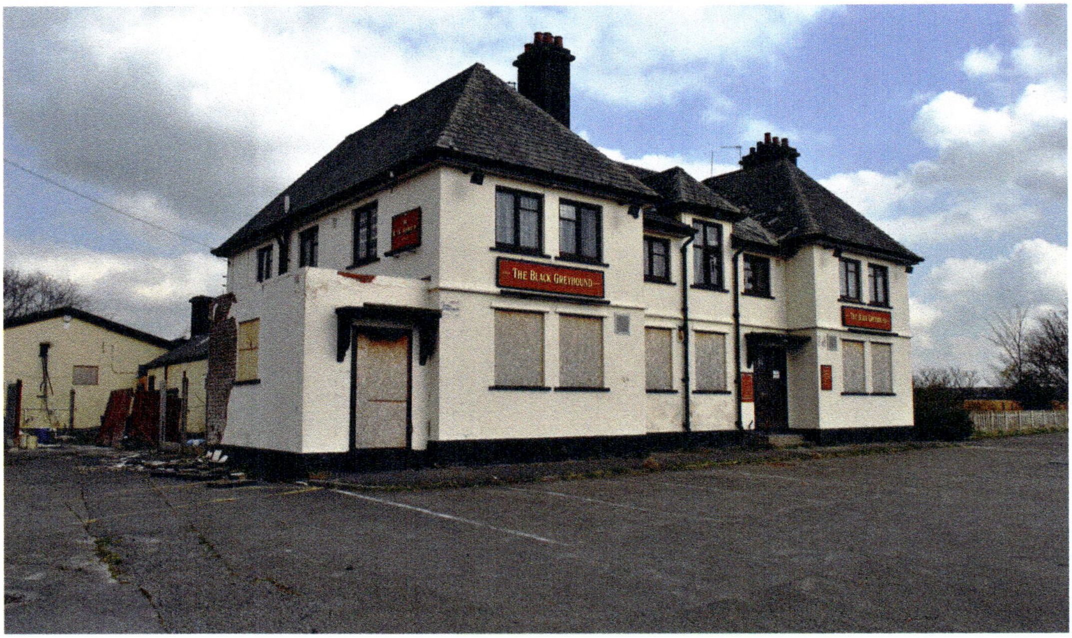

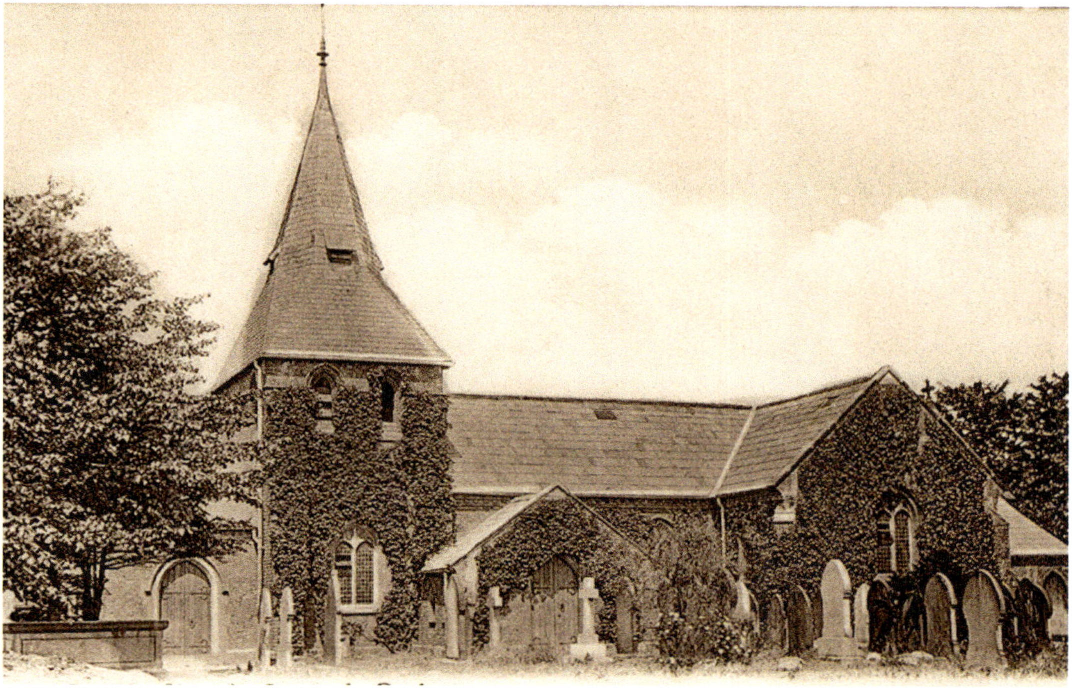

Lostock Church, Undated and 2015

St John the Evangelist at Lostock Gralam was built in 1845 to serve the villages of Lach Dennis, Birches, Hulse and Wincham.

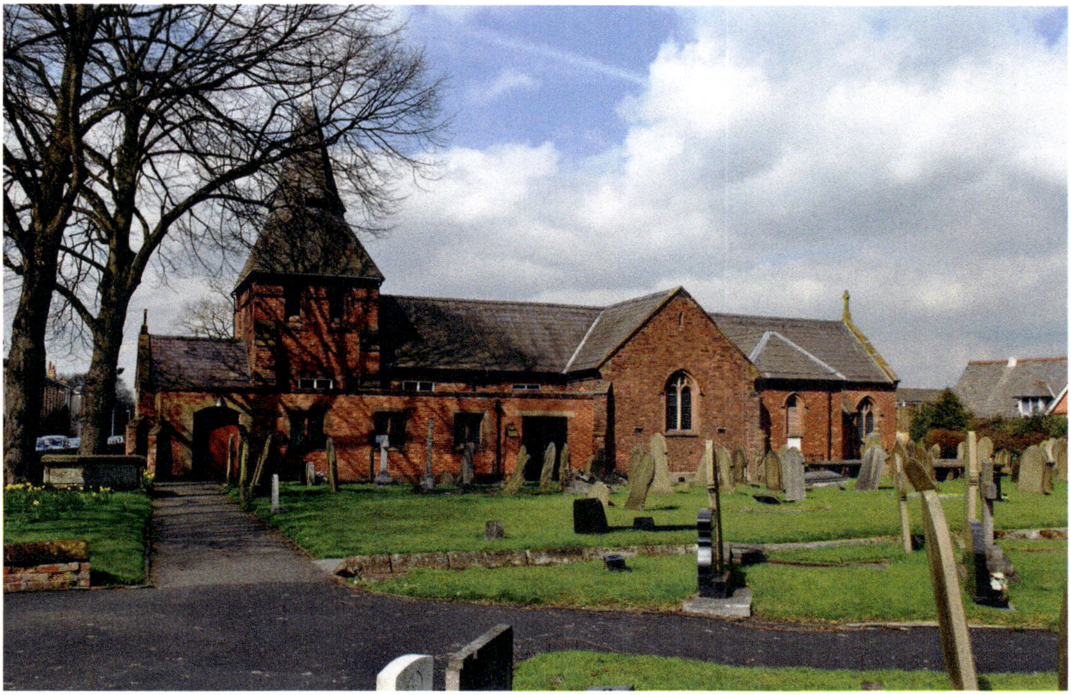

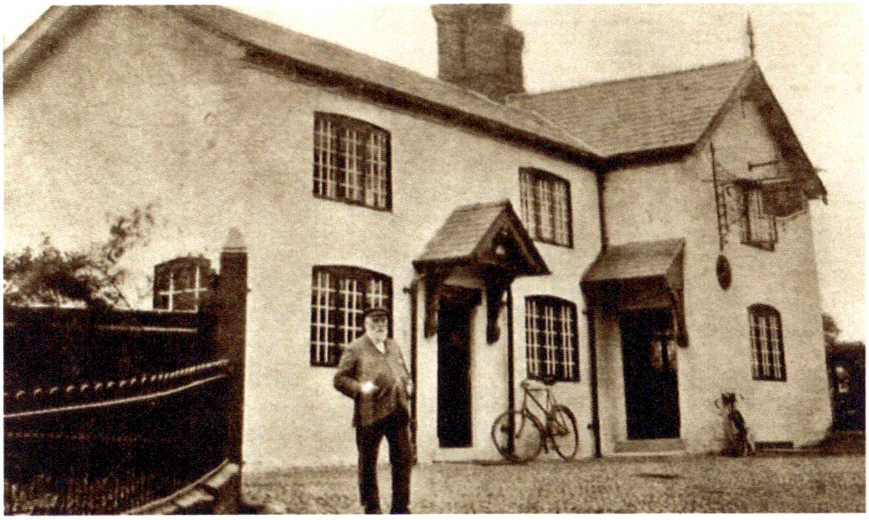

Spinner & Bergamot, Comberbach, 1900–1910 and 2015

The first licensee, Joseph Morris took over in 1770; it was formerly known as the Spinners Inn after one of J. H. Smith-Barry's racehorses. In the early part of the last century, the name was changed to the Spinner and Bergamot, Bergamot being another horse. The man in the old photograph taken in 1900 is the licensee whose rather flowery name was Albert Isaiah Coffin Lees; no wonder he looked miserable! He was tenant from 1898 to 1915.

Before taking over the Spinner, Albert had been licensee of The Druids Arms at the junction of Leicester Street and Gibson's Road in Northwich, an area of timber yards, industrial premises and poverty at the turn of the last century.

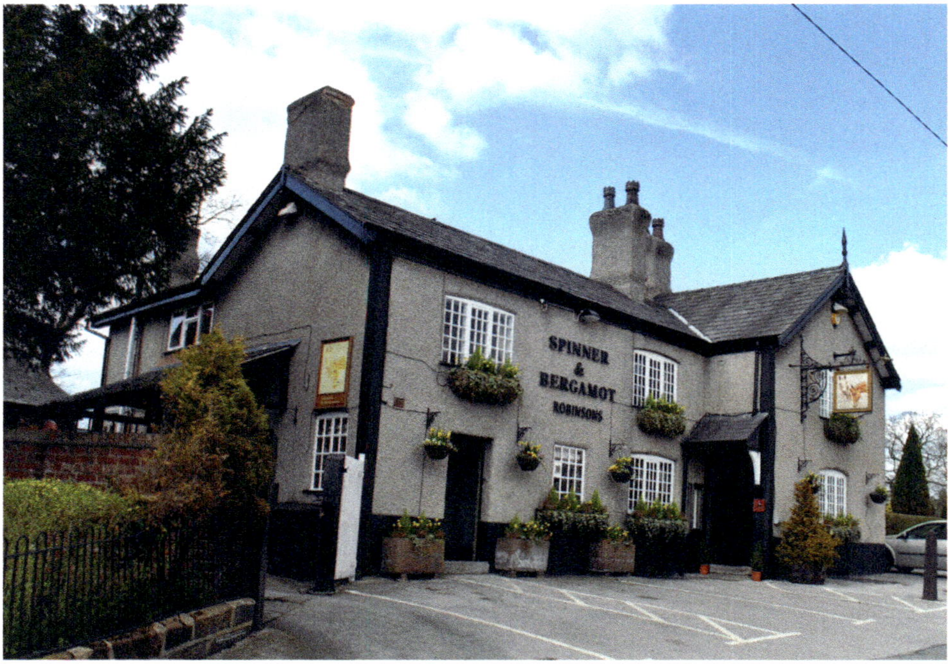

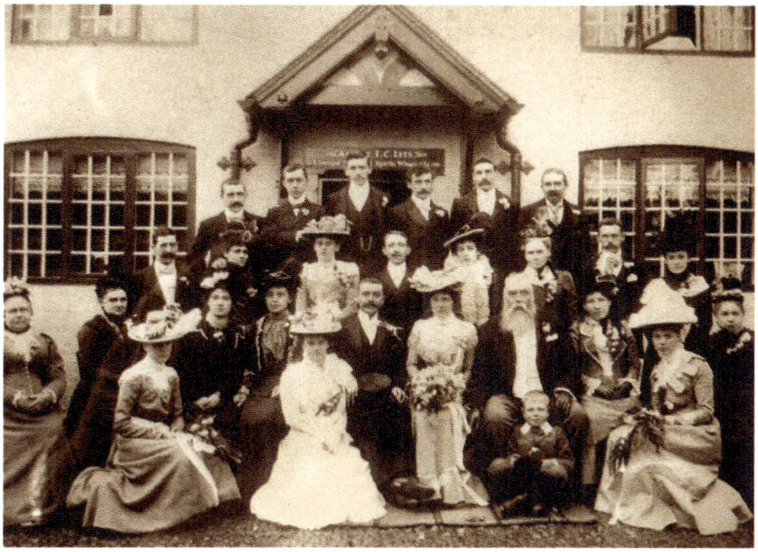

Spinner and Bergamot, 1900–1910 and 2015

A few years ago, I was contacted by Raymond Jones from Wrexham who, when browsing my book, came across the photo of the Spinner and Bergamot wedding shown here. Raymond is the great, great grandson of the licensee shown in the photograph, Albert Isaiah Coffin Lees, and the wedding is that of his daughter Edith, Raymond's great grandmother. An interesting fact here is that the bride had a child who was then three years old and illegitimate. This child was Raymond's grandmother Gertrude Lees. Gertrude was a pretty and happy little girl who was a favourite with the locals but, because of the strict puritanical Victorian prudery in vogue at the time, she was barred from the wedding ceremony by her mother. However, if you look at the photo carefully, you can see the top window is ajar and it is from there that the child was permitted to observe the scene. Gertrude went on to lead a long and fruitful life in Wheatsheaf Lane, Antrobus, where she and her husband brought up five children; she was also very active in the community.

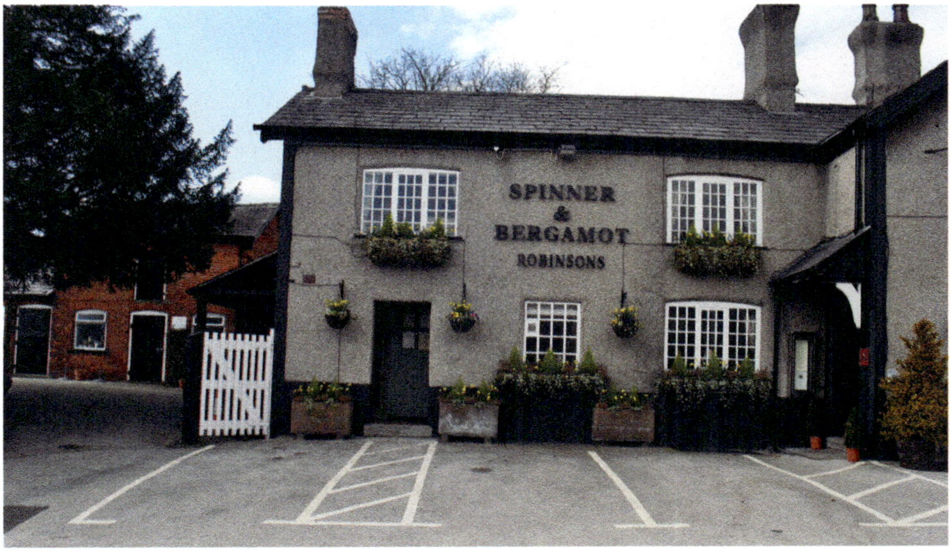

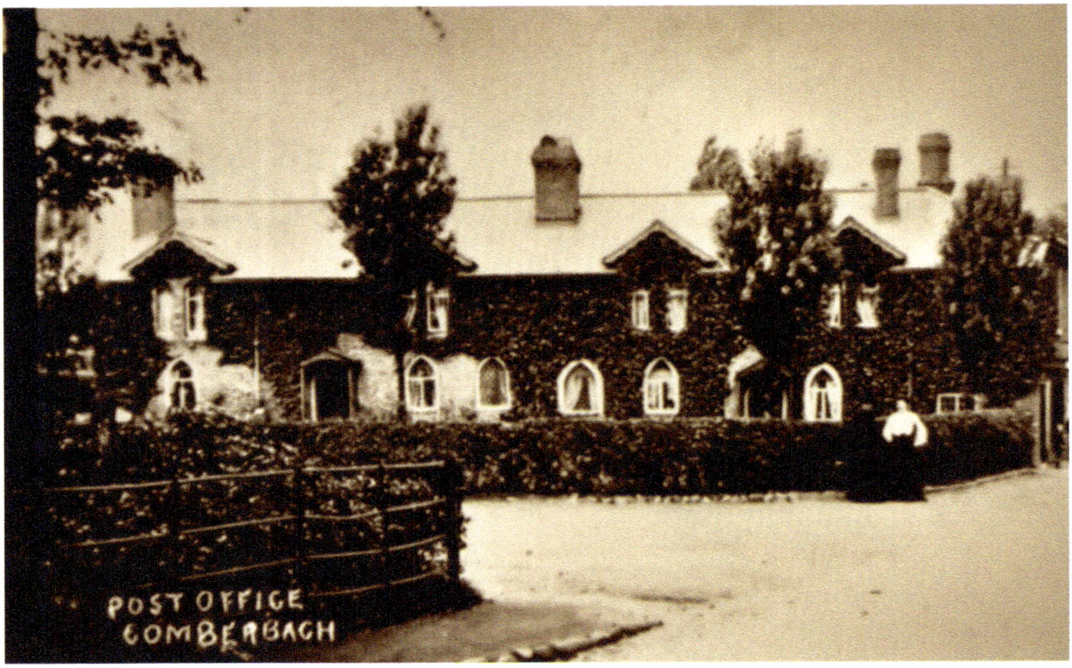

Comberbach Post office, Undated and 2014

This old photograph of a Comberbach building when it was the post office shows what can be done with refurbishment rather than demolition. The old ivy-covered building has been brought up to date both outside and in.

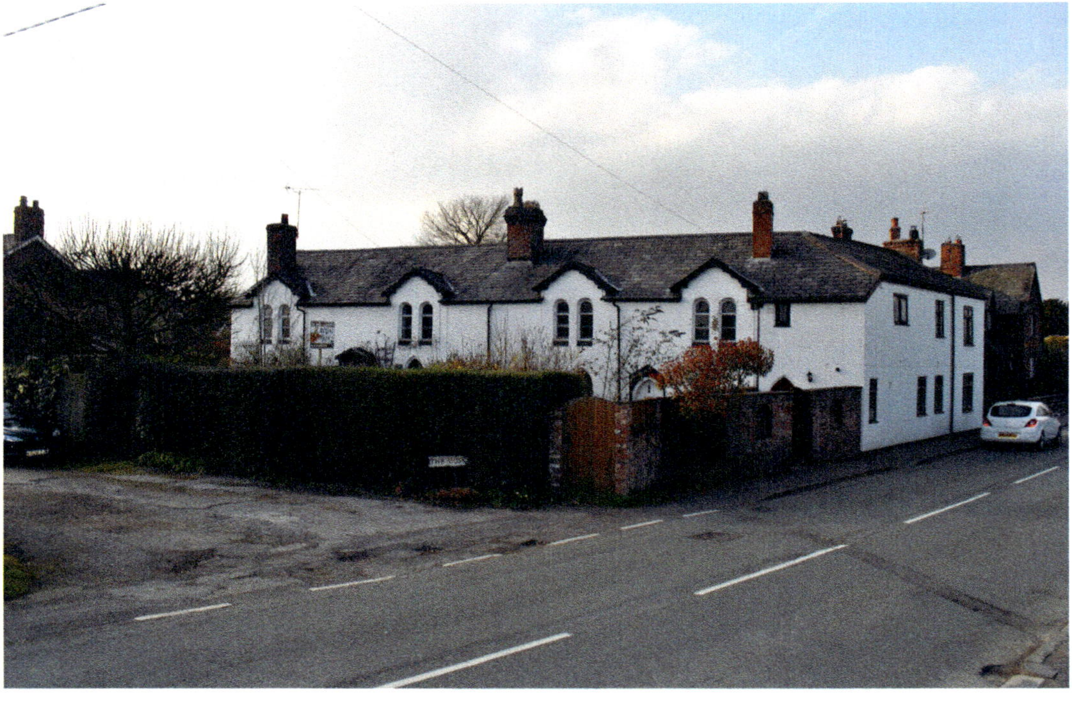

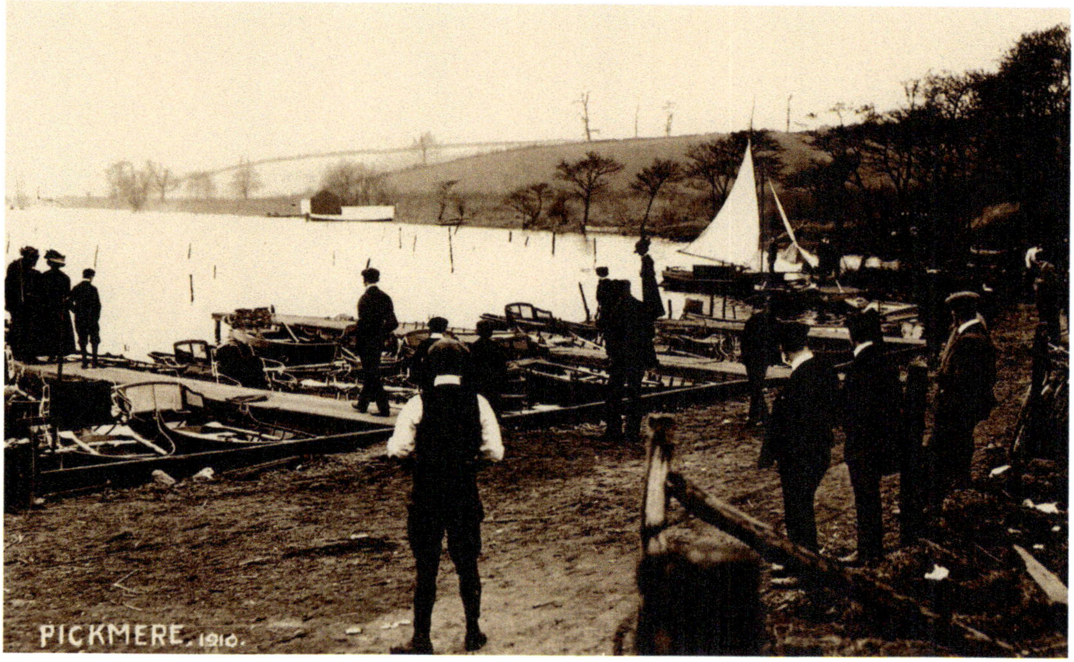

Pickmere Lake, Early 1900s and 2015

Pickmere Lake in Pickmere was for many years a holiday destination. In this 1900 photograph, boats are for hire and cruises on the lake by steam boat may be enjoyed. As time passed this entertainment included a permanent fairground.

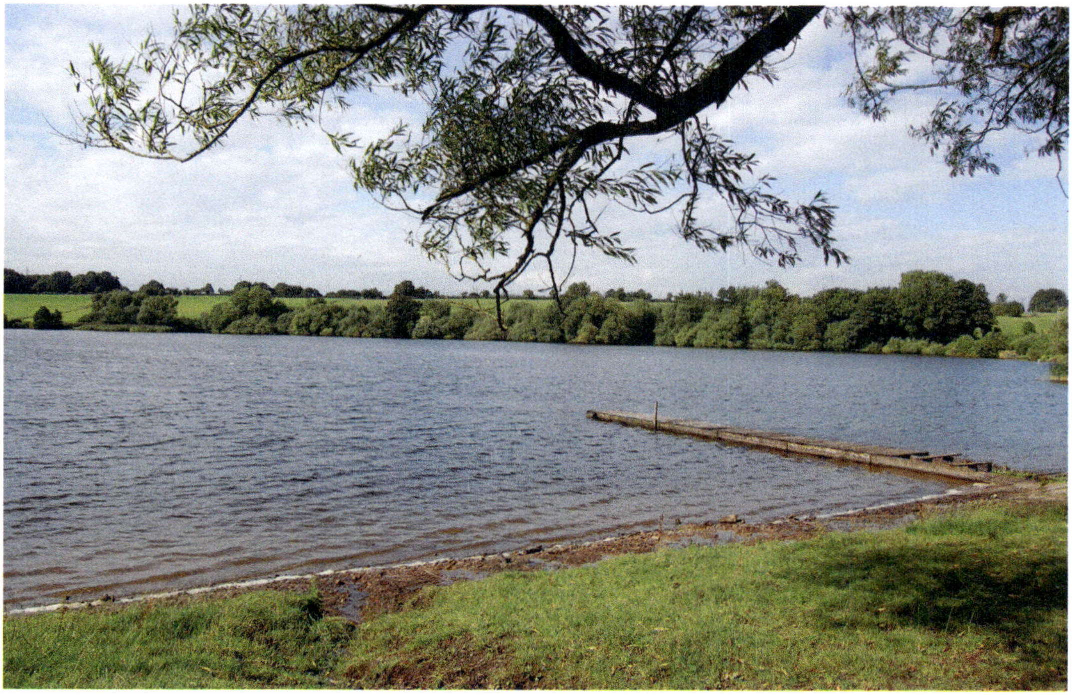

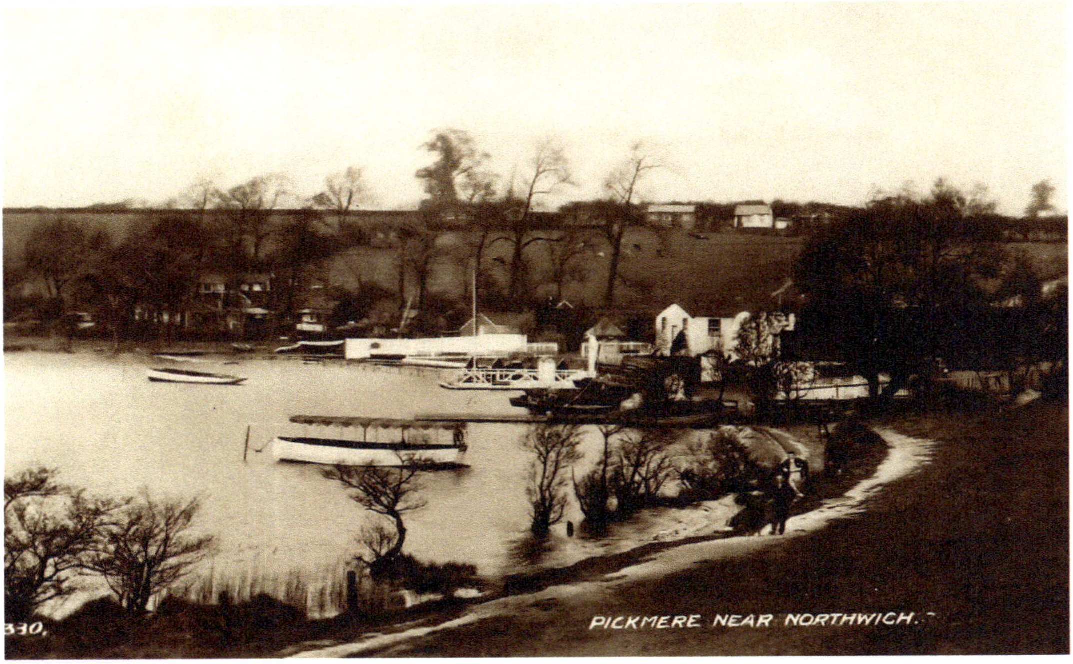

Pickmere Lake, 1910 and 2015

It is now 1910 and hire boats abound. Having evolved through the years as social fashions dictated it is now simply a pretty lake with pleasant walks around its perimeter. There are also strategically placed picnic areas.

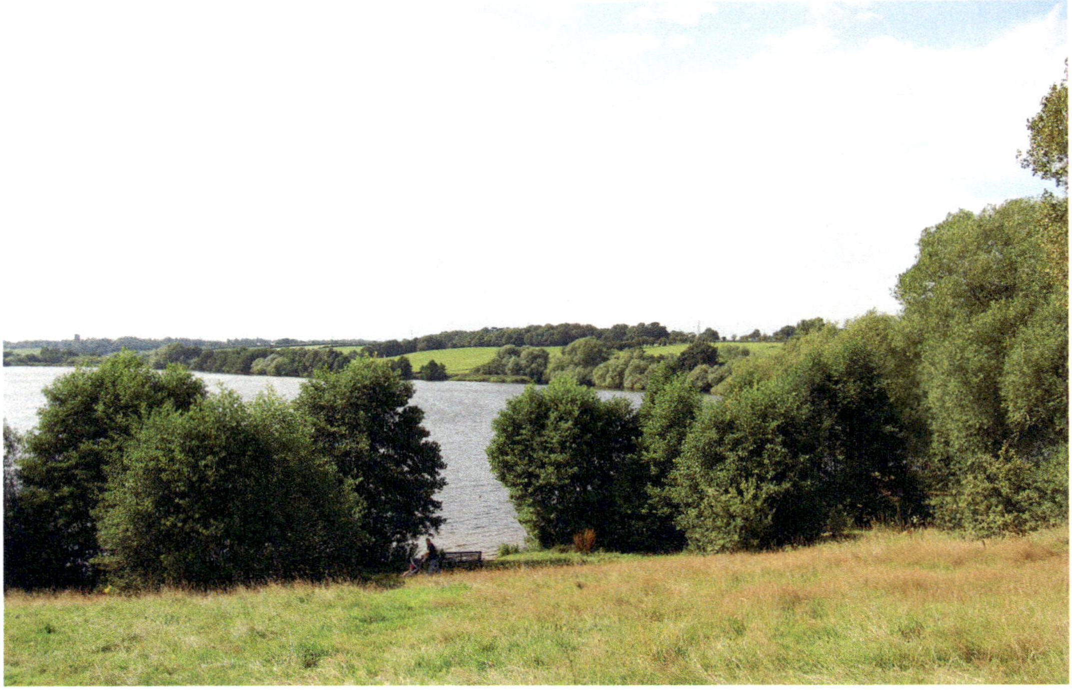

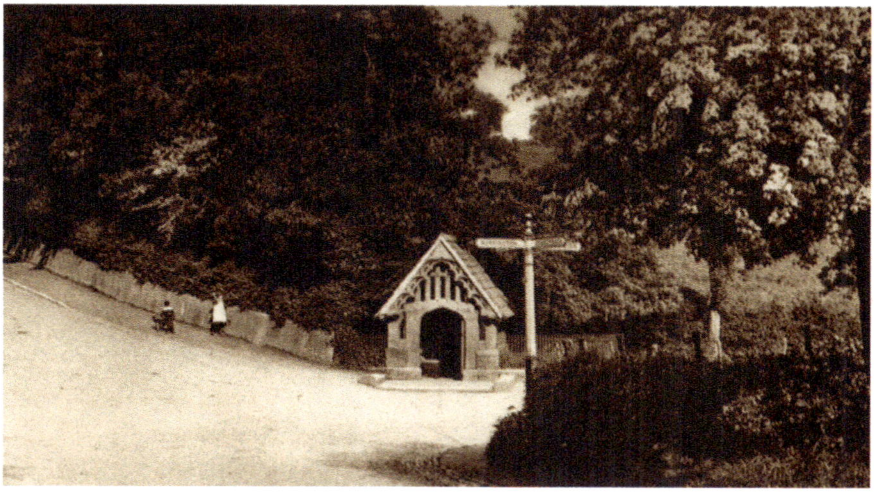

Great Budworth children, 1900 and 2015
One of the most famous villages in Cheshire is Great Budworth, a place where time seems to stand still. My wife's grandfather was the first policeman to reside at the then-new police house here. These photographs show the crossroads and the road that leads up to the village centre. The road is situated on the road from Northwich to Warrington, which is also the old coach road to London.

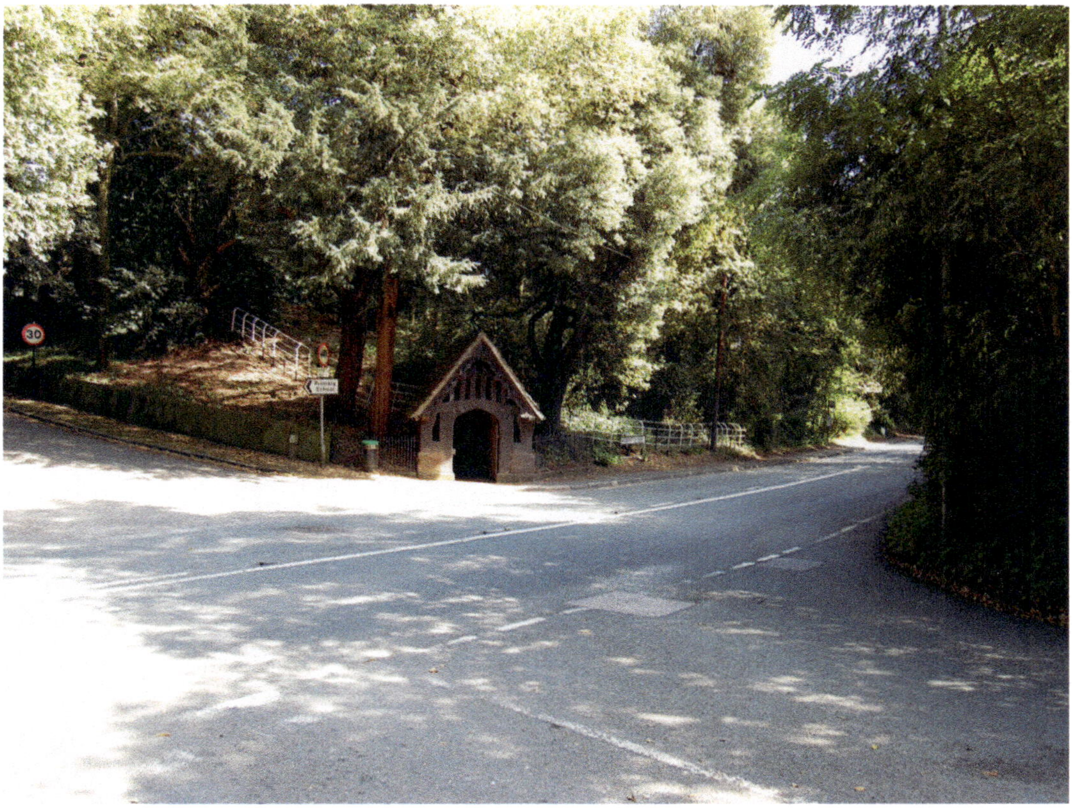

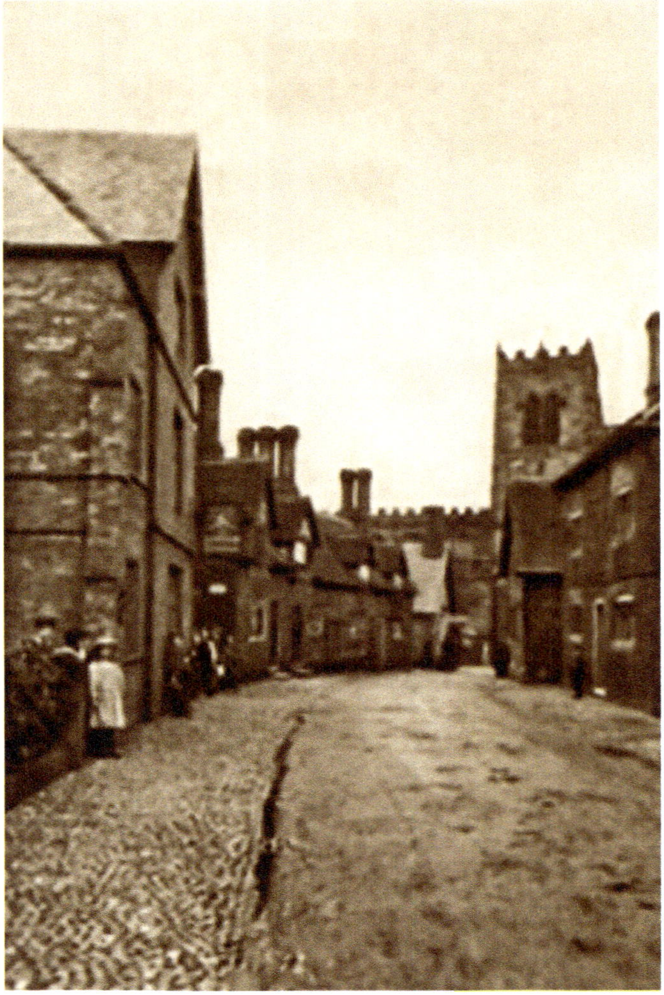

Great Budworth, 1890 and 1905

A hand-tinted view along High Street towards the church. The building sticking out on the right with the tree in front was the Ring o' Bells pub and was closed along with the nearby Saracens Head in 1856. This was to better control drinking in the village during those days of abstinence and moderation! Only the George & Dragon remained as the village pub. This time I have included a matching earlier photo.

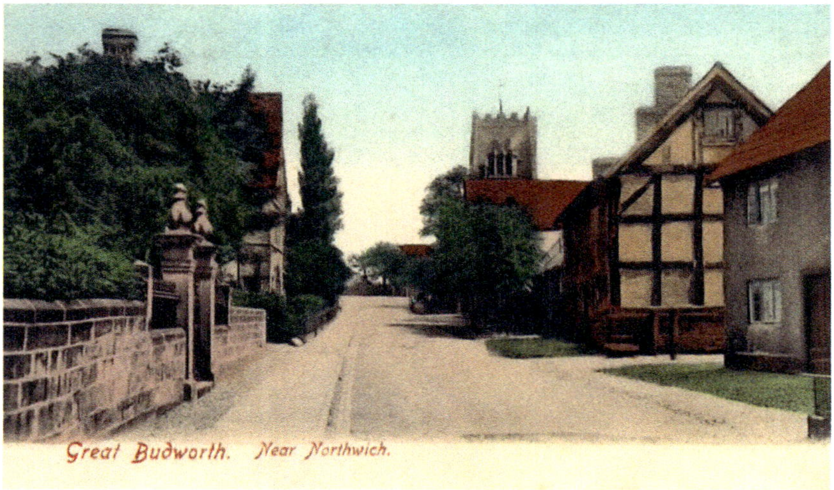

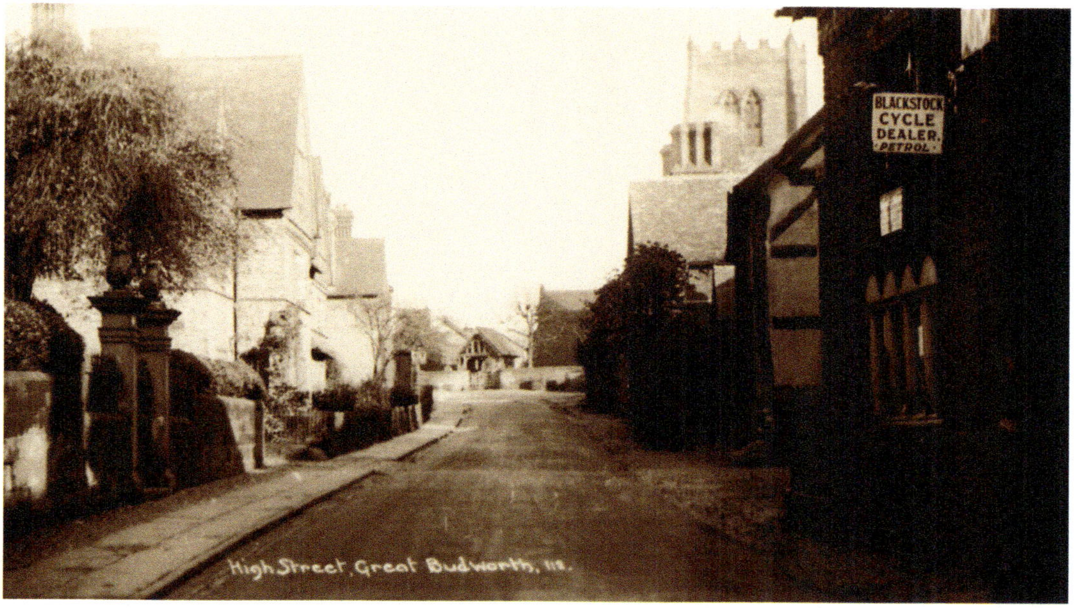

Great Budworth, 1900s and 2015

Now we see just how little has changed over the years and why the village is such a favourite with period film-makers. This is Church Street looking towards St Mary and All Saints' church. The oldest part of the church is the Lady Chapel, which dates back to the fourteenth century. The rest of the church can be dated to the fifteenth and sixteenth centuries. This is the same vantage point as the last view but inclusion of this image is worth it to see even more of what has remained, including the arched windows on the right. In the older photograph, the premises of Blackstock's cycle dealer also sold petrol to the early cars. This building also housed the post office.

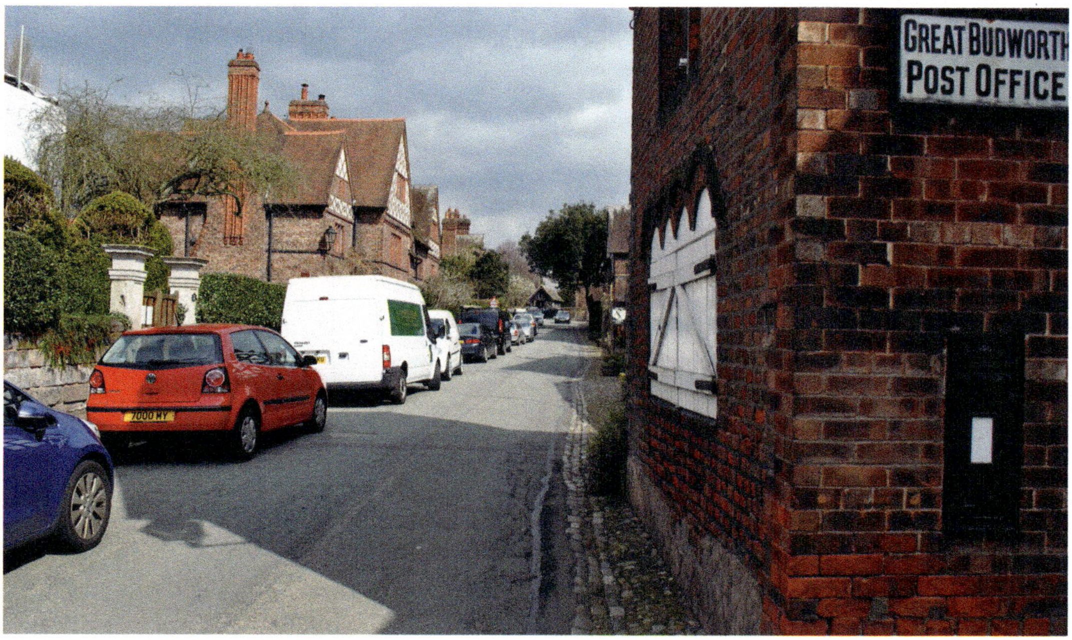

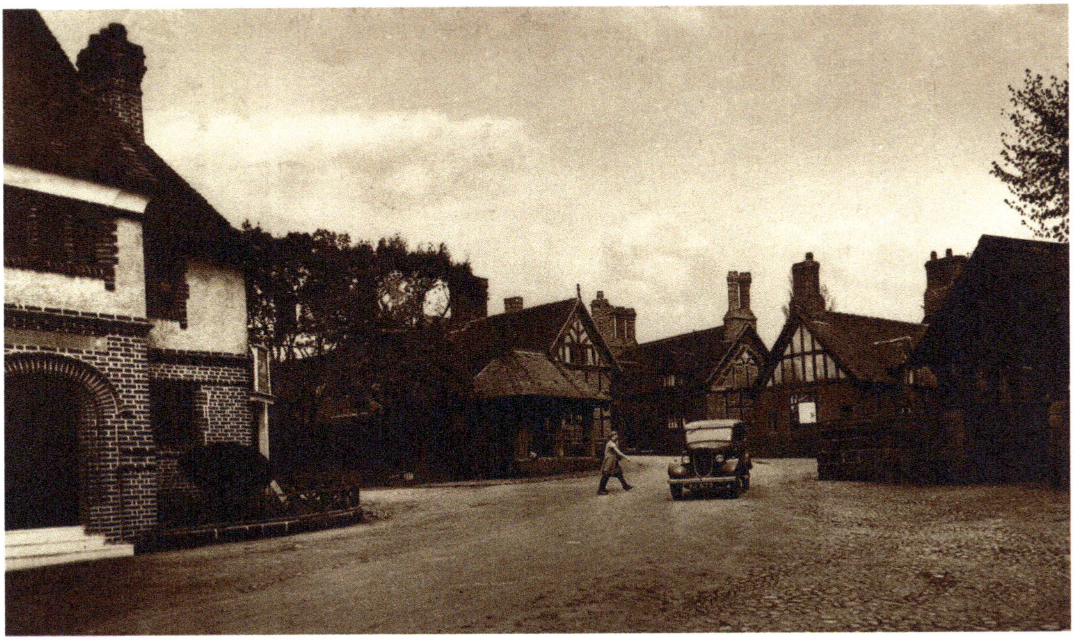

Great Budworth, George and Dragon, 1955 and 2009

Further up in the village centre showing the Lychgate to the church and the George and Dragon pub. After the forced closing of the lesser public houses in the village many years ago, the George and Dragon is the only one remaining. It is now under new management and has been refurbished back into a typical village pub, but with excellent food! The old Ford saloon sits well in the centre of the 1955 photo.

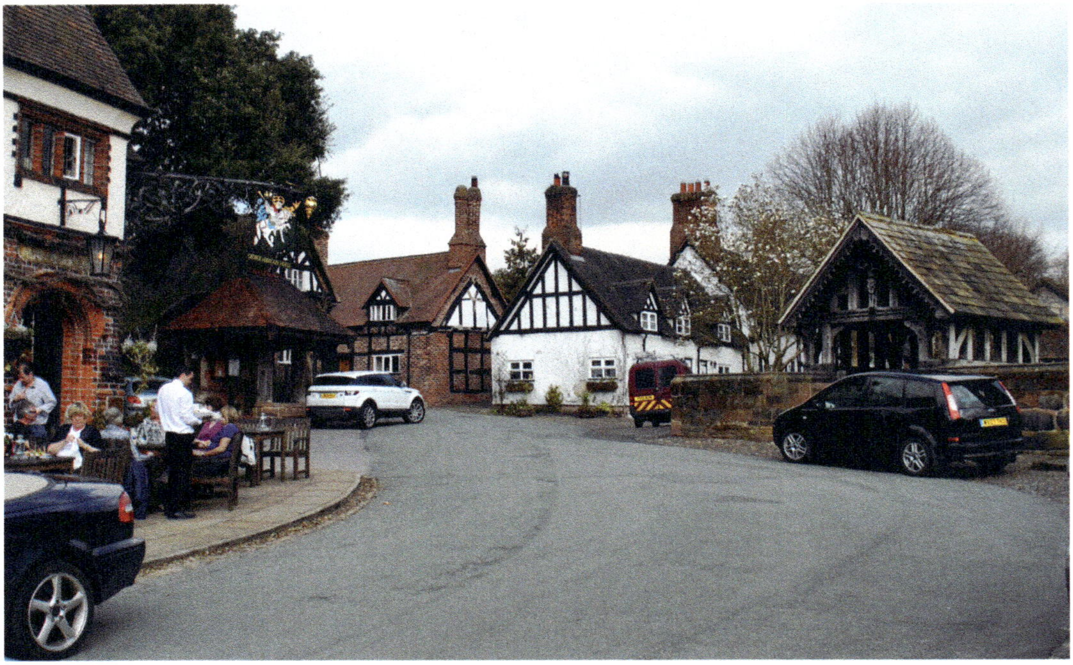

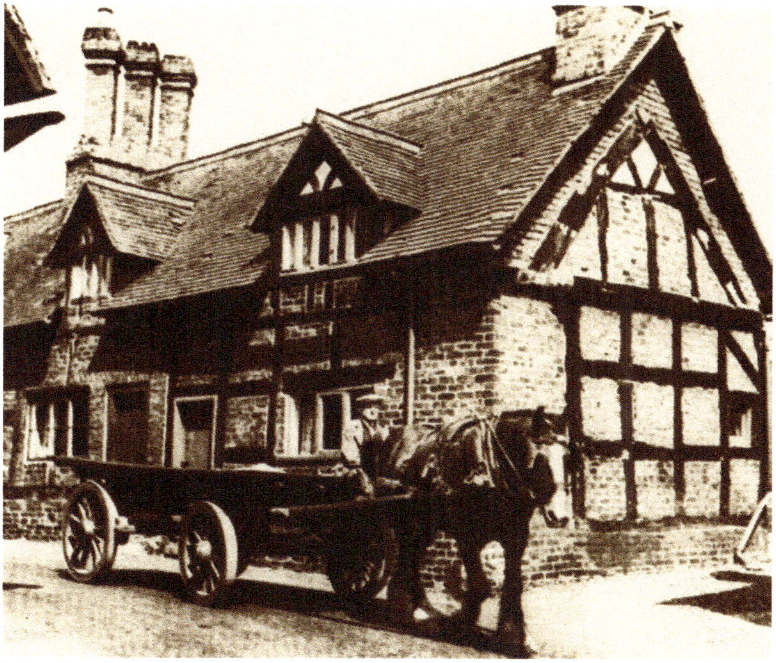

Great Budworth Horse and Lorry

This evocative shot of a horse-drawn lorry in Church Street also demonstrates how little the village has changed; the house has been tastefully modernized but has retained its ancient façade. The old photo is undated but will have been around the turn of the last century, although such transport was used well into the 1950s with supports at each end to convert it into a hay wain.

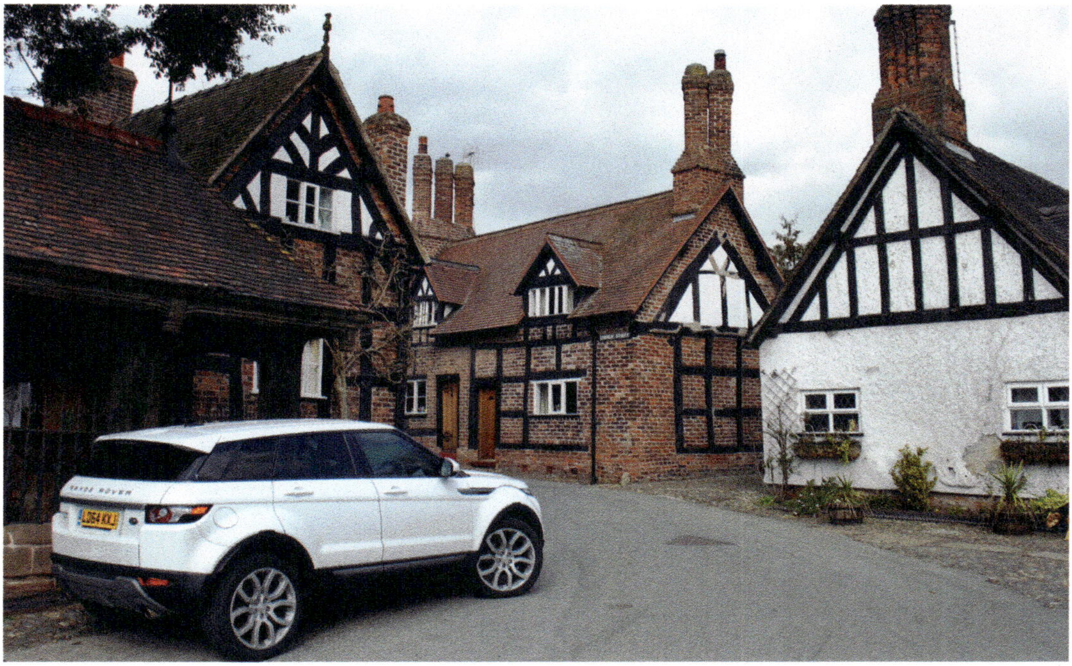

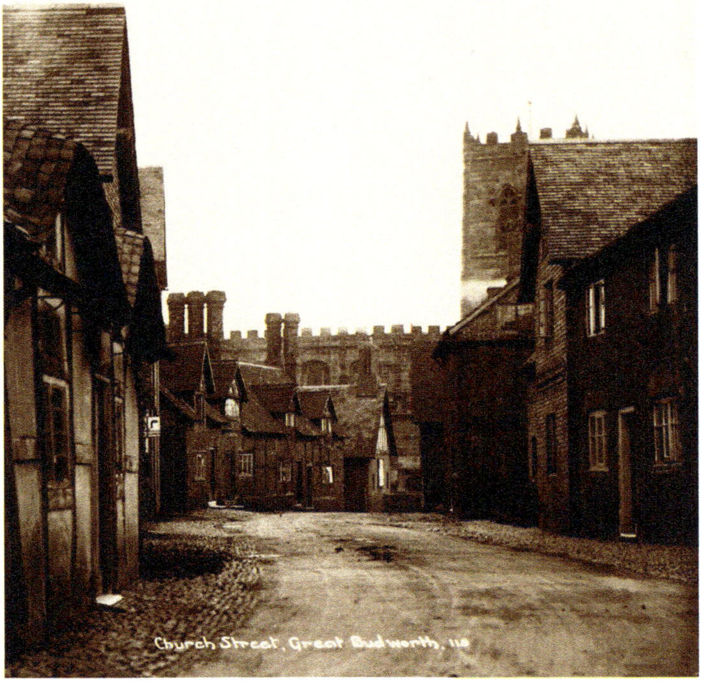

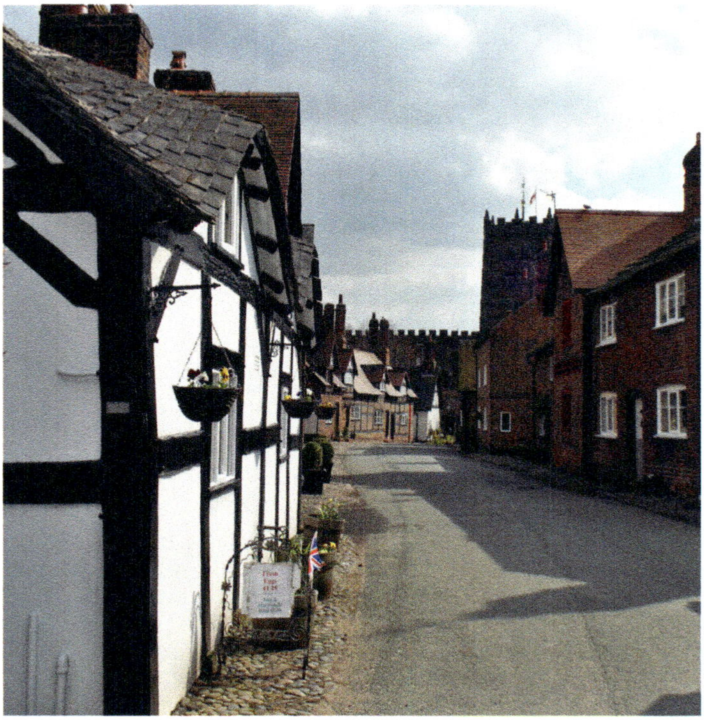

Great Budworth Towards the Church, Early 1900s and 2015

A view now into Great Budworth from the top of the village looking back towards the parish church. There is very little difference in the old and new views even though there is probably a hundred years between them. Outside the church can still be found the set of stocks. They were used up to 1854 to calm the village scallywags and deter those from other villages. To sit strapped into them for a while as rotten fruit is thrown at you is a deterrent that perhaps may work now!

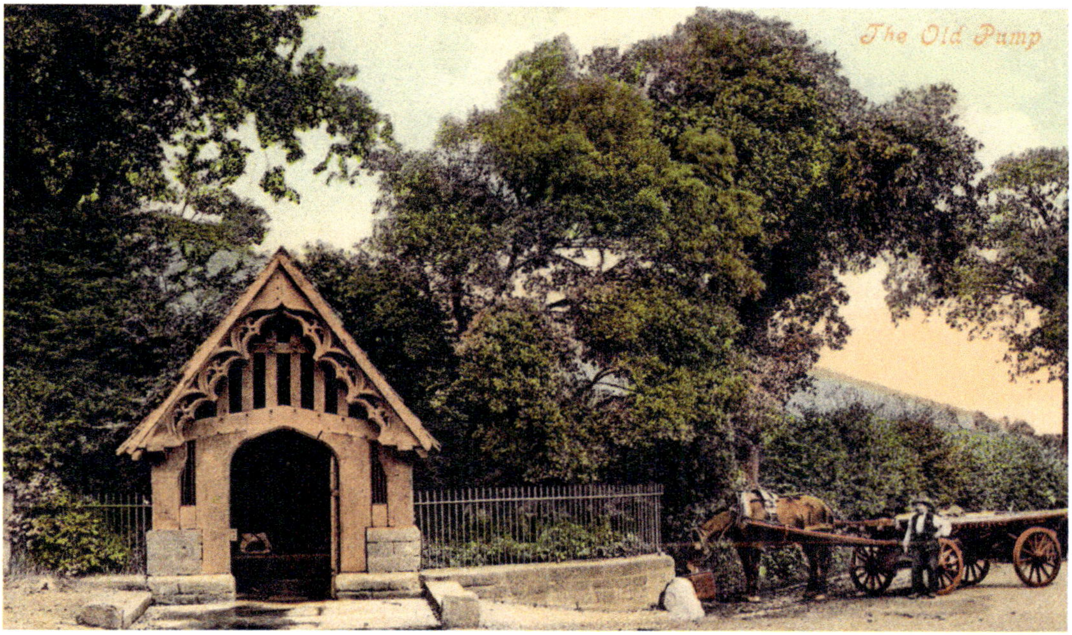

Great Budworth Pump, 1906 and 2009

This well-known landmark was built in 1869 to cover the well of the old Great Budworth running pump. This was the only supply of water available to the village from 1869 to 1890, after which five pumps were installed and remained the source of water until a mains supply was piped to the village in 1936. The pump still provides running water that is favoured by amateur winemakers and brewers who wish to avoid the chlorinated tap water.

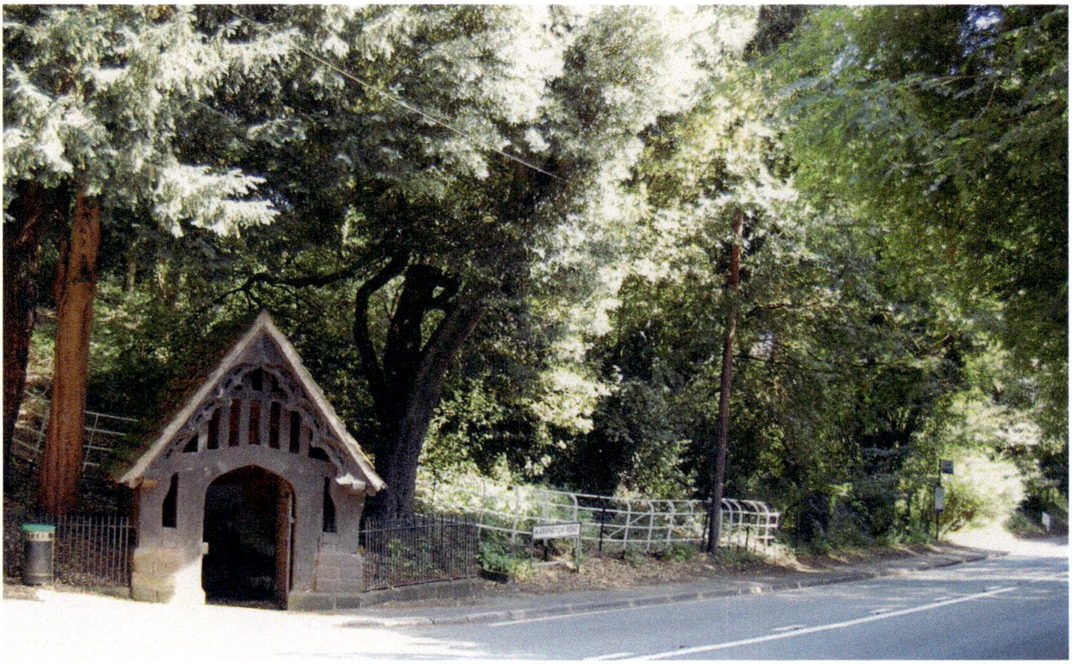

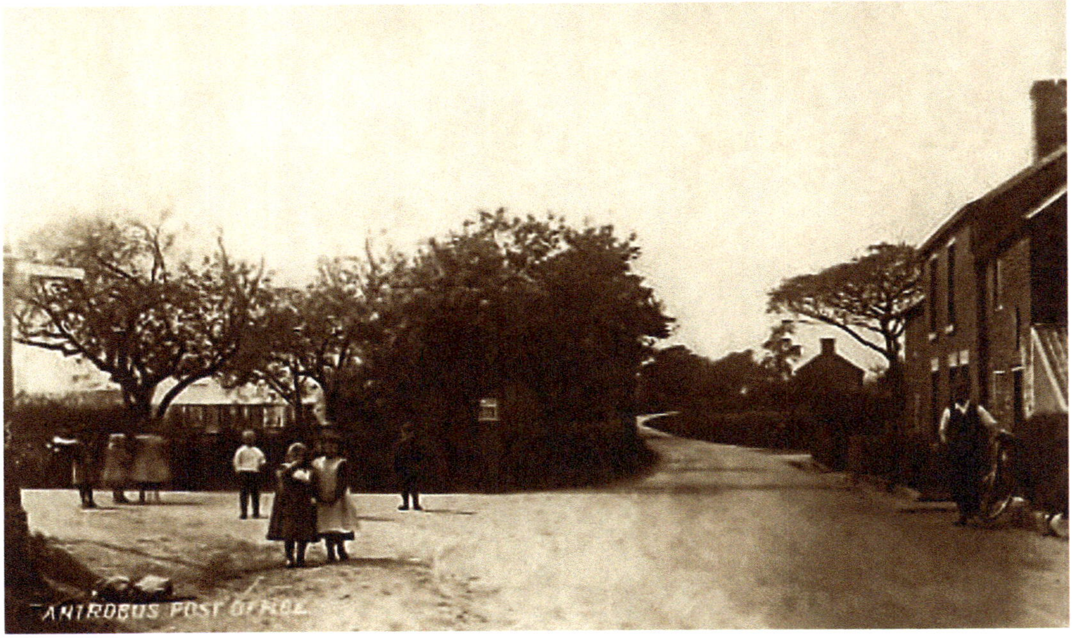

Antrobus Post Office, 1900 and 2014

This is a poor photo but shows that little has changed in this small village and even the post office is still open. This is a quite unique situation as it closed in 2002! The local community then got together and appealed for it to remain open. As a result a community shop came into being, staffed solely with volunteers from the village. It is open for seven days every week and has gone from strength to strength; profits are used for the benefit of the community.

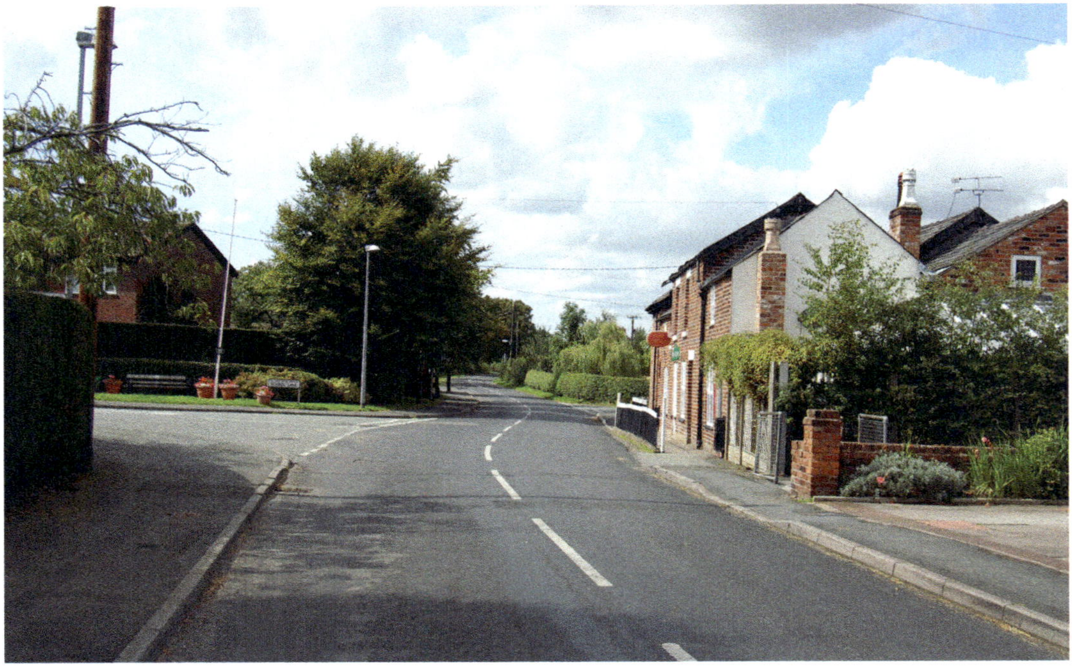

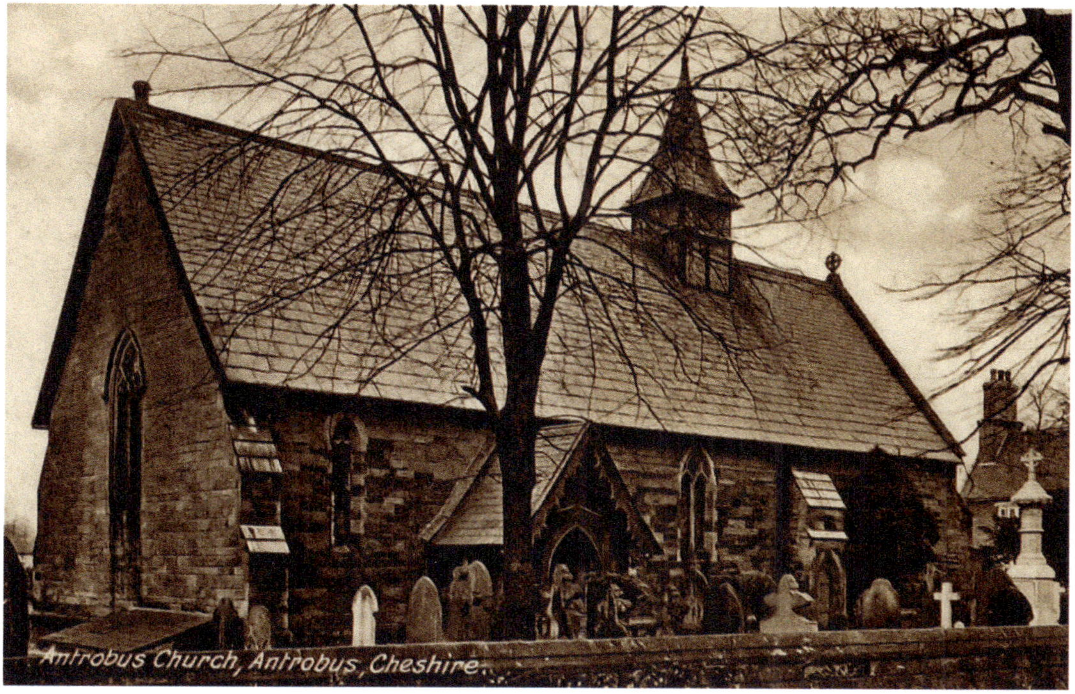

Antrobus Church, 1900 and 2014
St Mark's Church of England church was opened in 1848 to serve Antrobus and Seven Oaks, later taking in other villages.

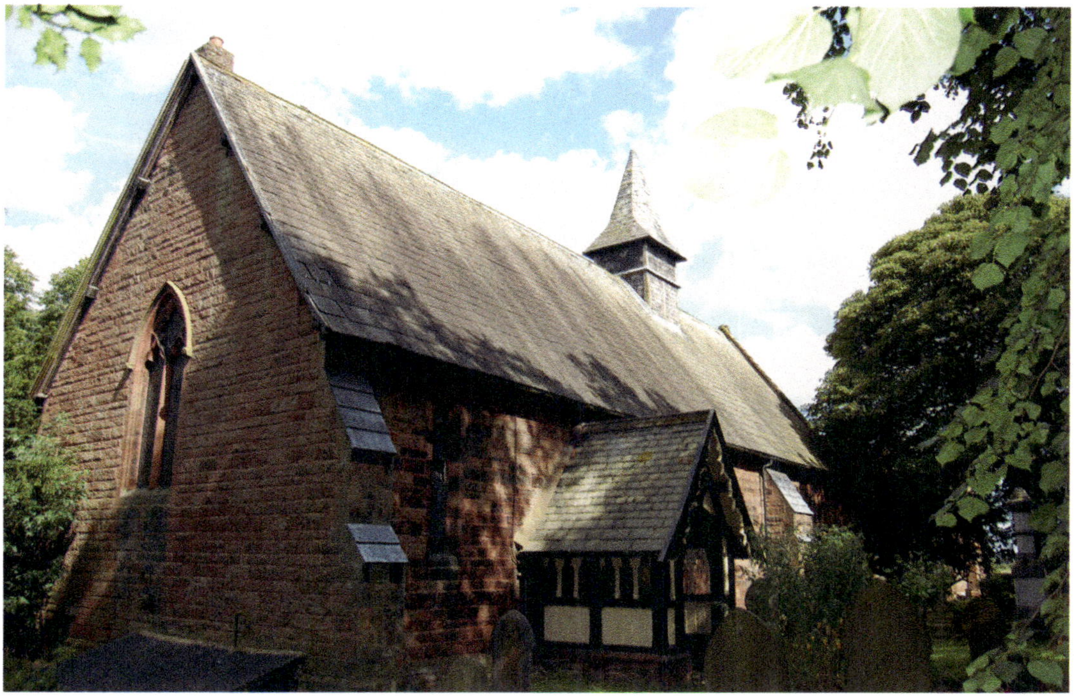

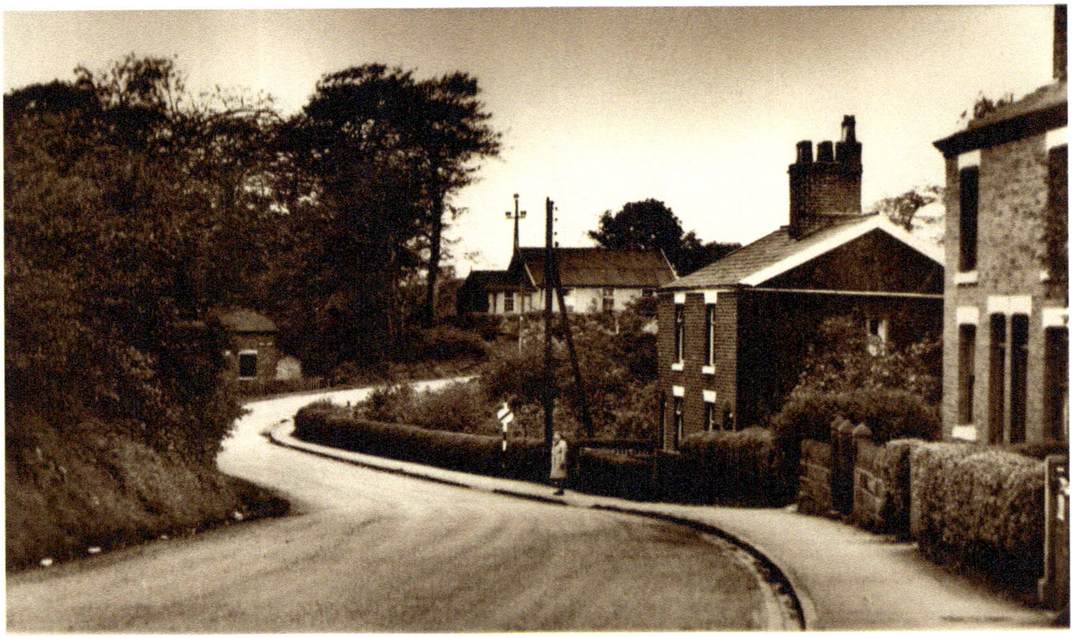

Gunnersclough Barnton, 1934–1945 and 2015

The old photo is dated to 1934 and beyond by the de-restriction sign just after the female pedestrian. These signs were erected to show the end of a restricted speed limit such as 30 miles per hour. They were then what the name states, de-restriction signs, as when passing them speed was not restricted at all until 1965. Gunnersclough or Gunner's Clough is on the outskirts of Barnton towards Anderton and was originally a small hamlet.

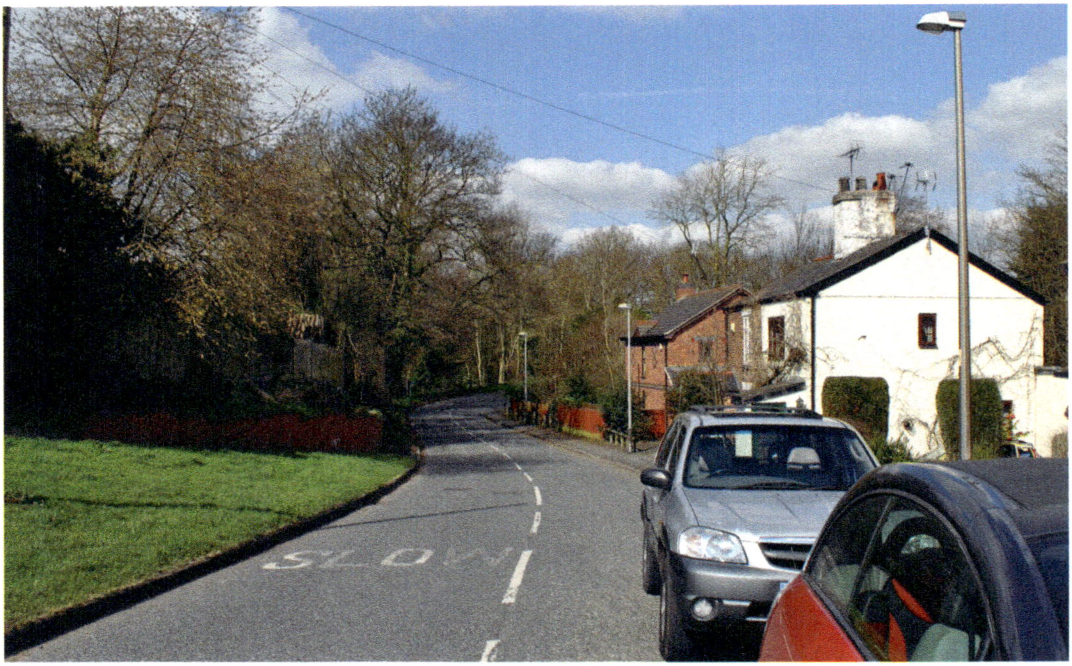

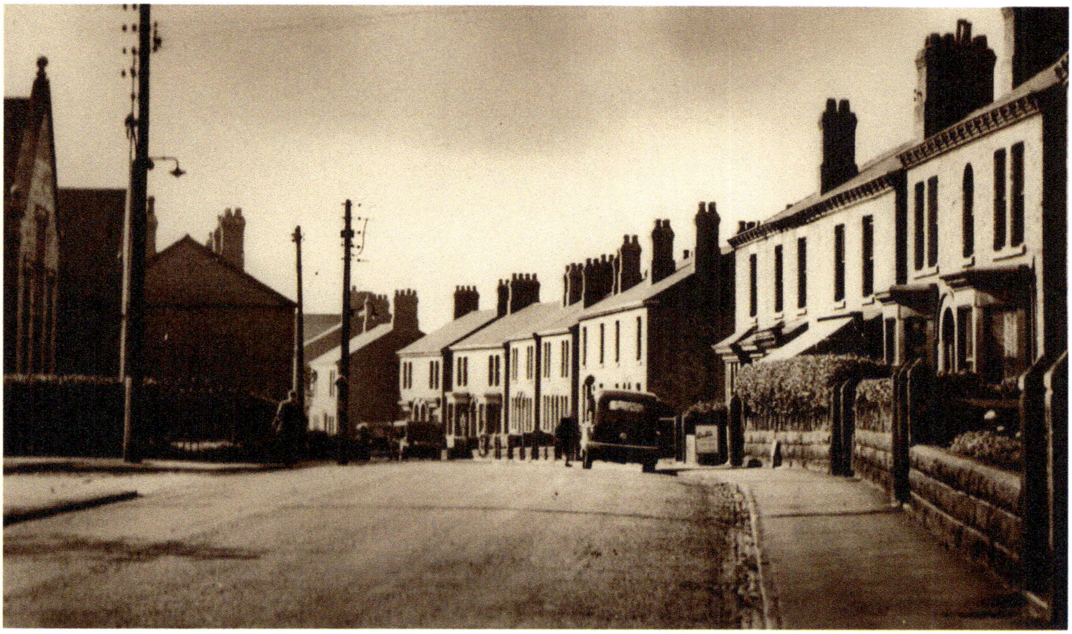

Lydyett Lane, Barnton, 1950s and 2015

Pictured is one of the main roads in Barnton, which leads down to Gunnersclough, looking back towards the Townfield Lane junction. The large building on the left in the old photograph has been replaced by a Co-op store. This building was the Brunner School built in 1895. In 1964 it was converted into a village hall, and in 2005 it was demolished when the new memorial hall was opened in Townfield Lane.

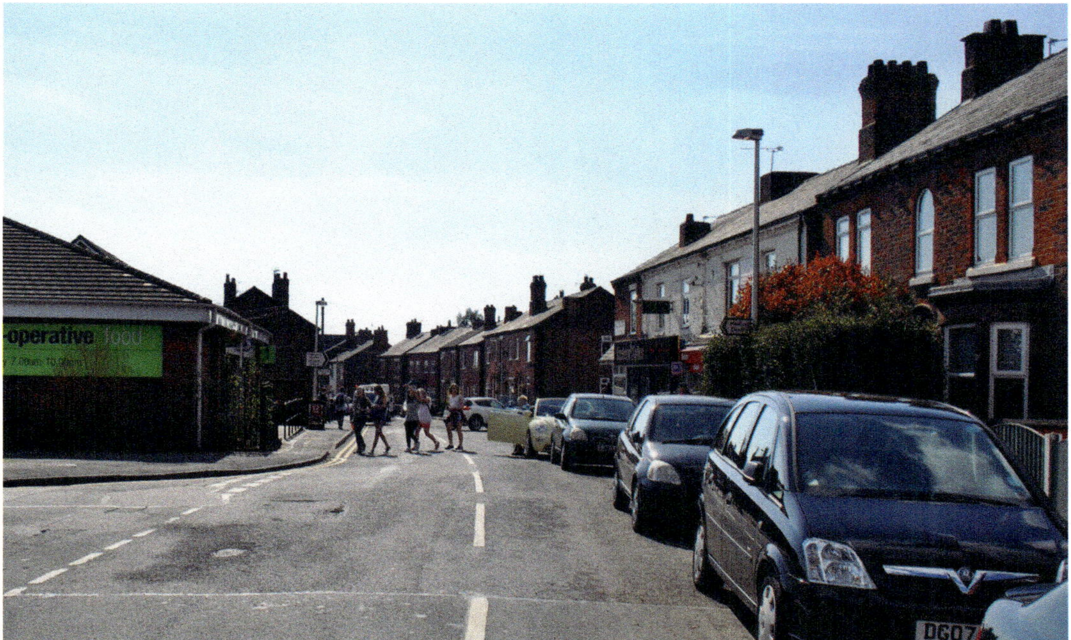

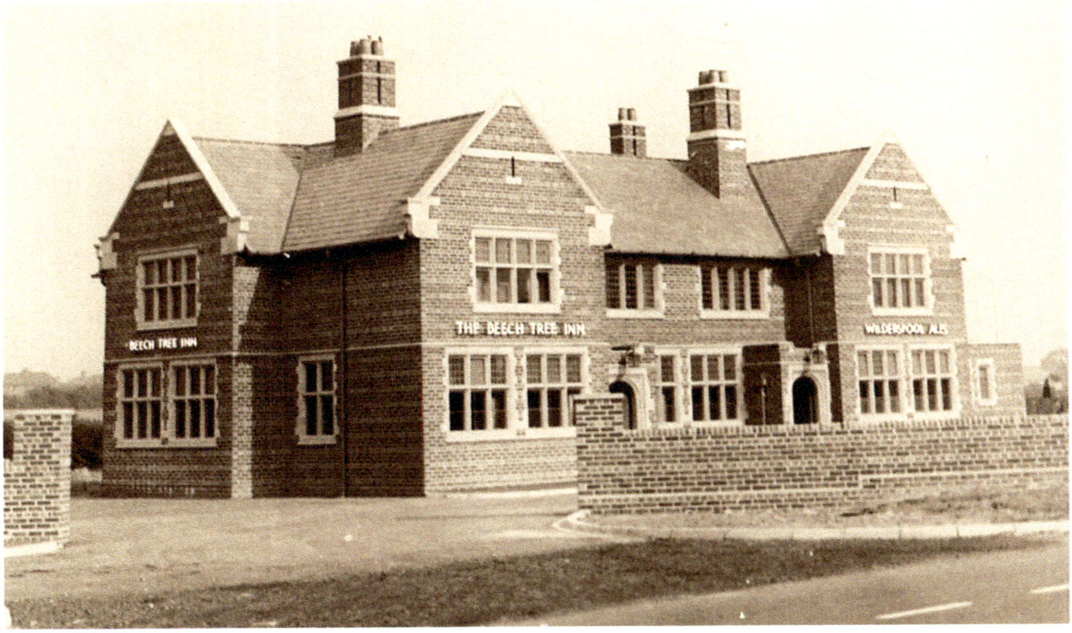

Beech Tree Public House, Barnton, 1939 and 2015

The 1939 photo was taken when the pub was new. The original Beech Tree was on the other side of the road and when the expansion of Barnton was planned before the war a suitably large pub was built. It was opened on the day that war broke out and took over the licence from the Eagle and Child in Northwich High Street. The pub was popular for a while but has now been closed for some time and is likely to be redeveloped.

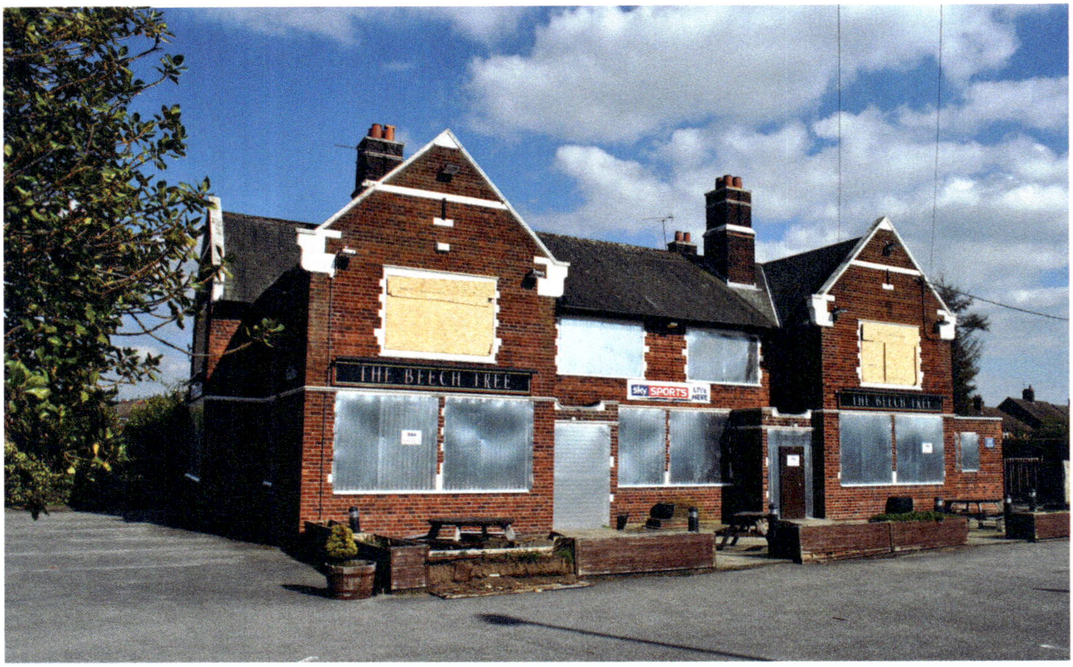

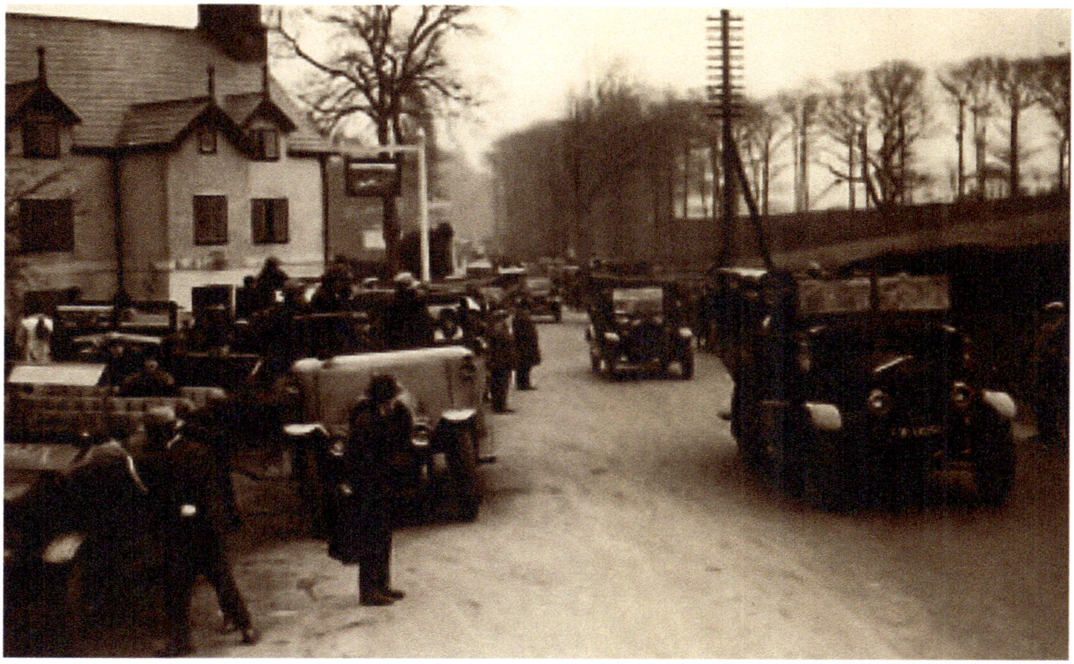

Blue Cap, *c.* 1895 and 2015

The ancient road from Chester to Manchester once carried the mail coaches that travelled between the two cities and onwards. Hotels were used as staging posts for this traffic and an important one was the Sandiway Head Inn. This famous old inn, which stood on the foundations of an even earlier one, was later to have its name changed to The Blue Cap.

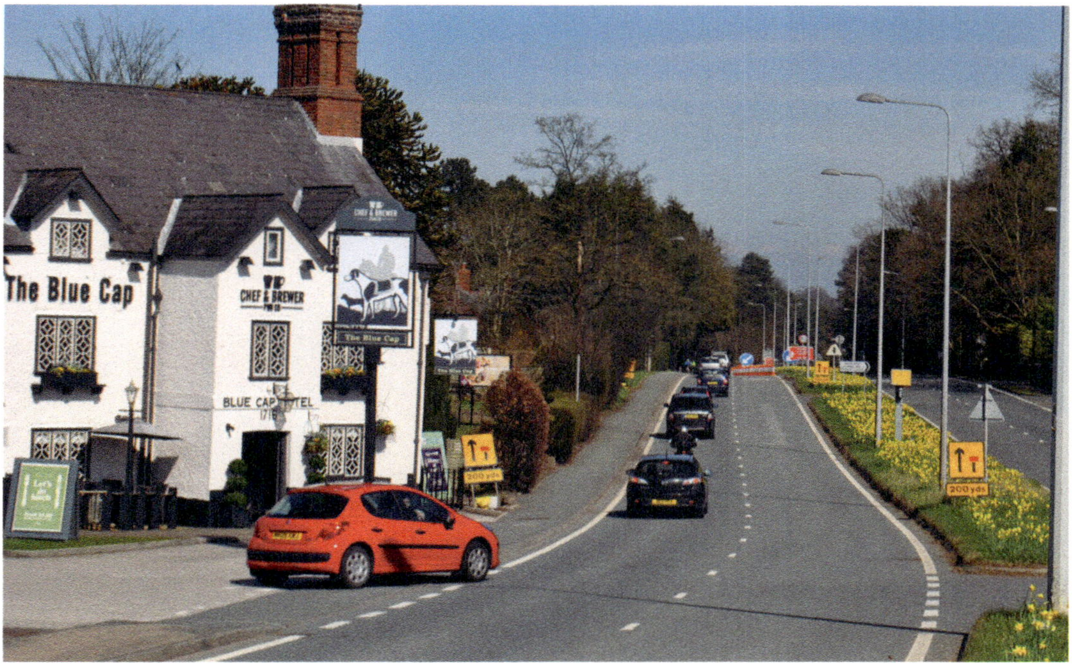

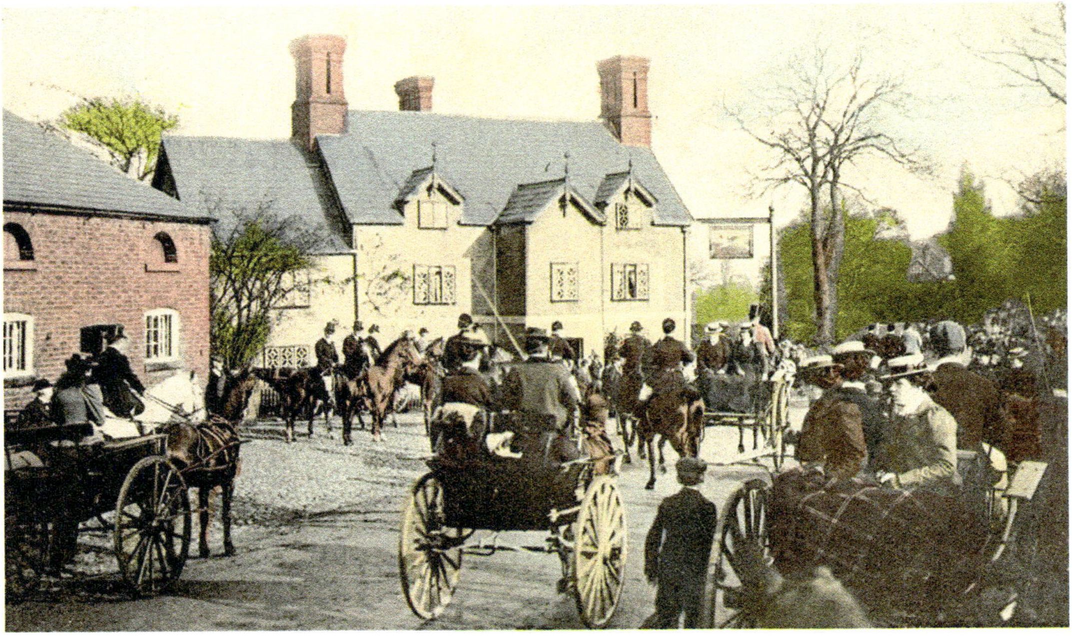

Blue Cap with Hounds, 1895 and Blue Cap, 1920s

For centuries, the Blue Cap Hotel was the starting point for hunt meetings, as can be seen from the old photograph. The second photo was taken in the 1920s. The name comes from a foxhound called Blue Cap whose owner was challenged to race him. The challenge was accepted and in the subsequent race at Newmarket, with a purse of 500 guineas, Blue Cap came first and his daughter, Wanton, second, winning 400 guineas and 100 guineas, respectively; after that the dog was a legend.

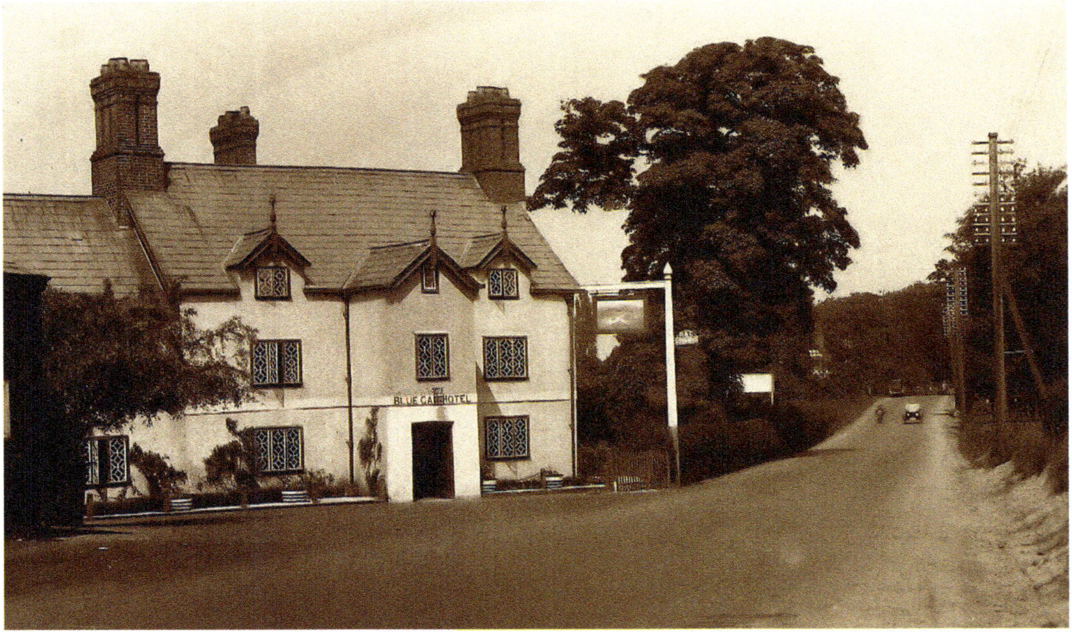

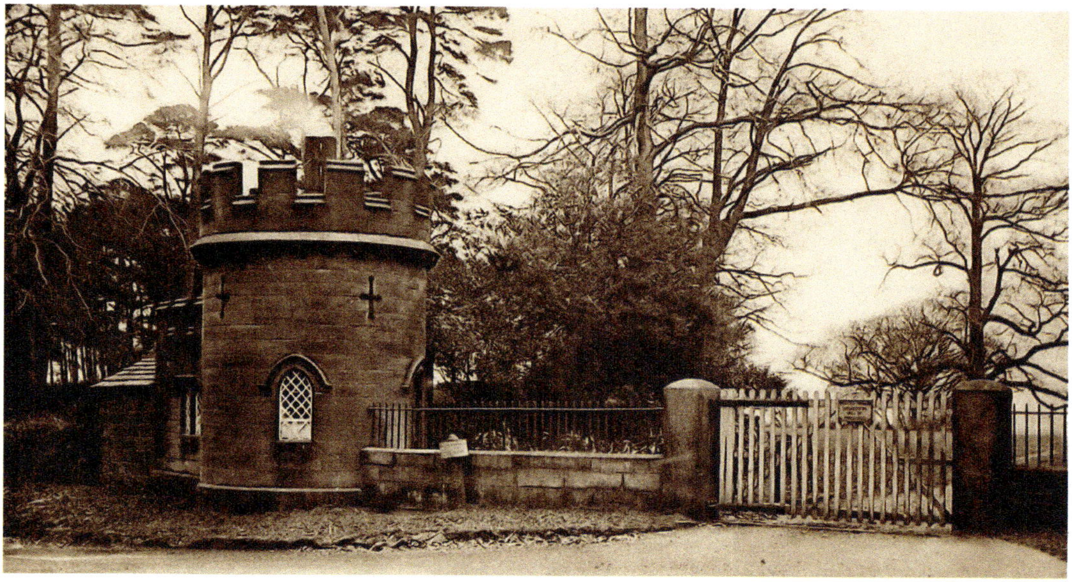

The Round Tower, 1910 and 2015 with inset from 2009

This tower, built in the early nineteenth century is now a well known landmark sitting astride the busy A556; it was once the gate house to a large manor via the later mentioned Monkey Lodge. The house was built from the remains of Vale Royal Abbey for the influential Cholmondeleys, later Barons Delamere. In 2002 this tower was completely refurbished after a campaign by local people. Until the 1920s it was actually a residence, the last tenants being Hughie Preston and his wife. Then in 2013 a traffic incident rendered it unsafe; rather than make it safe and rebuild it, the powers that be elected to demolish it completely! There was a massive public outcry and as a result the decision was made to rebuild it. This is in progress in this 2015 shot.

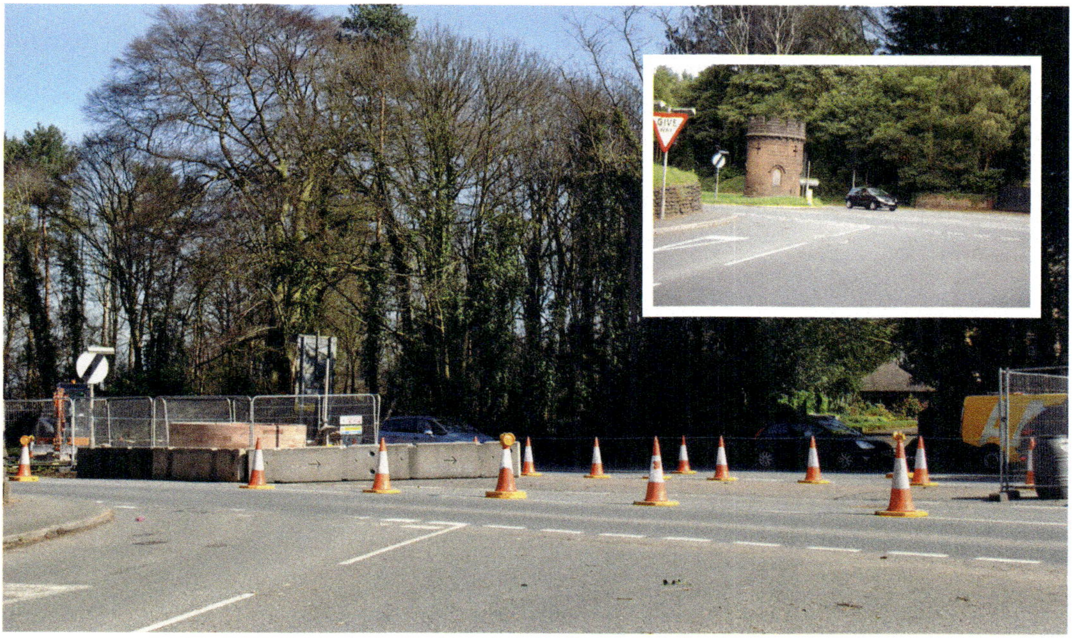

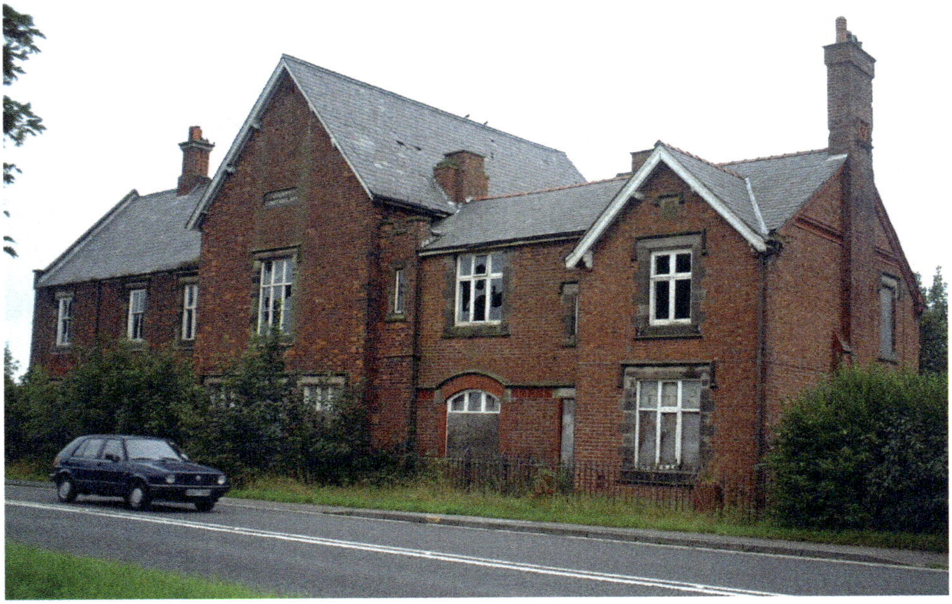

Oakmere Police Station, 2004 and 2015

Not such a gap between then and now here, but I believe that this building deserves a place in the book. It was built as a police station and court house to take over from the nearby Vale Royal Abbey Arms pub. Prior to its building in the nineteenth century, the court was held in the pub and felons detained in the cellar. It went on to be the divisional headquarters for Eddisbury Police Division and stables were built at the rear for the superintendent's horse and trap. Its last duties were as Oakmere Magistrates' Court and despite an appeal to save it, it has been empty and deteriorating since the 1980s.

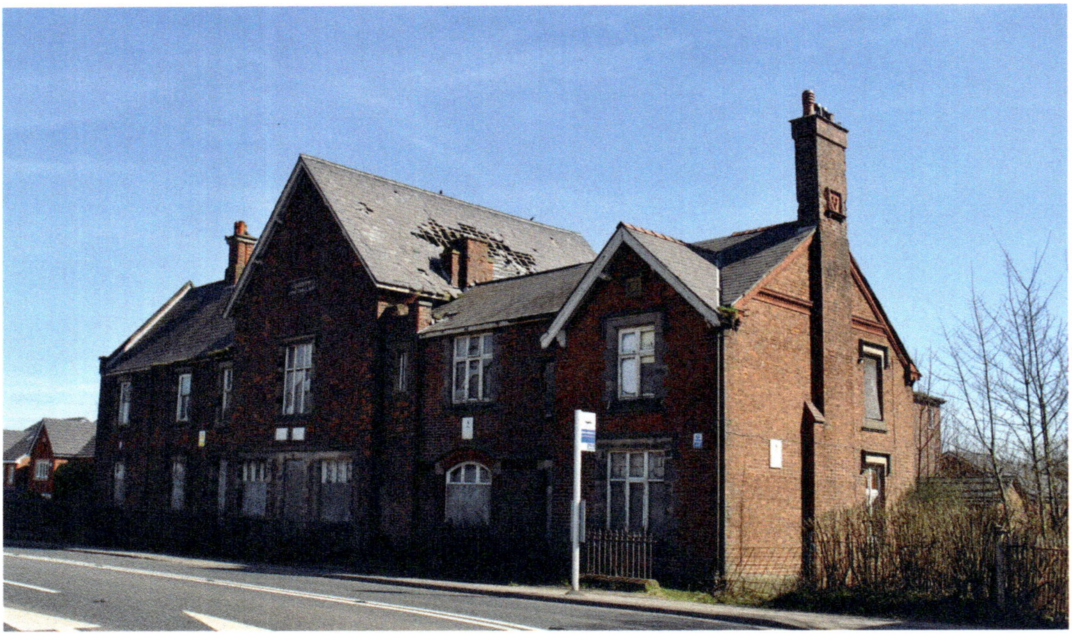

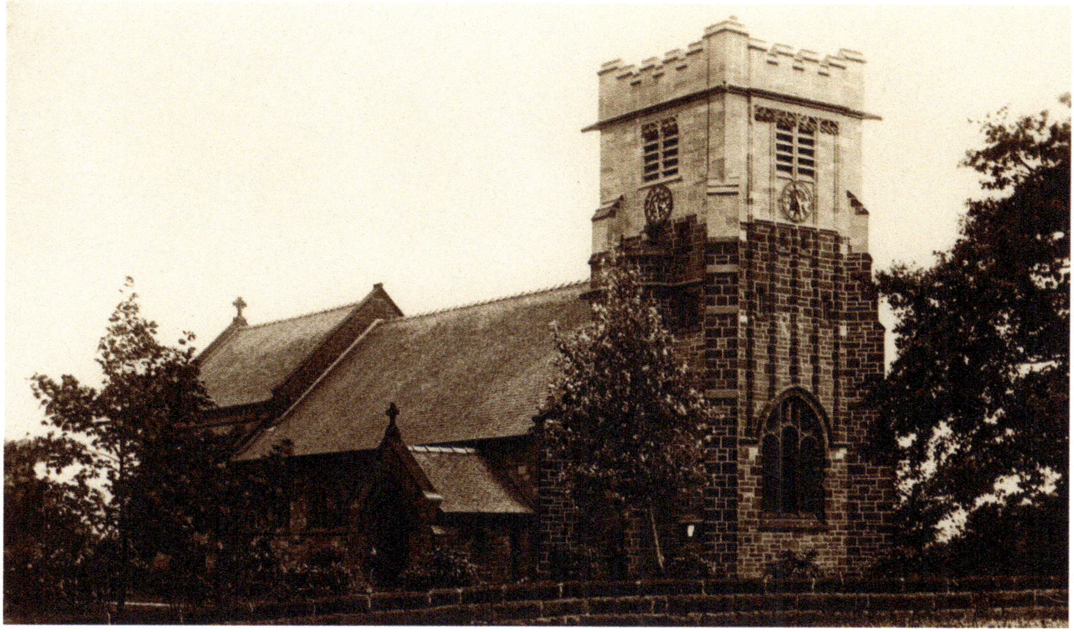

Sandiway Church, around 1910 and 2015

St John the Evangelist's church was designed by the famous Sandiway architect John Douglas who also donated the land. It was built between 1902 and 1903. The church was originally built without a tower but this was added in 1911. This can be seen in the old photograph where the newly completed tower can be seen as a different colour to the rest. The sandstone has weathered well in the 2015 photo.

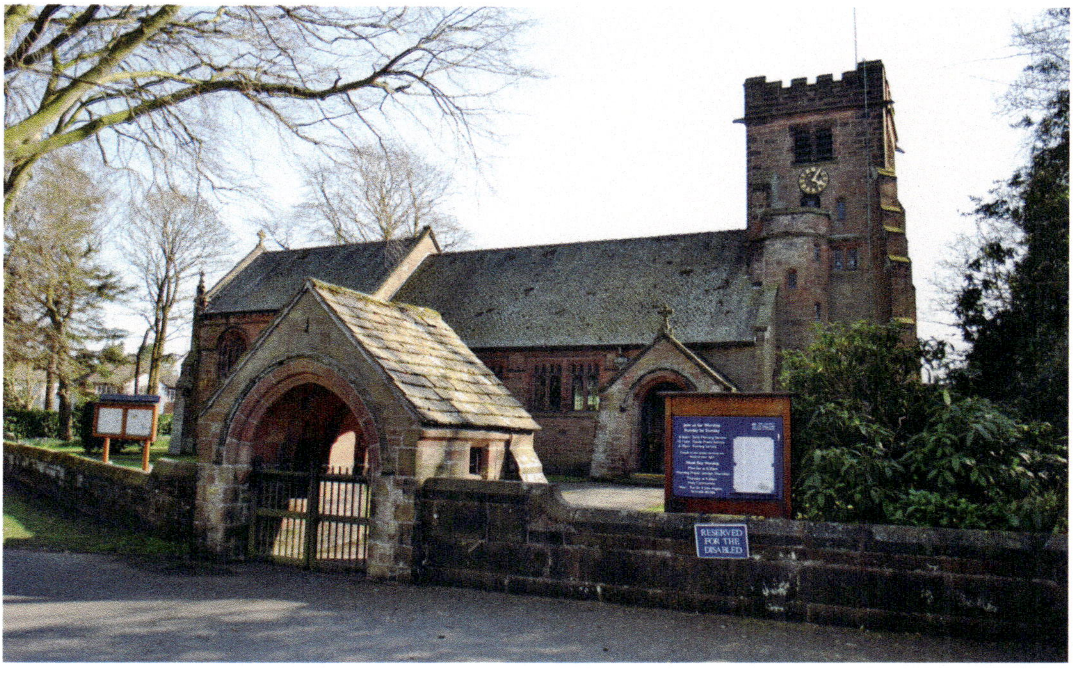

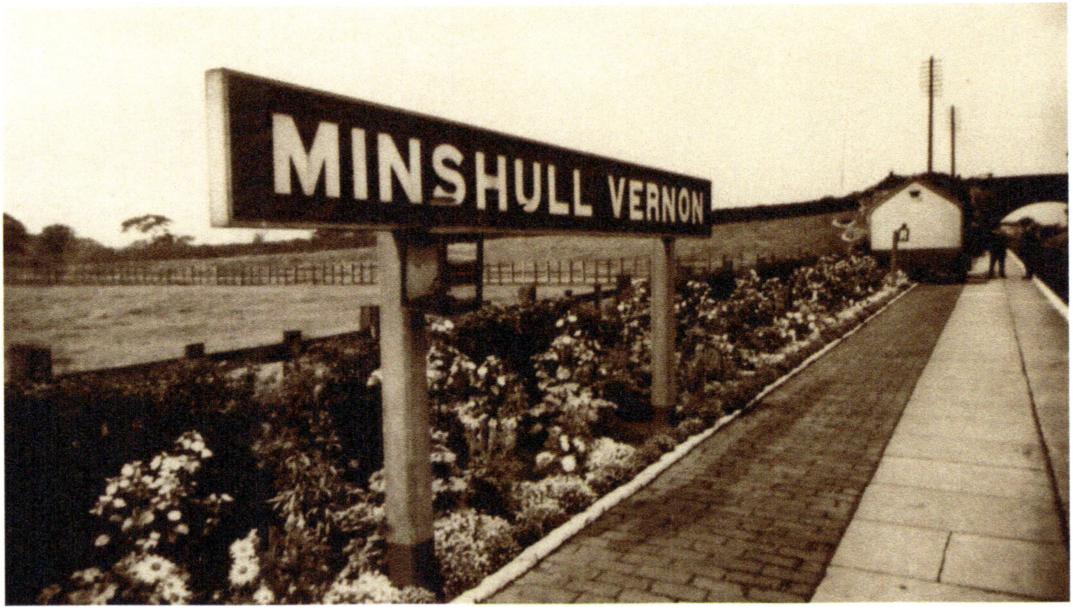

Minshull Vernon station, *c.* 1950s and 2014

This small station was situated on the west coast main line between Crewe and Winsford. In the late 1800s the station master was John Walker who was not exactly overworked as there were only three trains Up, two Down, and one on a Sunday. The station was built in 1837 and closed completely in 1942. All that is left now are a few loose bricks alongside the track. This was the site of a fatal rail crash that occurred on 26 December 1962. An express was stopped on the line due to frozen points and another express ran into the back of it, causing the deaths of 18 people and 34 injuries.

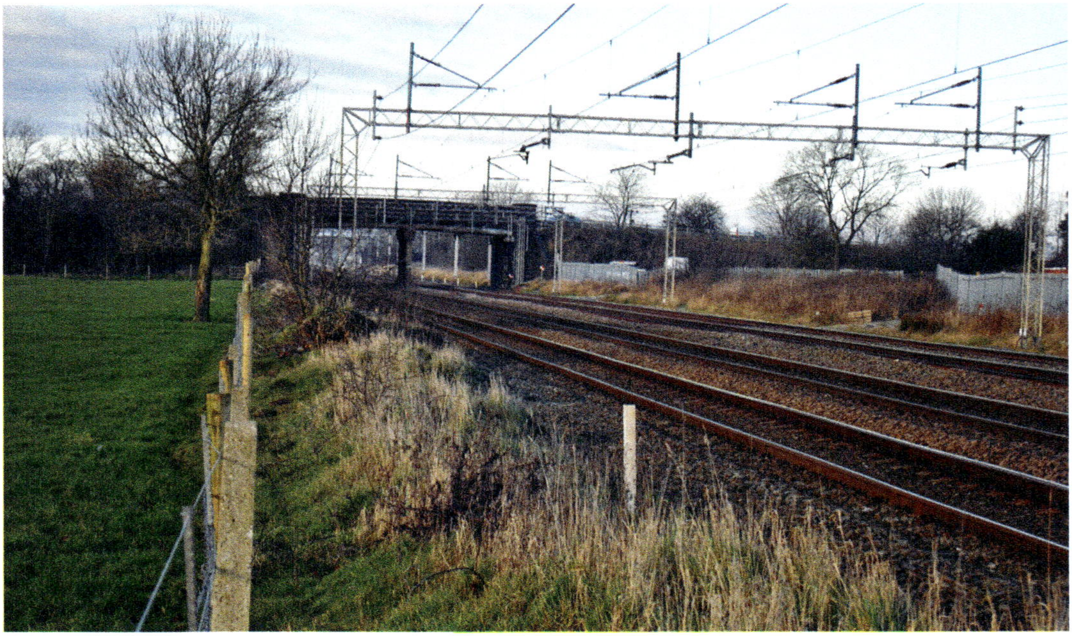

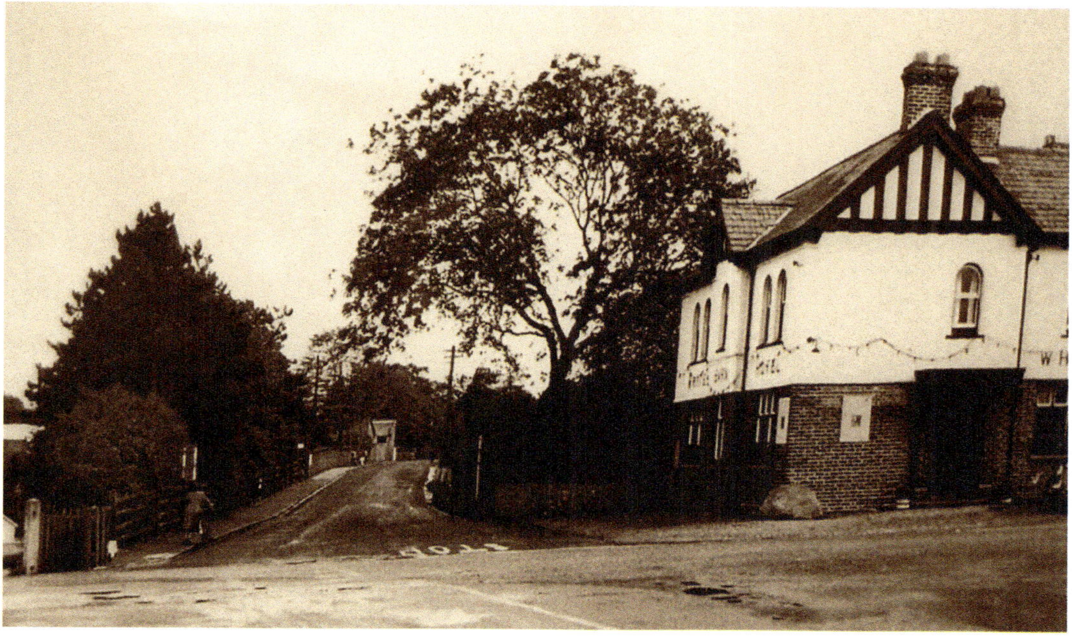

The White Barn, 1955 and 2015

This building dates from 1870, an earlier name being The Red Bull. Nearby Delamere Park housed Polish refugees and people awaiting re-housing. During the war it was an army camp. One of the divisions based there was the US 80th, better known as the 'Blue Ridge Division' who trained for and attacked at Omaha Beach on D-Day. Oh, what merrymaking went on within those walls!

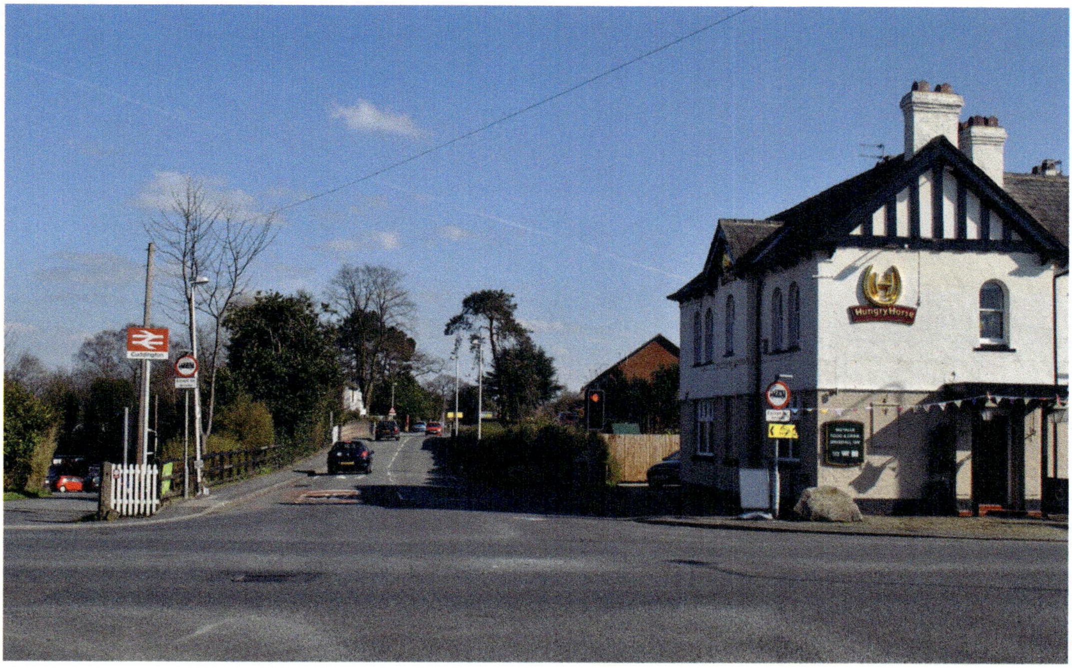

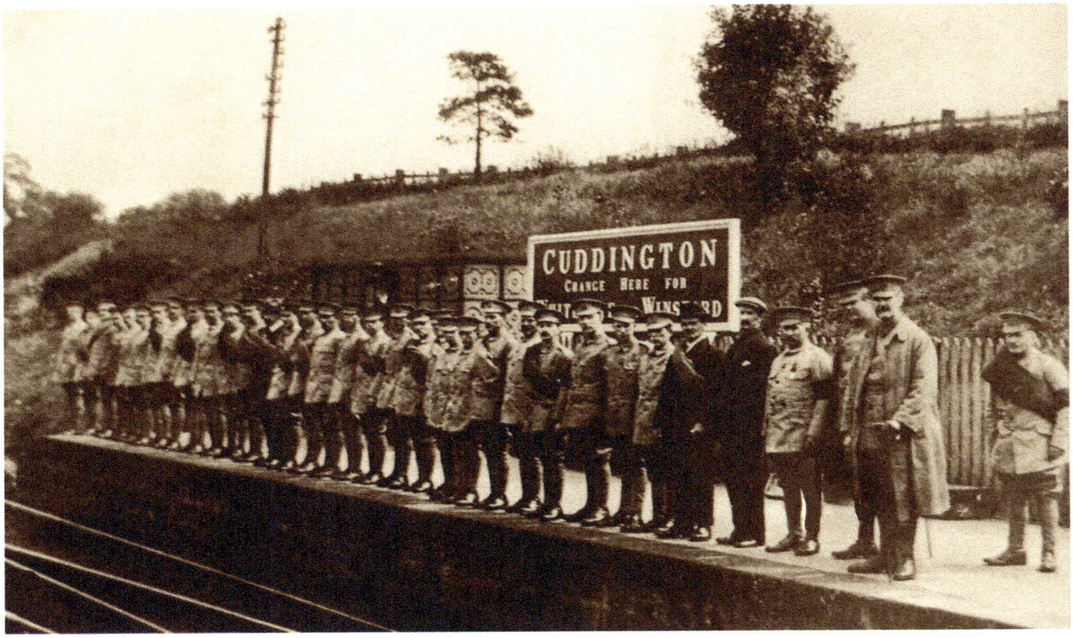

Cuddington Station, 1915 and 2015

I wonder how many of the soldiers in the old photograph returned? The likelihood is not very many as they were on the way to the mincing machine that was the First World War. It is quite likely that the soldiers were the Sandiway Local Defence Volunteers, one of the Pals Brigades comprising local men and estate workers at Delamere. Formations like this made the losses even harder to bear at home when the cream of a town or village would face slaughter together. The station sign advises 'Change here for Whitegate and Winsford'.

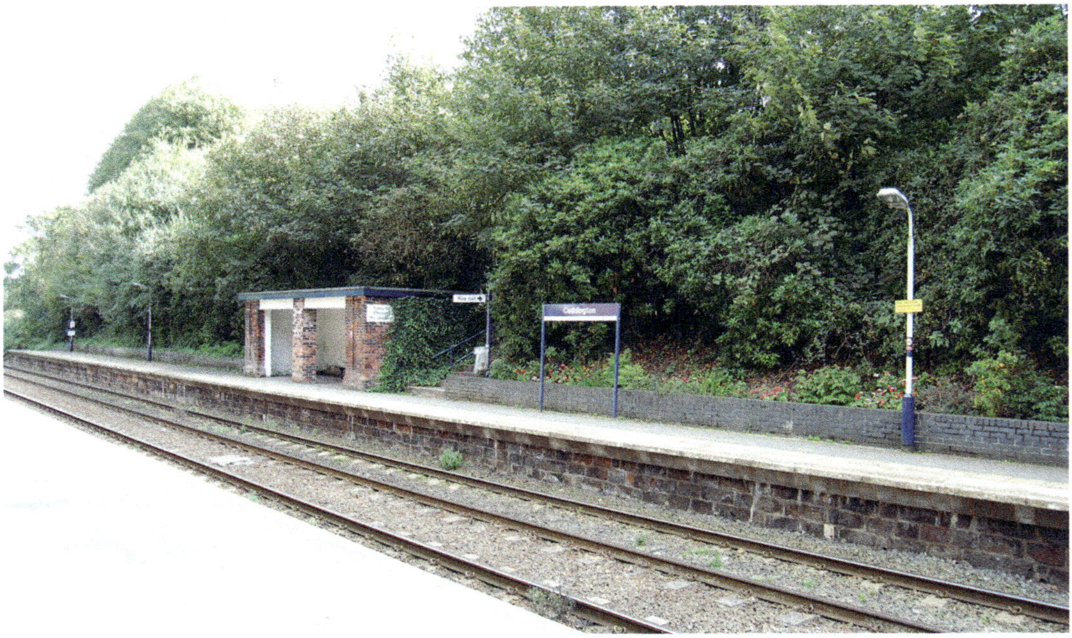

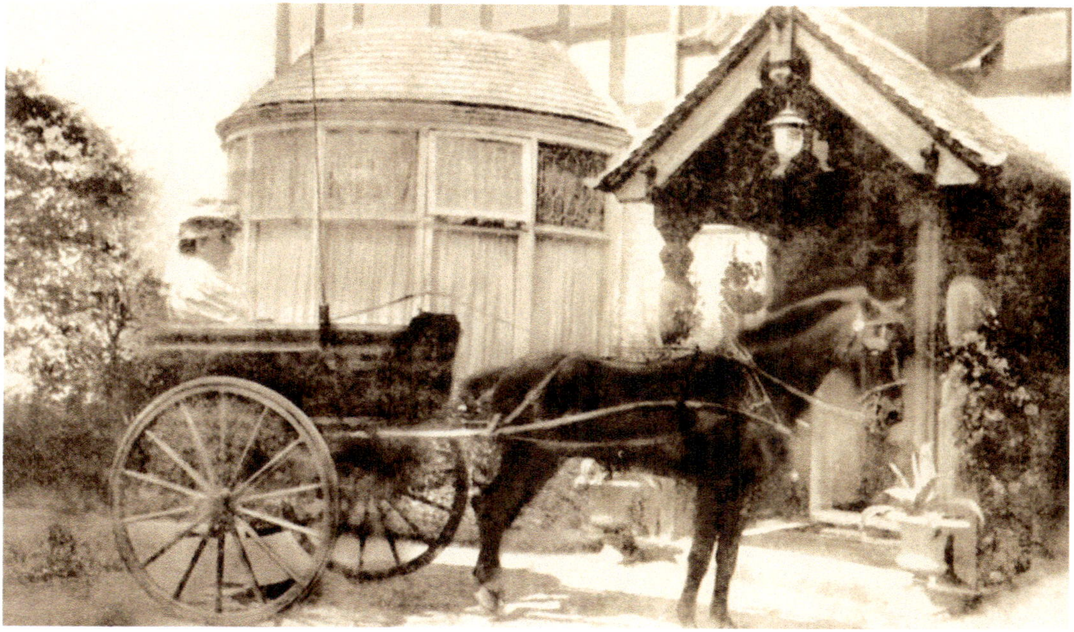

The Oaklands, 1910 and 2013

Not a particularly good old photo but atmospheric all the same. It shows a pony and trap outside the front of the building. Built in 1904, this prestigious house in Millington Lane between Weaverham and Sandiway was privately owned until 1947, when all of the furniture and fittings were sold to the highest bidder. In 1960 it was converted into a country club, and is now a pub with function rooms and hotel set in the glorious countryside.

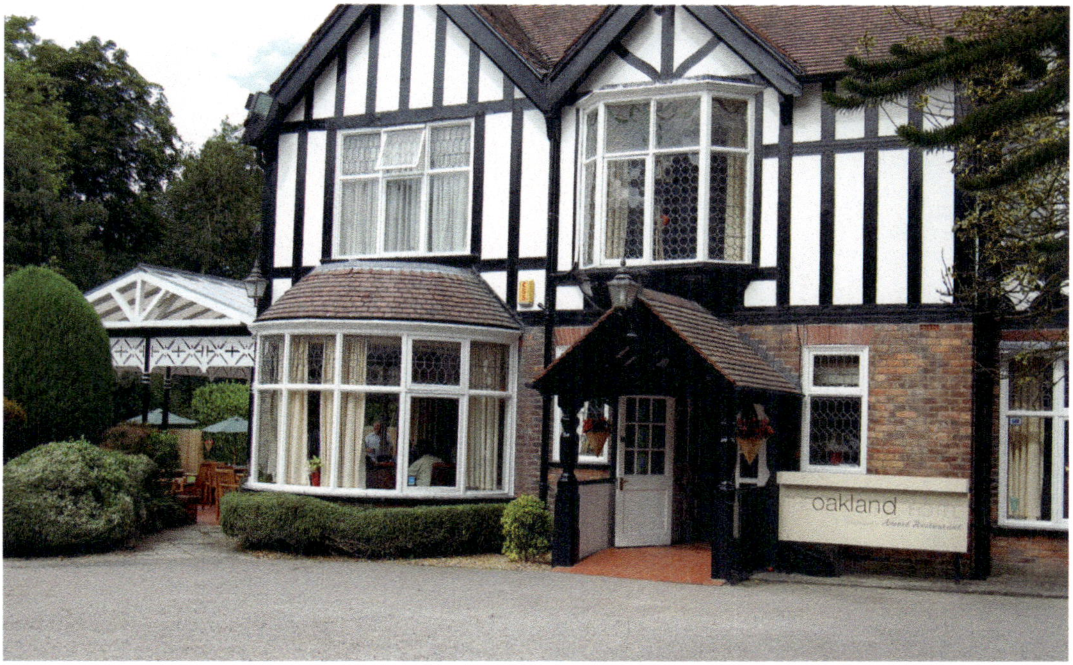

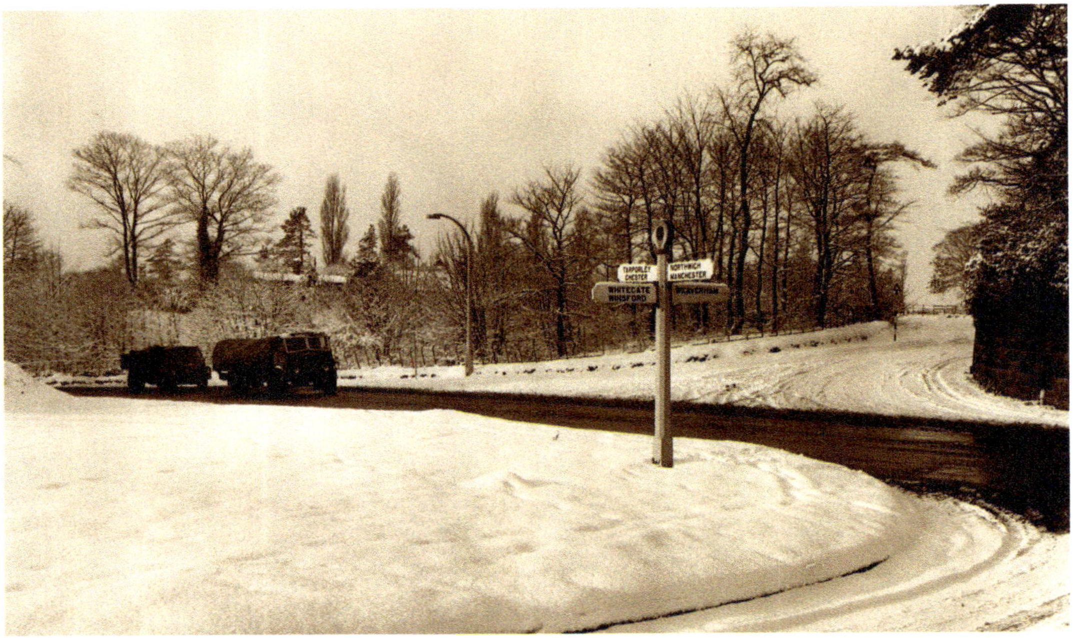

Lorries Leaving Northwich Bypass, 1950s and 2015

These photographs show the junction from the Northwich bypass at the bottom of Speedwell Hill towards Northwich with the Weaverham turn on the left. In the snowy mid-winter scene, an Albion flat back lorry leads a more modern Bedford tipper from the dual carriageway during the 1950s. This was originally the continuation of what became the Northwich bypass and took the traffic through Northwich before the bypass was constructed.

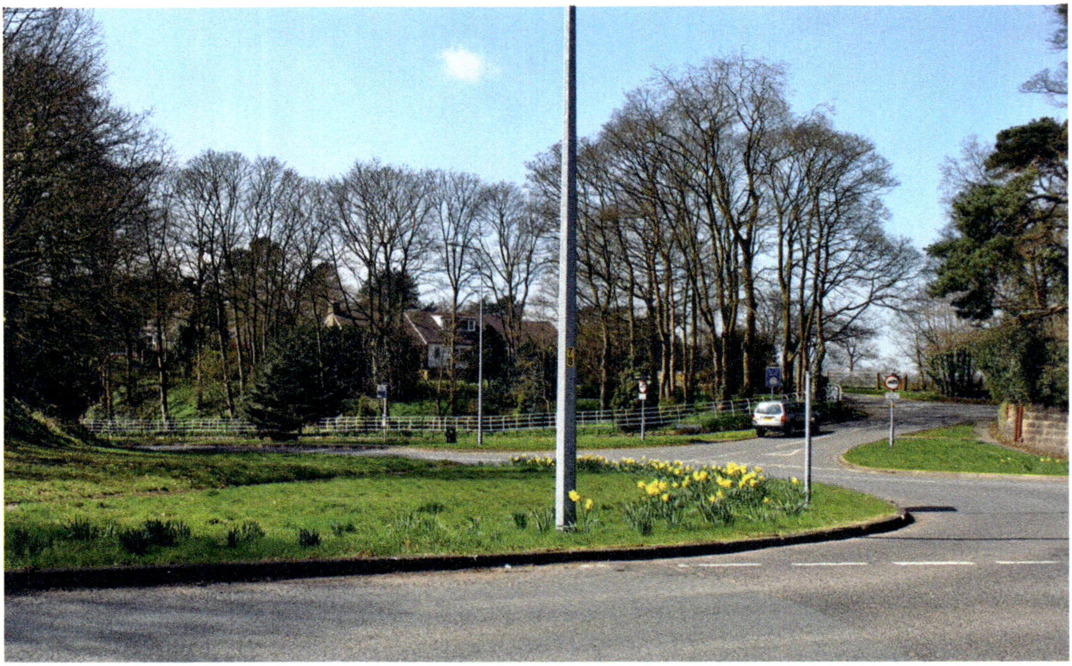

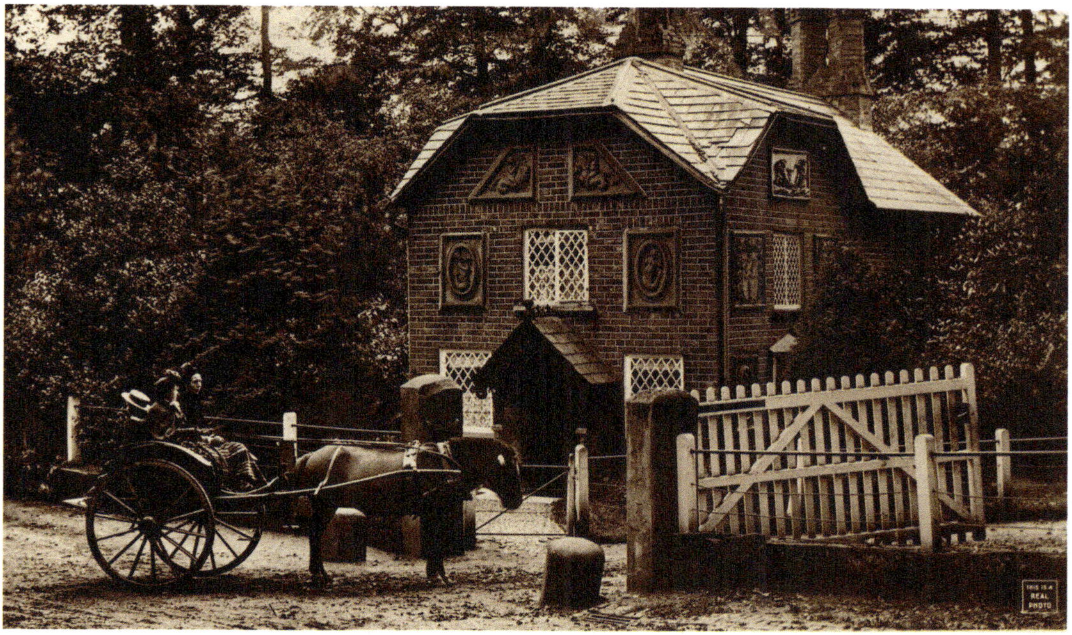

Monkey Lodge, 1890s and 2015

This unusual and clear photograph is of Monkey Lodge at Whitegate. At one time there was a drive from the round tower (see earlier caption) in Sandiway to this house and then into the mansion that had once been Vale Royal Abbey. The name comes from one of the many plaques on the building, one of which is of a monkey. The house is on the Winsford to Northwich road just before Whitegate and, as the 2015 photo shows, is still there but hidden by foliage and for sale.

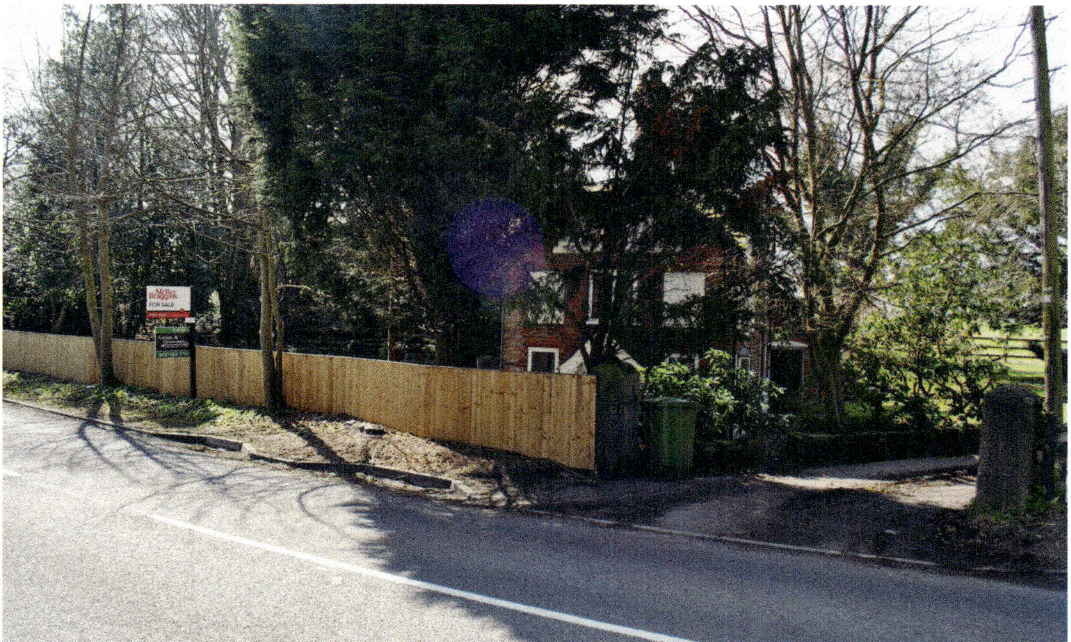

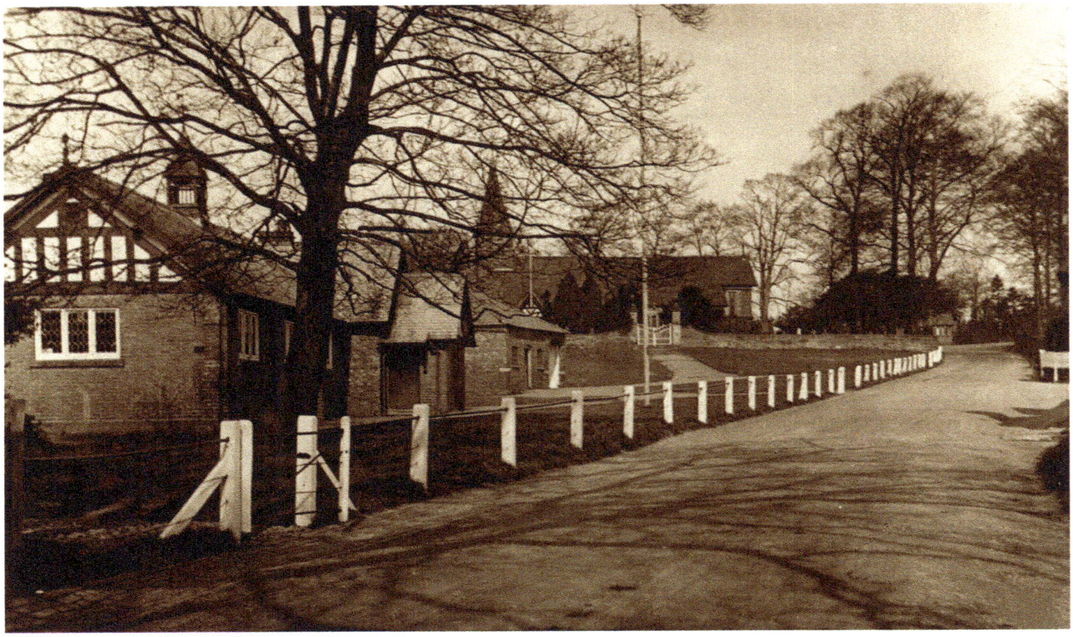

Whitegate Village, 1950s and 2015

In this pleasant village between Winsford and Northwich, we look up the main street towards the church of St Mary. This parish can be traced back to the building of the nearby Vale Royal Abbey. The abbey was named by Edward I *Vallis Regalis* (Vale Royal), hence the name. The monks moved to the Abbey in 1330 and it was completed by 1359. Following the Dissolution of the Monasteries, St Mary's became Whitegate parish church. The present building dates from the nineteenth century and was designed by John Douglas of Sandiway.

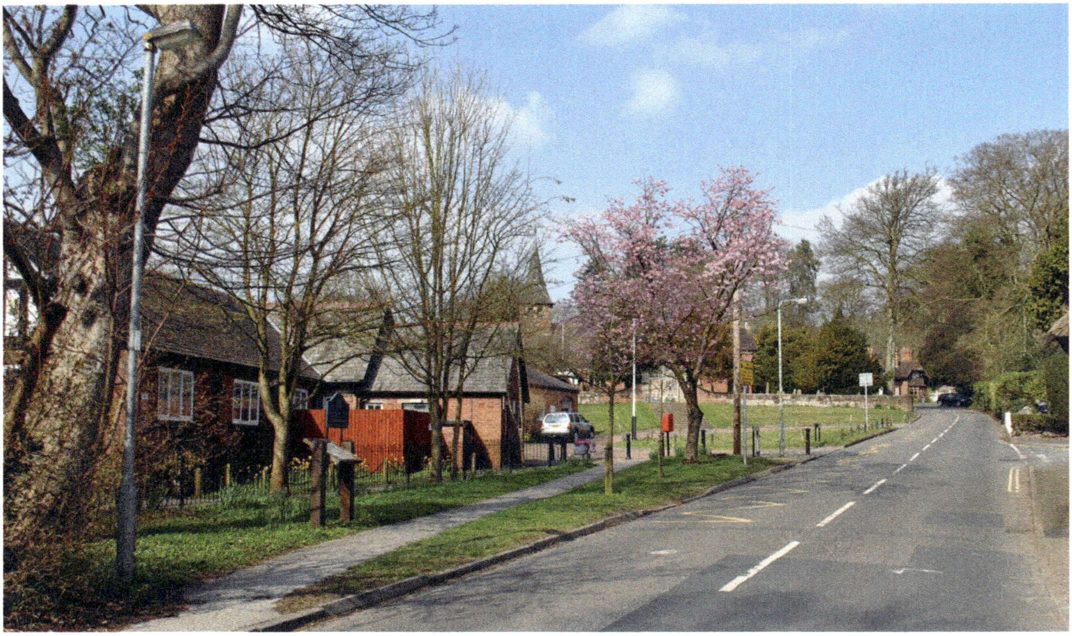

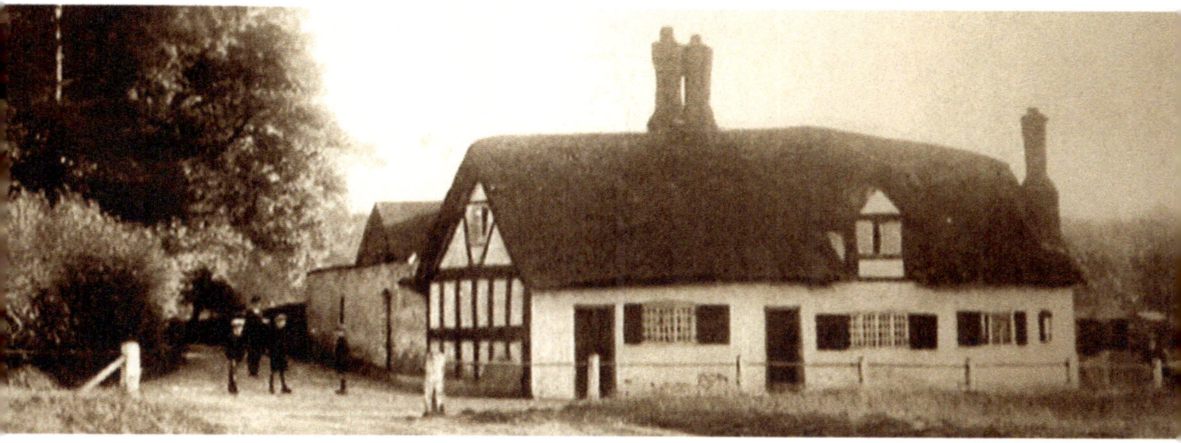

Whitegate Cottage, between 1890 and 1905 and 2015

This late seventeenth century cottage is known as Whitegate Cottage, and on the other side of the road is Whitegate House, which first came to note as a public house in 1841, it was The Rifleman, named after the formation of The Rifle Brigade in 1800. In 1870, on the orders of the Dowager Lady Delamere who was upset by the behaviour of the locals, especially on a Sunday, the pub was ordered shut and it became the home of the estate agent.

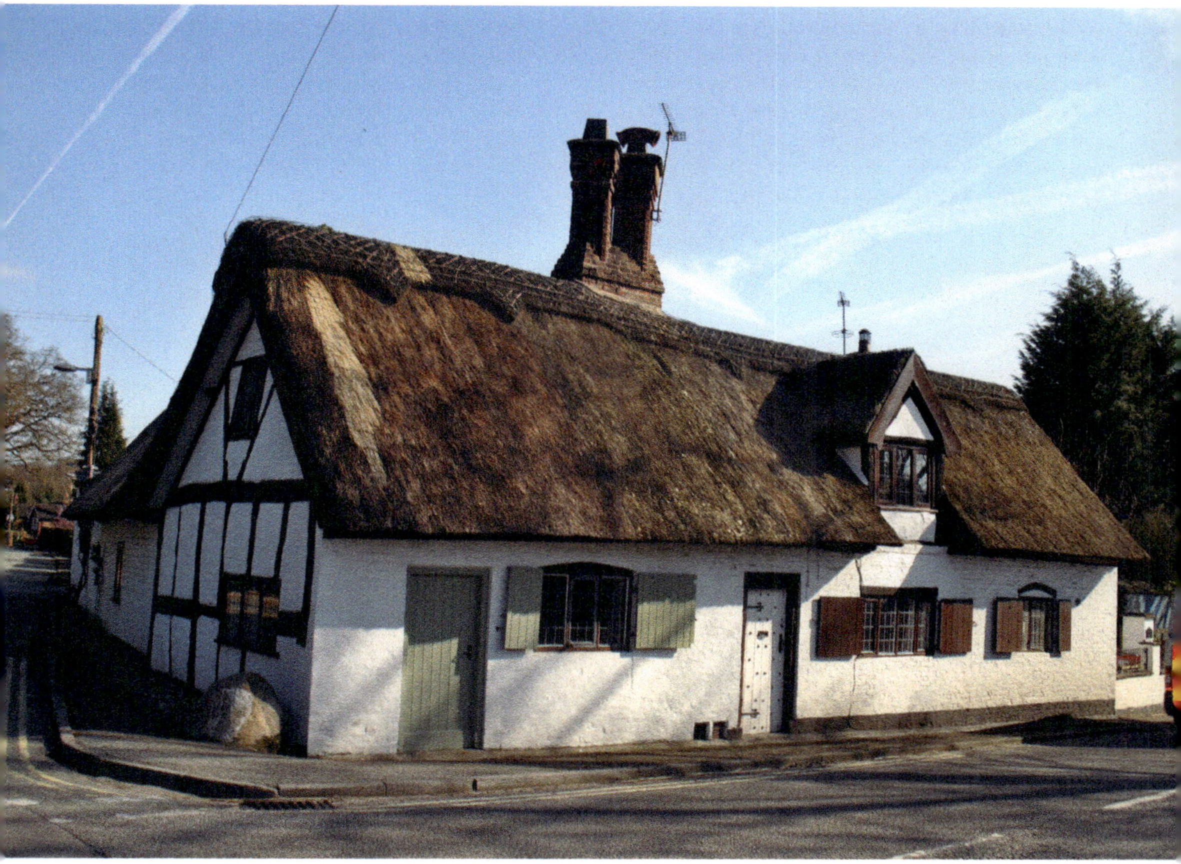

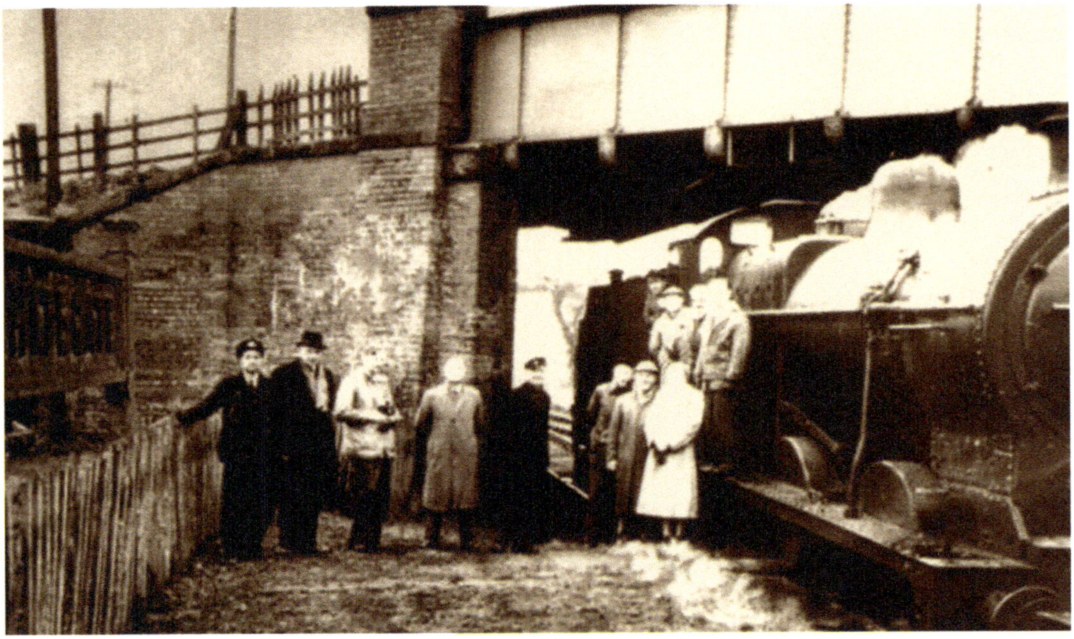

Whitegate Last Train, 1966 and 2015

Immediately to the west of Cuddington station a single track branch line was built by the Cheshire Lines Committee to a station called Winsford and Over with an intermediate station at Whitegate. This line was never a success for passenger working but as well as the terminus. The line crossed New Road Winsford to serve the many salt mines. This old photograph was taken as the last train stopped at Whitegate station. The branch closed on the 6 of June 1967 after which the track was lifted. In 2014 the bridge was completely rebuilt to a high standard.

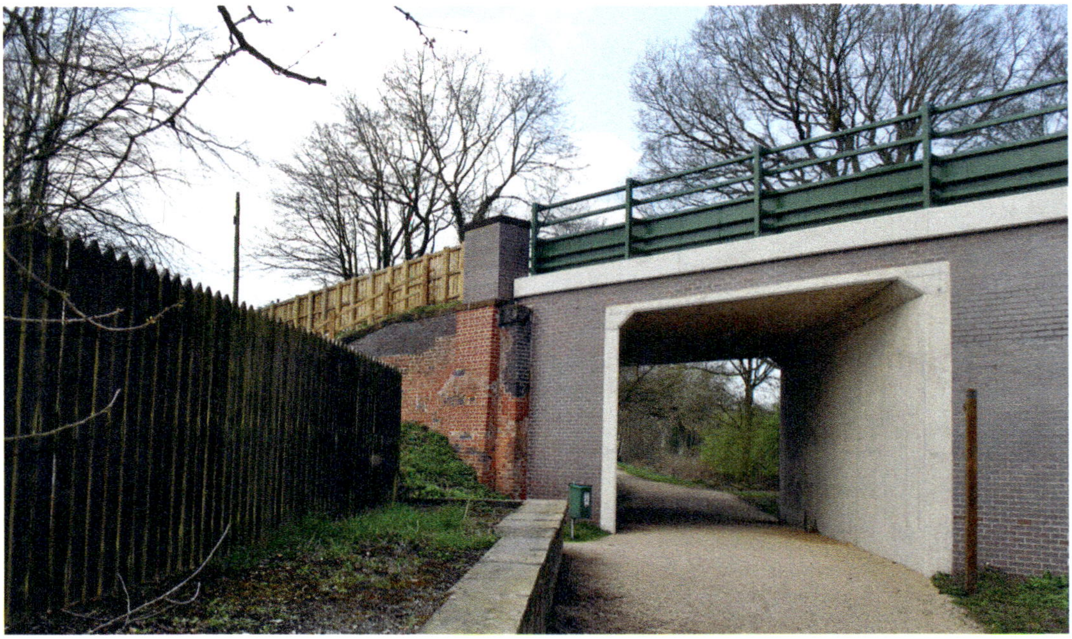

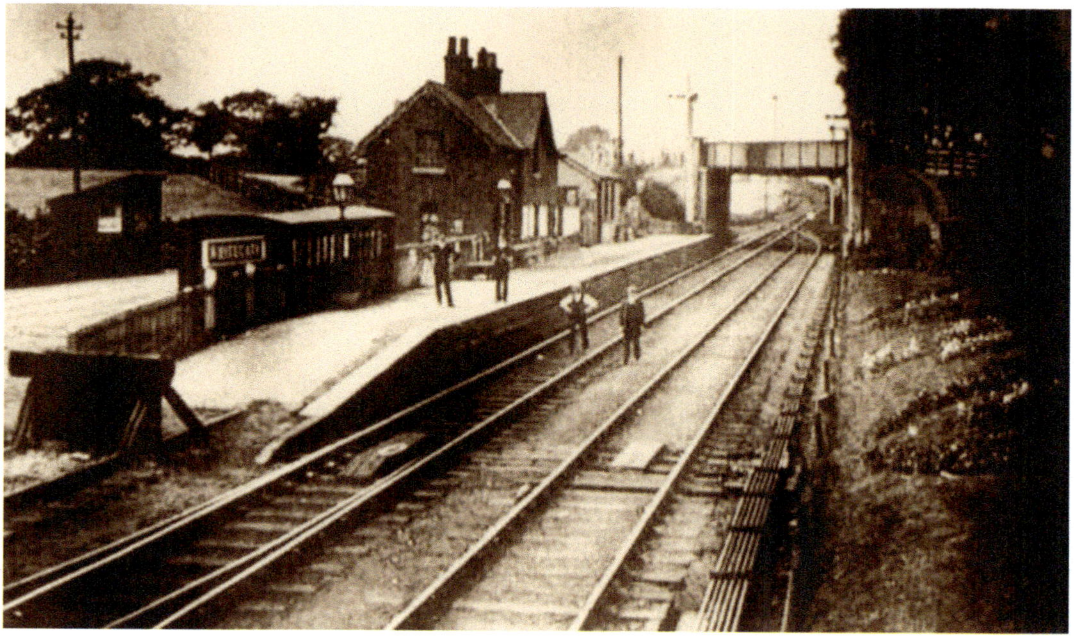

Whitegate Station, 1930s–1940s and 2015

An interesting view of the station and bridge in days when there would be at most about six trains per day calling at the station. The staff, as can be seen in the photo, would have had plenty of time to tend the gardens on the right. The grounded coach body is a CLC four-wheeled third-class saloon of 1874 to 1876. The track bed is now the Whitegate Way from Winsford to Sandiway and the station a picnic area and car park.

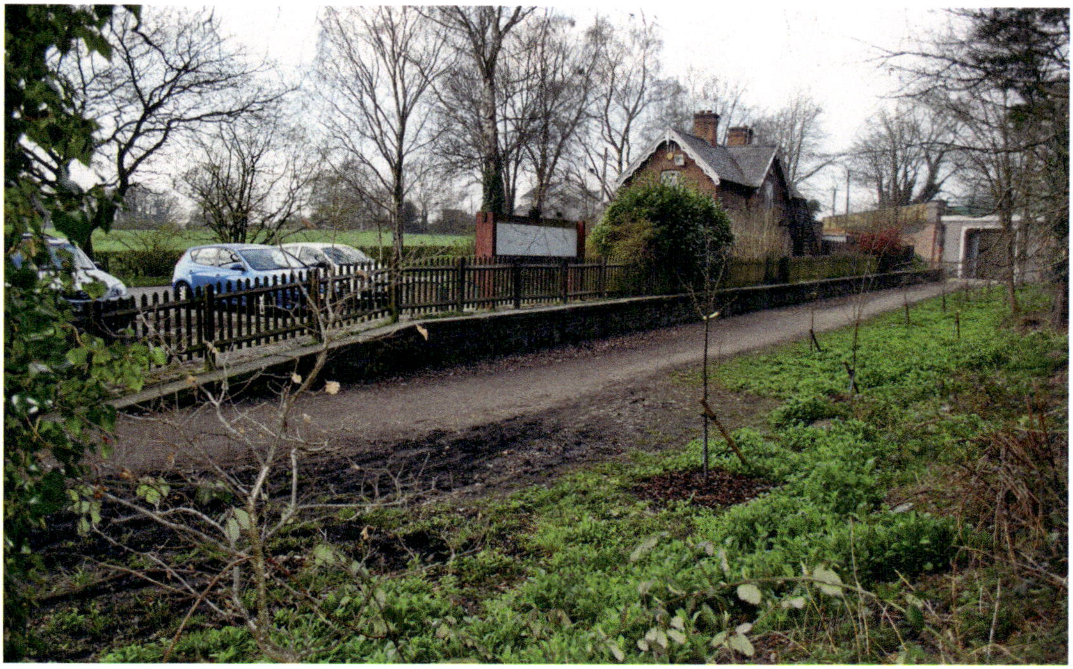

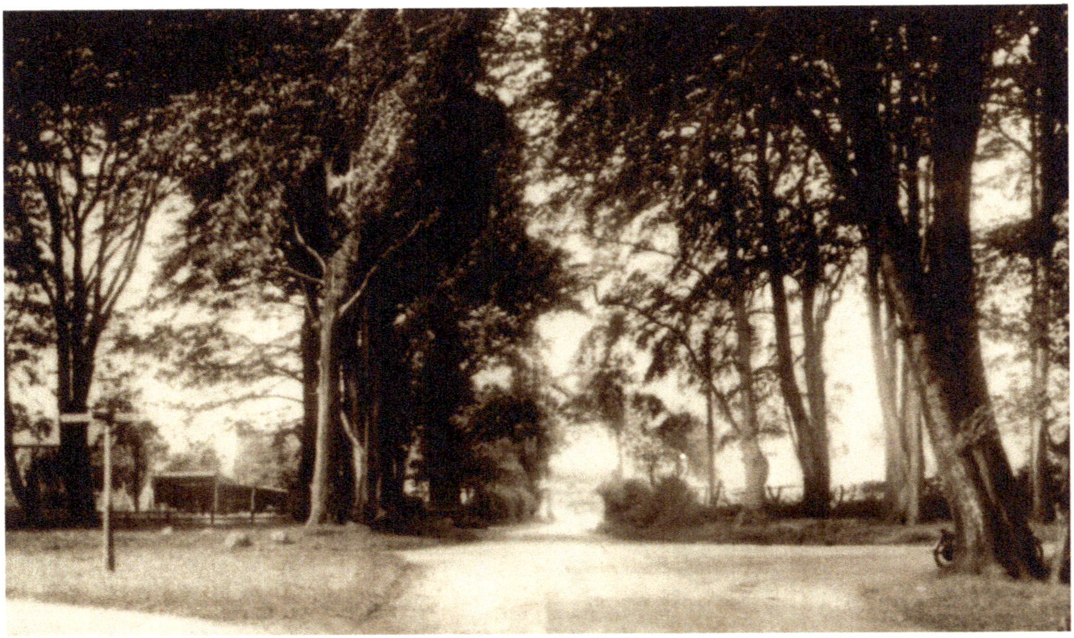

The Beeches Whitegate, 1910–1920 and 2015

This crossroads on the road from Winsford to Sandiway has always been a picturesque and shaded area. The large house on the left is called The Beeches and was the childhood home of Ellen Marion Irene Boyd 1907 1977. Although confined to a wheelchair she became a noted painter and author. The photographer's motorcycle can be seen partly hidden behind a tree on the right in the old photo.

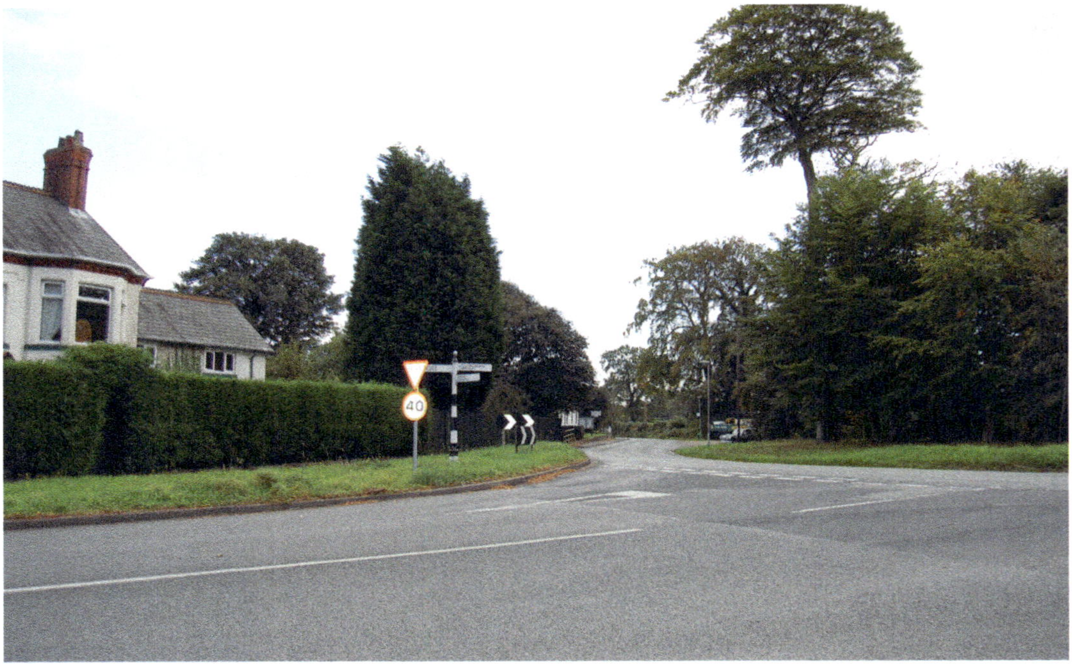

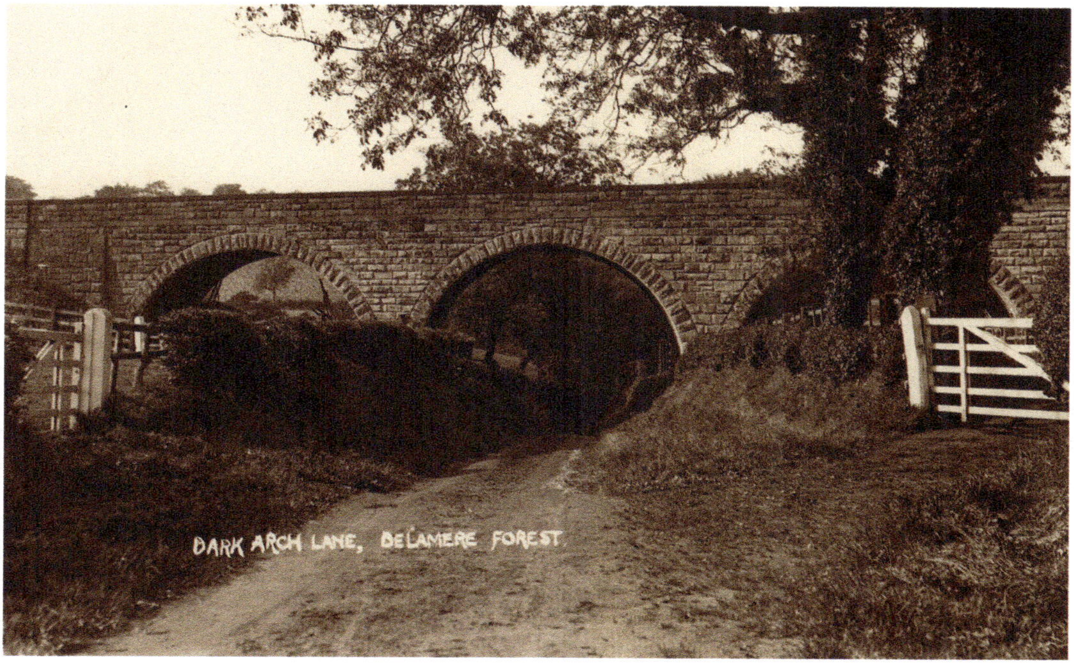

Dark Ark Bridge, Early 1900s and 2014

Now we venture into Delamere Forest, and on the road to Manley is the railway bridge across Dark Ark Lane (the name on the old photo is incorrect). This bridge carries the line from Manchester to Chester and is a good example of the build quality in the early days of the railway when labour was cheap.

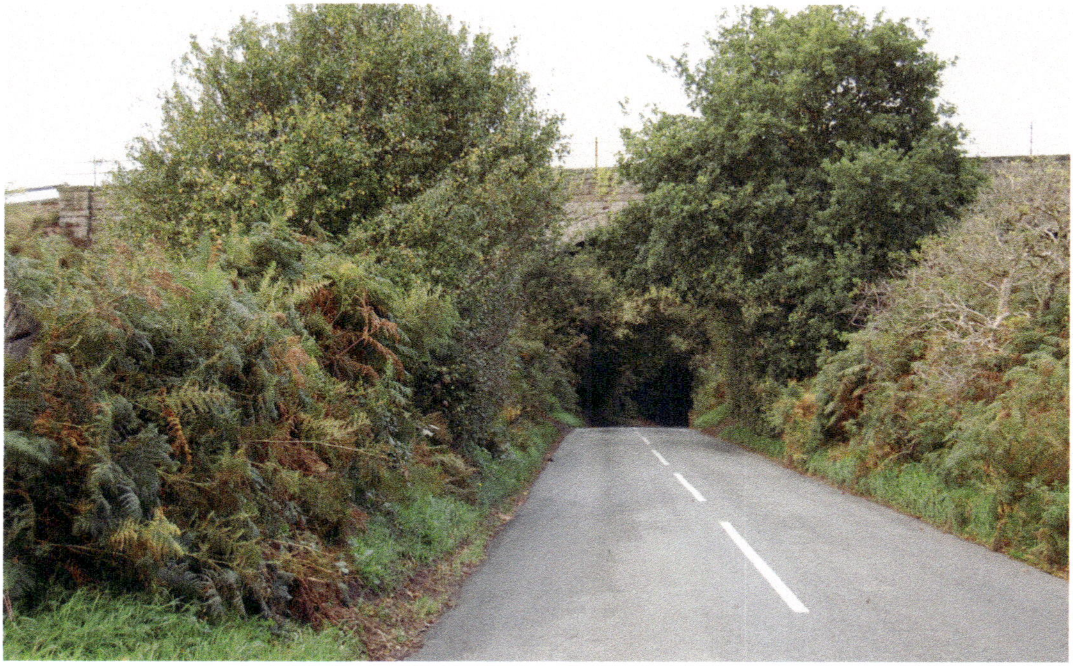

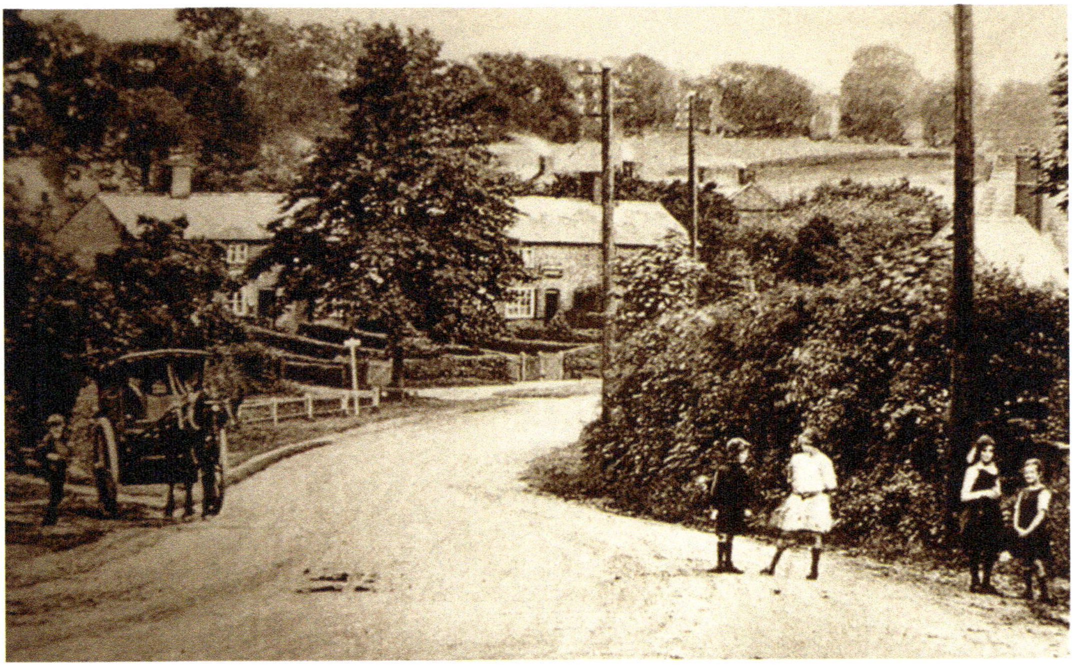

Cotebrook Downhill, 1895 and 2013

Back now on what is the A49 Tarporley Road and down the gradient through the hamlet of Cotebrook. Little has changed over the years other than the vast increase in traffic. Those children would not have been able to stand where they are. In fact, taking the new photograph meant risking my life on this fast and busy arterial road!

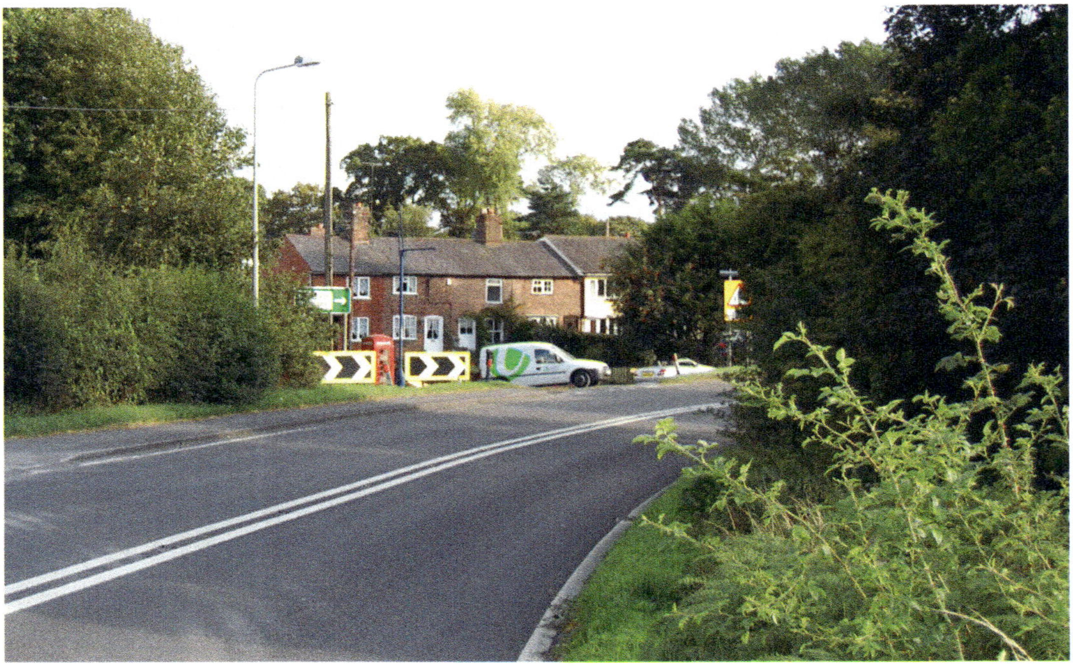

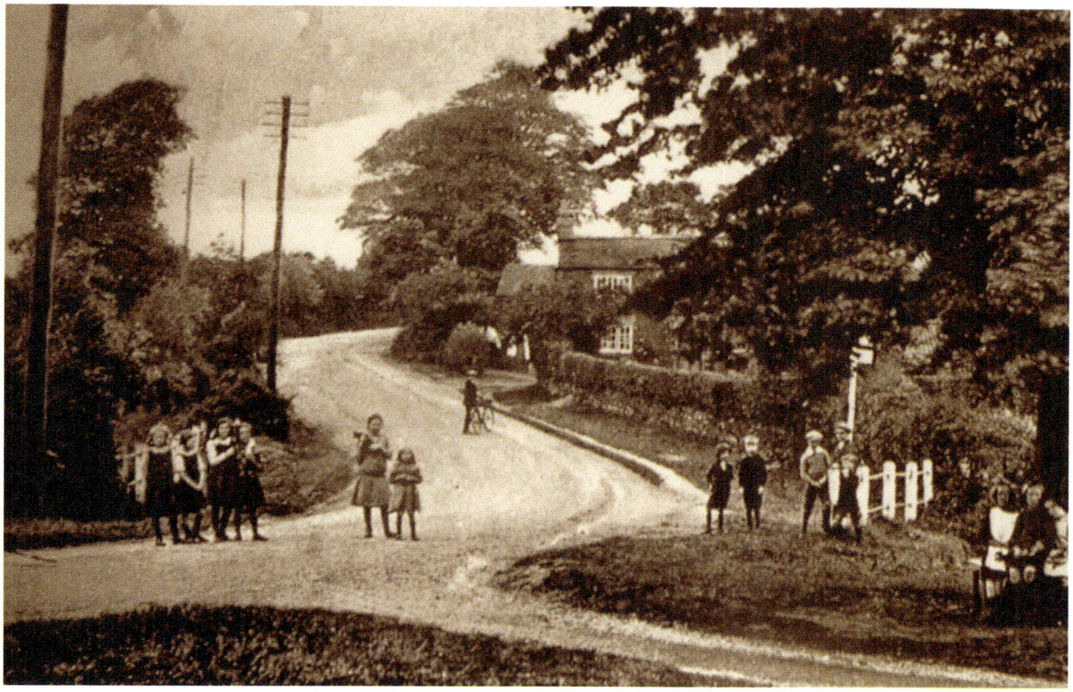

Cotebrook Uphill, 1895 and 2015

Just a look in the opposite direction with the same comments as the last caption and you can plainly see that this is a dangerous road and not suited to pedestrians, or taking photographs!

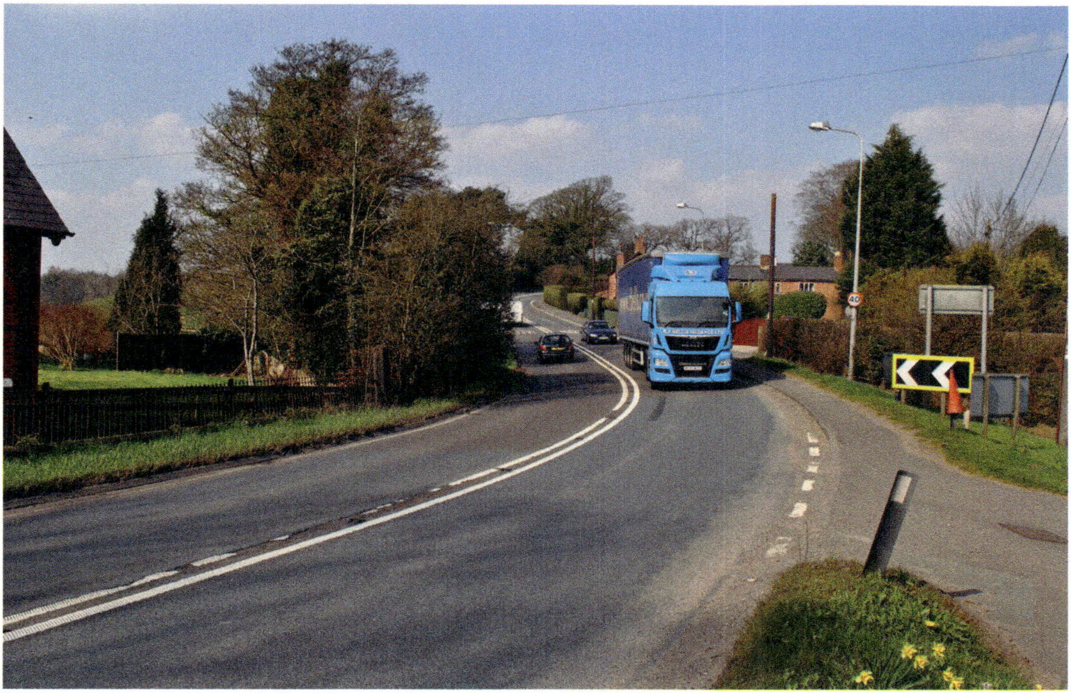

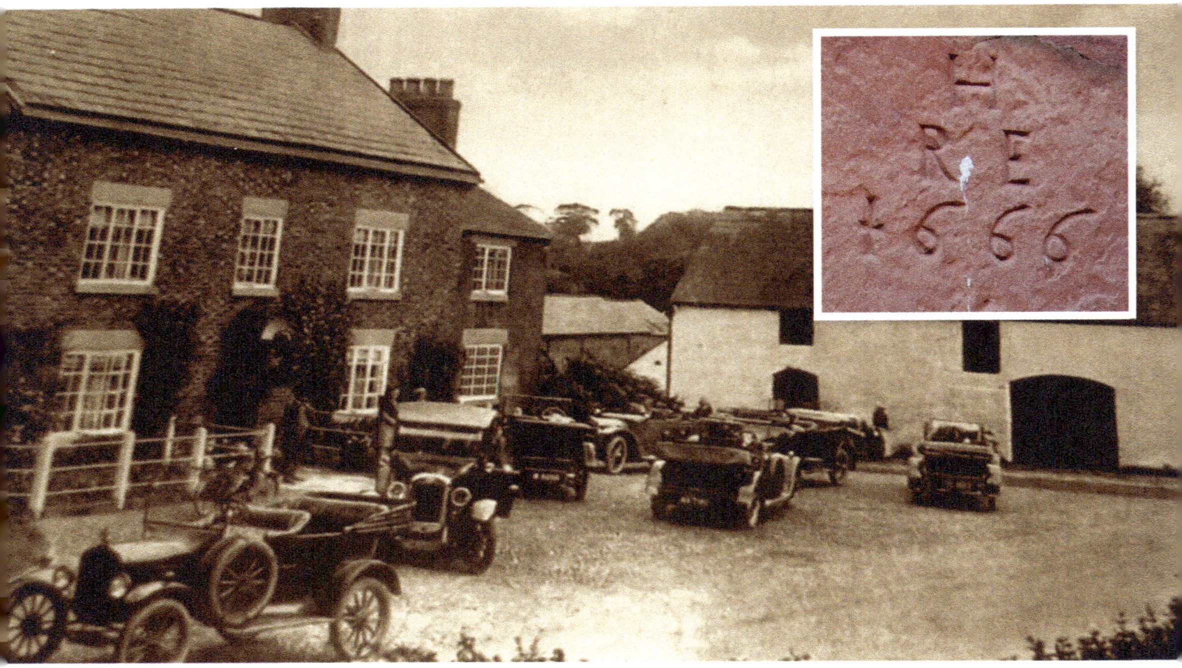

Alvanley Arms, 1910–1925 and 2013

Not the best of old photographs but it provides an interesting look at the forecourt of the Alvanley Arms at Cotebrook. Landlords at the pub are listed from 1666 to the present day. Until 1888 it was called The Ardern Arms, which is one of the family names of the Earl of Haddington, the one-time owner. The inset shows the building date over the door.

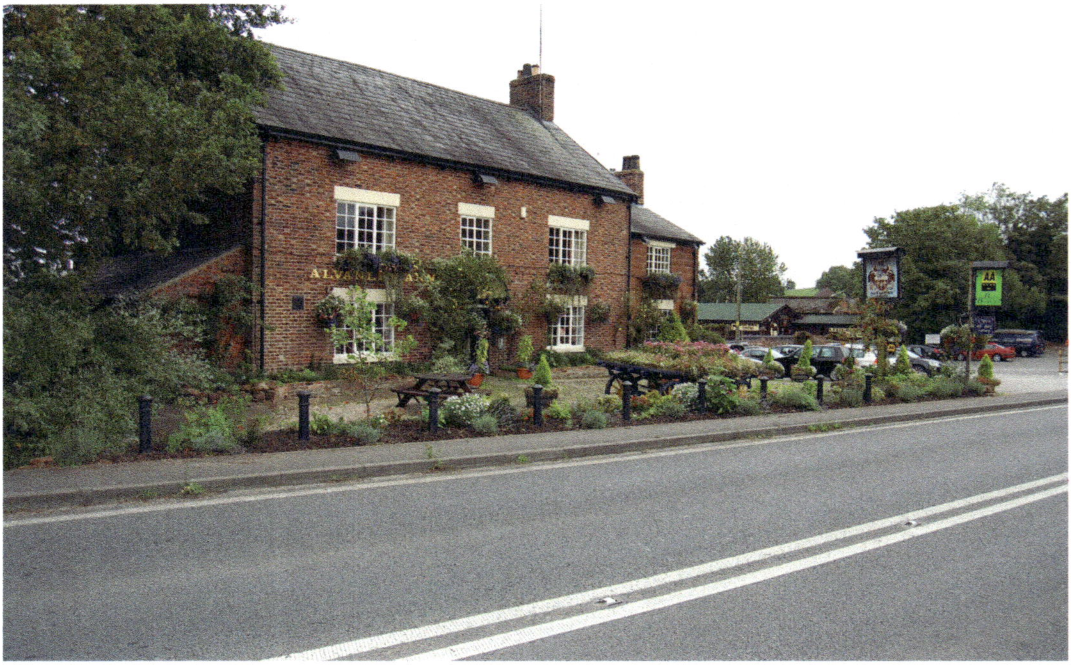

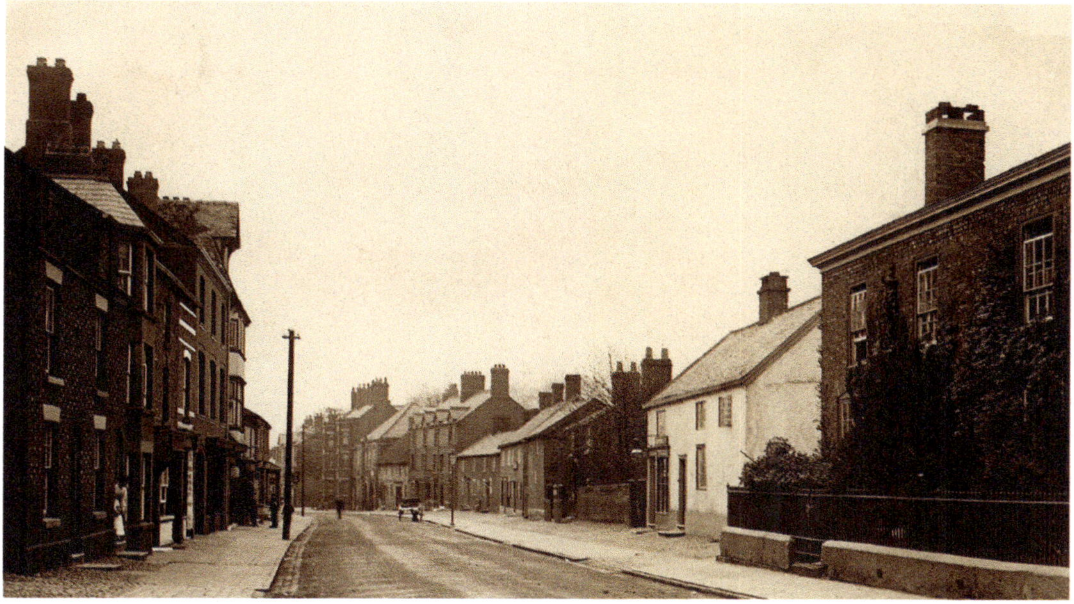

Tarporley, 1900 and 2009

We now take a quick look at the ancient town of Tarporley. This photograph looks down the main street. There is considerably more traffic than in the old photograph. This was once a main trunk road but has now been bypassed, albeit that the traffic is still heavy! My copy of Ormerod tells me that 'Tarporley town consists chiefly of one long street, a considerable thoroughfare on the London Road, broad, cleanly and well paved, with respectable buildings and is by far the most sightly of the towns of the western hundreds.' And so it is; Tarporley is a wealthy town and one of Cheshire's hidden gems.

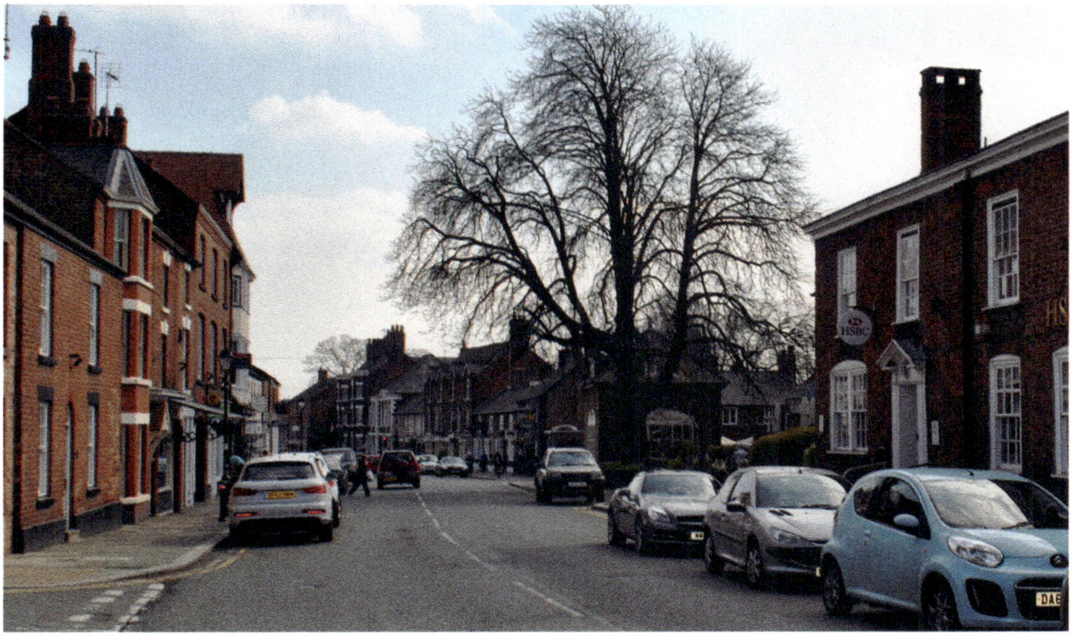

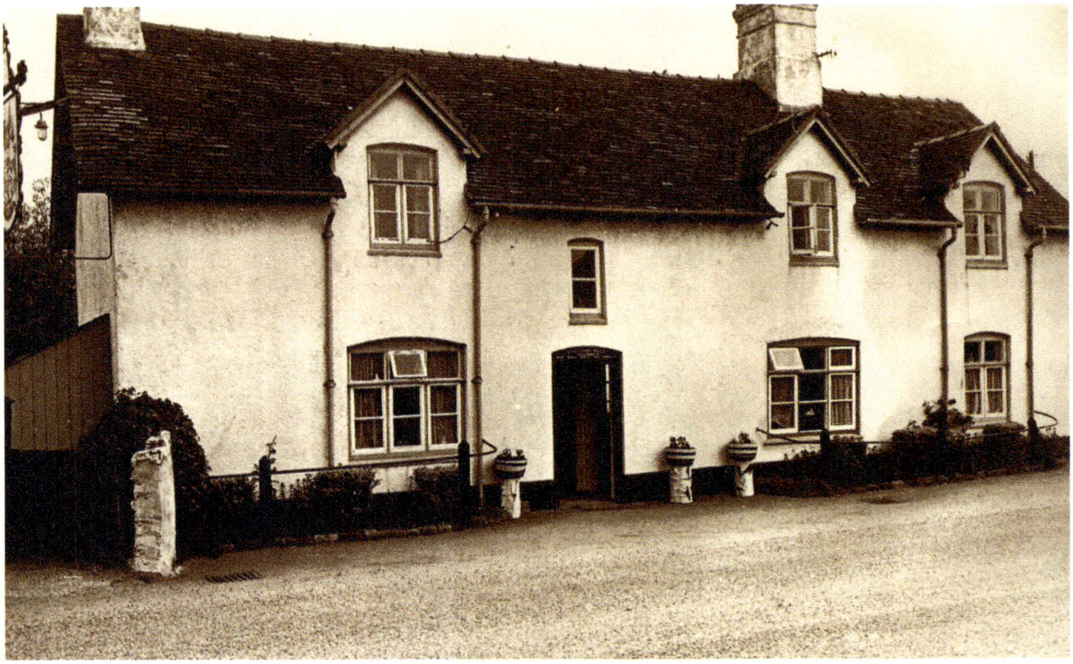

The Shrewsbury Arms, 1900 and 2014

The Shrewsbury Arms in Little Budworth, is another pub owned originally by the Earl of Shrewsbury, and after whom it is named. Licensees go back to 1872, but it is believed that prior to that it was The Bears Paw but there are no licensees listed between 1834 and 1872. At one time there was a racecourse at the pub's rear.

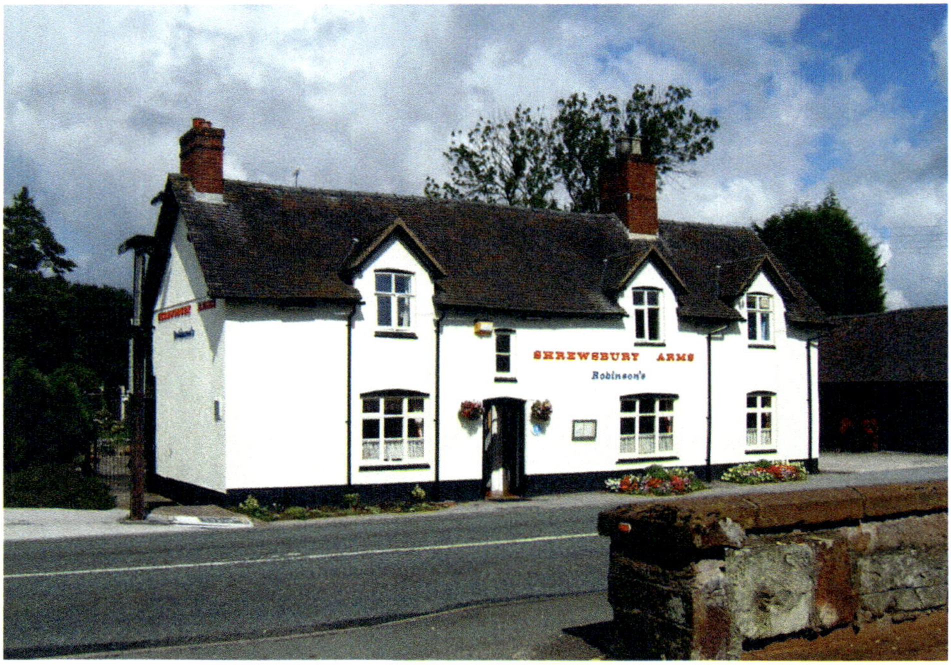

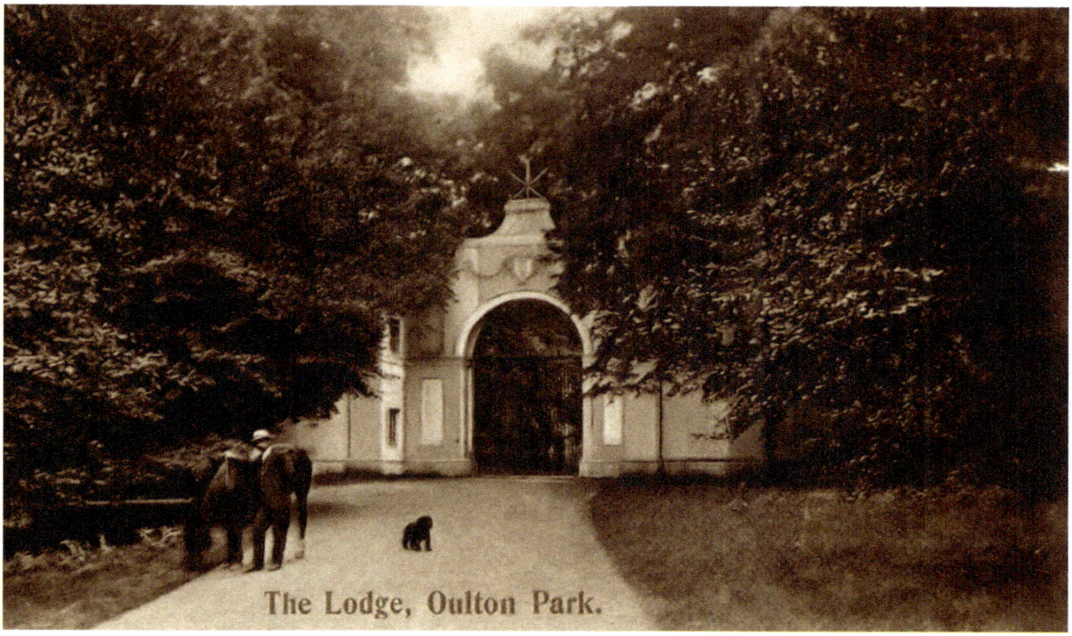

Oulton Park Lodge Gates, Undated and 2015

These gates originally formed the entrance to the Oulton Park estate and hall. The hall was commissioned in 1731 by Philip Egerton who had inherited the estate from his uncle. In 1752 a brick wall was constructed to enclose the 231 acres of the estate and the lodges, of which this is one, were designed by Joseph Turner. In 1926 the house was destroyed by fire causing the deaths of a number of local workers and then during the Second World War it was an army camp and the house suffered again by being bombed. General Patton and the boxer Joe Louis were stationed there at the time.

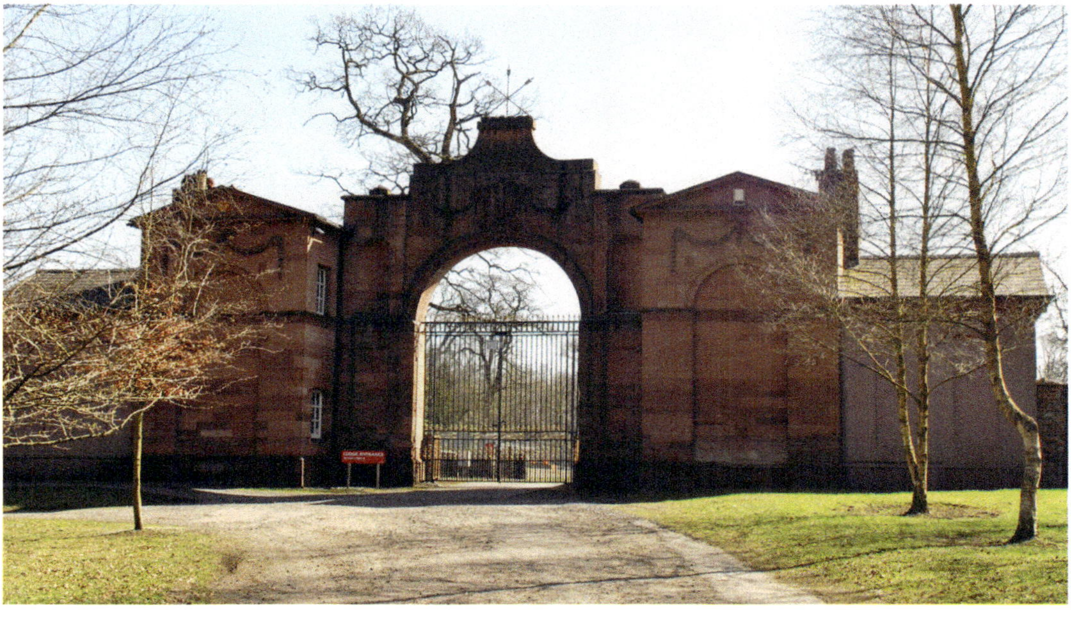

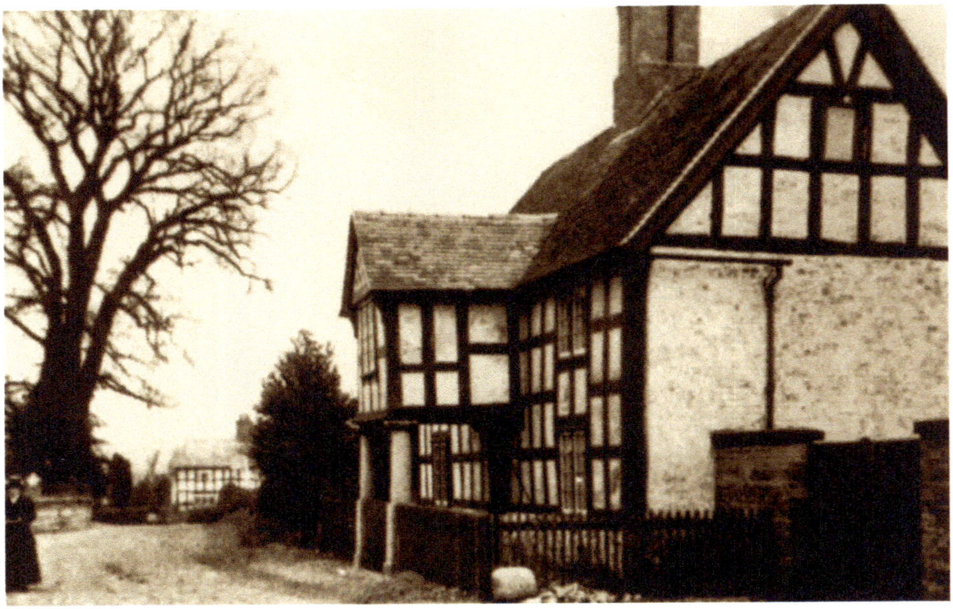

Church Minshull, 1895–1910 and 2014

This is the last of our villages and we are on the road from Winsford to Nantwich in the pretty village of Church Minshull. Black-and-white buildings predominate and the photographs show Church Farm, which is opposite St Bartholomew's church. The building has a 'magpie porch' and at one time was the vicarage. It is believed that it was once the home of Elizabeth Minshull, the third wife of the poet John Milton. They married on 24 February 1663 and he died in 1674. She was thirty years his junior and lived to the age of eighty-nine. Opposite this building is The Badger, filled with antiquity and now a very pleasant pub with excellent food.

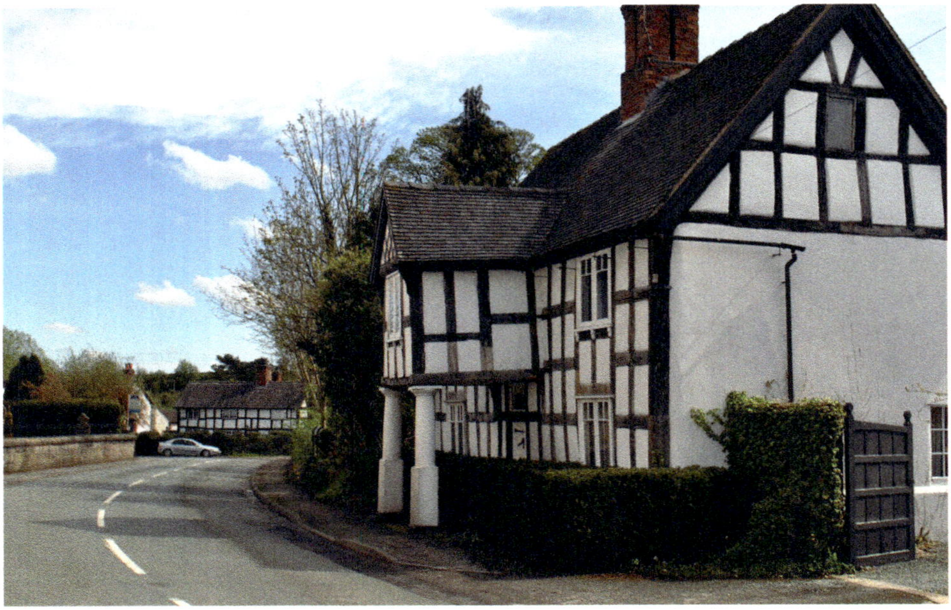